Edmund Heward

LORD DENNING

a biography

D0556901

Weidenfeld and Nicolson
London

Contents

	Illustration Acknowledgments	vii
	Acknowledgments	viii
	Preface	ix
1	Early Days, 1899–1923	1
2	The Bar, 1924–44	19
3	High Court Judge, 1944–48	34
4	Deserted Wives	49
5	Construction	58
6	Common Law	67
7	Appeal Judge, 1948–62	78
8	Precedent	91
9	Abuse of Power	99
10	Master of the Rolls, 1962–82	110
11	The Profumo Affair, 1963	124
12	Trade Unions	134
13	New Procedures	150
14	A Leaky Umbrella	161
15	Ambassador at Large	172
16	Author	183
17	Disaster	193

Contents

18 Retirement   202
19 Legal Influence   ·213
   Notes   222
   Bibliography   234
   Index   236

Illustration Acknowledgments

The photographs in this book are reproduced by kind
permission of the following:

Express Newspapers 9 above; Hulton Deutsch 7 below;
News International 11 above; Oxford Mail & Times Ltd
14 below; E.A.Sollars 15 above; Sport & General 4
above; Universal Pictorial Press 10 above, 16;
Westminster Archives 9 below.

Acknowledgments

My greatest debt is to Lord and Lady Denning for their patience and kindness in helping me. Apart from Lord Denning's books and judgments reported in the Law Reports the source material is to be found in the letters, press cuttings and other documents deposited at the Hampshire Record Office at Winchester. I am very greatly indebted to Rosemary Dunhill, the Archivist, for her help and guidance in the use of this extensive material. Also to her staff for their willing assistance, in particular to Sarah Lewin for her work on the photographs. Butterworths have very kindly granted me permission to quote from Lord Denning's books published by them.

I have seen some of those who have known Lord Denning over the years and acknowledge with many thanks the help given to me by Lord Ackner, John Baker, Hume Boggis-Rolfe, John Bradburn, Lord Bridge, Sir Simon Brown, Sir Denys Buckley, the late Edward Clarke, Robert Denning, Tom Dinwiddy, Lord Edmund-Davies, Lady Fox, Roger Gray, Antony Harwood, Sir Desmond Heap, Lord Havers, Tom Kellock, John King, Sir Frederick Lawton, Geoffrey Lock, Norman Marsh, Sir Robert Megarry, John Monckton, Peter Post, Sir Thomas Skyrme, Sir Robert Somerville, Sir John Stephenson, David Webster, Sir Max Williams and Sir John Whitford. I am most grateful to my wife for all her help.

Preface

In the nine hundred years of the common law Lord Denning is a phenomenon according to legal biographer Professor R.F.V. Heuston. Circumstances and natural abilities have combined to this end. Great powers of memory and comprehension, together with formidable legal learning, had been exercised over a period of thirty-eight years as a judge. Not only was he a great judge but a judge who is held in respect and affection by his brother judges, the Bar and the public. Never has a judge been better known to the public; he is well-known for his restless energy and has always enjoyed the excitement of appearing on television and giving his views no matter what the topic.

In his career as a judge he was bold and innovative, wished to restate the law in accordance with established principles and hated the restrictions imposed by precedent. He was astute enough to circumvent awkward precedent so that justice could be done in the individual case before him; he did not wait for Parliament to amend the law. Some legislators applauded his actions as the sitting time of Parliament is limited and Denning's decisions freed them to concentrate on major legislation. His priority has been to do justice and he has been more clearly aware than others of the limits of logic. Despite his zeal for justice he is conservative by nature and although his instinct is to help the little man he is always on the side of law and order. He believes that the offender should be punished and not be given the opportunity to get off on a technicality.

His pungent style is simple and direct, intended to arrest and interest. Writing a foreword to Fenton Bresler's biography of Lord Goddard, Denning's description of the subject could be applied with equal force to himself:

Famous for the lucidity of his judgments. Forthright in speech. He was clear and forceful. Never long winded. No long and confused sentences. No parenthesis. No shilly-shallying. Simple sentences in words which everyone could understand – straight to the point.

One outstanding characteristic of Lord Denning's career was speed. In the Profumo Inquiry he took evidence from 160 witnesses over a period of 49 days and wrote a 70,000 word report during the two months of the Long Vacation. He was very quick to take the point and dealt with litigants courteously but with exemplary speed. Many have remarked that he was a tiger for work and when Master of the Rolls set a fast and furious pace. He would never take time off from his work as a judge during term time and all his public work was done during the legal vacations and after the courts had risen for the day.

Lord Denning has made countless lectures and speeches. Never has a judge given so many lectures nor written so many books. He gave the lectures and wrote the books in order to spread his idea of how the law could be improved; however he also took seriously the judge's duty to help in the legal education of the young. From 1954–77 almost every long vacation was spent abroad lecturing and he has done much for the development of the law in the Commonwealth. He has always been interested in and studied other systems of law, particularly the American and common law systems.

In Lord Denning's many battles with the House of Lords as a judicial body he has frequently been defeated. Nevertheless Parliament often legislated in the way that Denning had marked out and the House of Lords, with its different composition, sometimes came round to his way of thinking. He remains disappointed that the House of Lords will never adopt the role of a body able to restate, expand and develop the law. He feels that this would be the proper function of the highest court in the land and that the House of Lords obstructs justice by putting fetters on the Court of Appeal with its strict rules on the subject of precedent. He echoes the words of the great sixteenth century lawyer, Edmund Plowden, who often said. 'Blessed be the amending hand.'

One

EARLY DAYS
1899–1923

Finality is a good thing, but justice is better.
Lord Atkin[1]

On admission as a judge of the High Court the new judge swears to do right to all manner of people after the laws and usages of the realm. He is appointed to the High Court of Justice and sits in the Royal Courts of Justice. He is addressed not as 'Judge' but as 'Mr Justice'. On promotion he becomes a Lord Justice of Appeal. Denning's passion for justice caused him to make every effort to avoid doing injustice to the parties before him. Too often this element in judgment is forgotten and the judge will sit back with folded arms and say that there is nothing that he can do for the party injured as the law is against him. Denning often said that he had not sworn to do injustice according to law. In his coat of arms he took as his motto '*Fiat Justitia*' (Let Justice be Done) and a large part of this book is taken up with the strategems and techniques used by him to avoid doing injustice.

A judge is not a passive machine which responds automatically when the penny is put in the slot. If this were the case no special skill would be required. He has to weigh up competing claims and for Denning the overriding claim was that of justice. To him the claims of justice have had a higher priority than going by the book. All judges want to do justice but most have a greater respect for the book. Denning believes that justice is what right-thinking members of the community believe to be fair. Professor Peter Stein, Professor of Civil Law at Cambridge University, said in this regard: 'Men are said to have an inborn sense of justice, but it is probably more accurate to say that they generally share a sense of injustice, in as much as certain types of conduct universally provoke anger on the ground that they are unjust.'[2] Giving an interview in 1978 Denning said:

If I give a decision that I think wrong or unjust I'm always unhappy about it, whereas I sleep well at night if I give one that is just. Because if I've given anything which I think is wrong or unjust I just can't stand it – it goes against the grain. There's something inbred in that. Other people would rather not take this responsibility. They say: 'It's not for me to alter the law, let Parliament do that.' But I say, why wait for Parliament? They can't ever correct the particular case. You've got to wait three or four years or whatever it is, but the particular person who suffered the injustice will never get it right.[3]

Justice for Denning is one of the basic ingredients in judgment. What is there in Denning's ancestry and background which makes him lay such emphasis on the prevention of injustice?

Hampshire has played a large part in Denning's life. He was born in Whitchurch, went to school in Andover and has always retained his Hampshire burr. In 1963 he returned to live in Whitchurch where he supports all the local activities. William Cobbett wrote about this part of Hampshire in his *Rural Rides*:

There are not many finer spots in England; and, if I were to take in a circle of eight or ten miles of semi-diameter, I should say there is not one so fine. Here are hill, dell, water, meadow, woods, corn-fields, downs: and all of them very fine and very beautifully disposed.[4]

The first church in Whitchurch was built by the Saxons before the year 800. There are round Norman pillars and an oak stair turret leading to the bells. There is a full octave of bells; the last two were installed in 1919 and Denning helped to raise the money for them as a memorial to the men of Whitchurch killed in the First World War.[5]

Denning believes that the family's true origins are in Somerset, however, where the name Denning is more common than in any other part of the country. 'Ing' means 'son of' so Denning is 'son of the Dane'. In the ninth century Somerset was peopled by the West Saxons and was invaded by the Danes. Perhaps a Dane married a West Saxon to produce the first Denning.[6] The Danes were a litigious people and the word 'law' is Danish. Maybe this is the source of Denning's love of argument.

More certain it is that the Dennings are descended from the Poyntz family who were given manors in Gloucestershire by William the Conquerer. There is firm evidence regarding these ancestors during the Civil War. Sir Sydenham Poyntz was for Parliament while his brother Newdigate Poyntz was for the King. Newdigate was killed fighting at Gainsborough while Sydenham was one of Cromwell's most famous generals. In about 1720 Sir Sydenham's granddaughter eloped with Richard Denning. Ever since the eldest son of the family has been named 'Newdigate Poyntz Denning'. Denning's great-grandfather, Thomas Newdigate Poyntz Denning, was born at or near Frome, Somerset, in 1798 and, when he was only a few weeks old, he was taken to Dursley, in Gloucestershire. He was christened in the Parish Church at Dursley, grew up and was married there in 1820. He was an organist and teacher of music who had three sons and two daughters. Denning's grandfather was the third son, William. He was, like his father, an organist; he played at the church in Cheltenham and taught music at Cheltenham Ladies' College. He left Dursley and moved to Leckhampton where he made his home. William and his wife Anne, née Browning, had three sons and four daughters. One of the sons, Charles, was Denning's father.

Denning's father was a very well read man with an extensive knowledge of English literature and a good verbal memory. He could quote poetry and prose extensively, particularly from the works of Shakespeare, Byron, Scott, Wordsworth and Bunyan. He tried his hand at writing poetry and some of his poems were published in the *Andover Advertiser*. Denning's excellent memory came from his father, a generous and sensitive man who made his living as a draper in Whitchurch. Although not a good businessman he took a great interest in his customers and many also became his friends.

Denning's mother came from Lincolnshire and her grandfather was a sailor. Her father, John Thomas Thompson, lived in the Bail Gate, near Lincoln Cathedral. He built up a prosperous business as a coal merchant and had six daughters and a son. Denning's mother, Clara, was the eldest child and became a schoolteacher. On a visit to friends in Whitchurch she met Charles Denning and two years later, on 17 October 1888, married him in Lincoln. Charles was twenty-nine and Clara twenty-three. John Thompson bought for his daughter two old houses in Newbury Street, Whitchurch; one was a chemist's shop, and the other provided Charles Denning with a draper's shop. Clara Denning was the driving force behind the family, very intelligent and hard working, ambitious for her children. Denning believes that his father and his mother each provided qualities that the other lacked.

They had fifty-two years of married life together until Charles died in 1941.

There were six children of the marriage: Marjorie Evelina (Marjorie), John Edward Newdigate (Jack), Reginald Francis Stewart (Reg), Charles Gordon (Gordon), Alfred Thompson (Tom), and Norman Egbert (Norman). They were brought up in a house built in the seventeenth century with oak beams, low ceilings and narrow stairs; cellars below and attics above. It stood opposite the White Hart Hotel. Denning has described the house as follows:

Although it looked attractive, our house would have been condemned today as totally unfit for human habitation. It had no indoor sanitation. The WC – or, as people call it nowadays, the toilet – was a deep pit, covered by a seat. At the end of the garden path – 25 yards from the house. No running water to flush it. It stank in hot weather. Flies swarmed there. The night-cart came every three or four weeks to clear it out. It was hidden from sight by a corrugated iron fence. Next to the WC was the manure dump and rubbish heap. You would think it would harbour diseases of all kinds. Yet we all kept in good health – except for childhood complaints.

No water from the mains. No water at all except that which we pumped up from a well just outside the back door beside the drain. To fill the iron kettle to put on the kitchen range – to fill the jugs with water to drink or to wash in – or to clean the floors.

No electric light. No gas except in two of the downstairs rooms a few flickering gas mantles which continually gave out. A paraffin oil lamp as a stand-by. Only candles to take us up stairs and into bed.

No daylight in the kitchen. No light got into it at all except through a glass panel in the door – or when the door was left open. Mother had to cook the meals for us children in that dark kitchen. It wore her out. Bath night was on Fridays. In a small zinc bath. In front of the kitchen range.

No living room except a makeshift affair, a long narrow slit of a room, with no window – only a skylight in the roof and a glass door at the end. We boys sat on a long bench screwed on the wall – for our meals – and our homework. Mother sat there every afternoon making up the books of the business.

The front part of the house was the shop. One side was the men's. The other was the ladies', where there was a girl assistant. Father was in the shop in the morning, serving the few customers, but in the afternoon he went on his 'journeys'. He went with his horse and trap filled with parcels – for his customers in the villages. The stable was at the end of the garden, just beyond the WC. It was built of stout oak. It had two stalls and a hayloft above. It housed Sam, the big white cob, and Queenie, the little brown mare. We bedded them down with straw at night. We cleaned out the dung in the morning. We took them to be shod. We harnessed them up into the trap. We got the lamps ready with the candles – on springs to keep them moving up. We boys went with father whenever we could. Off we would go with Sparkle, the rough-haired terrier, running beside the wheels. Father would go to different villages and hamlets every day – three, five or eight miles away – to call on the cottagers and supply them with their needs. They were not able to come into the town. None of them had any transport except for 'Shanks's pony'. They were supposed to pay by instalments regularly when he called. Some were good. Others were not. He never pressed them for payment. He was too kind. No holidays except that the shop was shut on Wednesday afternoon and Sunday. On Sunday father put on his best clothes. He went to church and sang in the choir – for 50 years.

None of the complications of modern business. No telephone. No typewriter. No adding machine. No paper money. Only coins. 'Coppers' – pennies, halfpennies and farthings. 'Silver' – threepenny bits, sixpences, shillings, florins, half-crowns, and some crowns. 'Gold' – sovereigns and half-sovereigns. But not many of those in our till. (The father of our good Dolly was a head carter. His wages were 15 shillings a week – and he had to keep a wife and six children on it. He also had his Michaelmas money, £5.)

No motor cars. Only horses and the railway. No wonder that we hardly ever went out of Whitchurch – except by train to school at Andover or with father on his 'journeys'. I did not go to London until I was eighteen in the Army.[7]

Denning was born on 23 January 1899, two months earlier than expected, and nearly died. His mother's friend Mrs Roe, who lived opposite, rushed across the road, wrapped the baby in a blanket and gave him some brandy. As she wrapped him up she said: 'That's one we could have done without.'[8] His baptismal name was Alfred Thompson Denning, but he was always known as Tom, a shortened form of his mother's maiden name of Thompson. He was baptised on 23 April 1899 at All Hallows Church, Whitchurch, by the vicar, the Rev J.H. Hodgson; his sponsors were Mrs Roe and his parents. His sister Marjorie claimed that she chose the name of Alfred as she had seen the statue of Alfred the Great in Winchester. His mother regarded him as the weakest of her brood, needing special care. When off to school she insisted that he had cod-liver oil in a cup of milk.

Denning wrote: 'I was so tiny and puny that I could be put in a pint pot. They called me Tom Thumb.'[9]

Mrs Roe's husband was a brewer and Denning wrote of him:

Opposite us was John Roe, the brewer – with his brewery alongside his house. The men of Whitchurch drank much beer. There were nineteen public houses in the town. He was a big, fat man. Vigorously against the temperance movement. It was he who opposed the Salvation Army when they determined to play their band in the Square. There was a riot. Three of the Salvationists were sent to prison – and became the heroes of the place.[10]

Denning also wrote about their friends, the Geer family:

Equally great friends were the Geers – Charles Henry Geer, the school-master, his wife, his daughters and one son. They ran a small private school in their own house beside the river. It was regarded as somewhat superior to the elementary school. The tradesmen and farmers sent their children there – paying as much as they could afford. Never more than 20 or 30 children all told. My sister and two of my elder brothers, Jack and Reg, had their entire education there ... He [Geer] had never taken a degree but wore a scholar's gown – torn and tatty – to show his learning ... His prime concern was to build character, and next to teach his pupils to write good English and speak it. He always saw to their cricket, urging them in the game – as in life – to keep a straight bat. He played the organ, too, in church. His wife, lively and smiling, supported him. She taught music to the girls – and to a few of the boys. She taught me all I knew ... But I had no ear for music. My elder brothers all sang in the choir in church. But I never did. I was given a try but the Vicar said I wasn't good enough.[11]

Gordon and Tom did not go to Geer's school as their parents could not afford the small fees. They went to the local elementary school but after taking examinations were awarded free places at Andover Grammar Shool, then in New Street. Denning describes the routine of going to school in Andover:

Each morning we set off. Mother had put up our sandwiches. We had them in our satchels with our exercise books. We walked up the steep hill. It was half a mile to the station. The station staff were all our friends. We went into the signal box with the signalman. We went into the cab of the shunting engine. The driver used to boil his egg in water in his big shovel in the fire-hole. We got into the train. It had one stop – at Hurstbourne – two miles. The next stop was Andover Junction – another five miles. We made our way round the road by the river – dawdling by the stream –

through the churchyard – till we reached the school. Always late by a quarter of an hour. We had a good excuse. The train was late.[12]

Andover Grammar School was then a small school with about eighty boys and five masters. There was the Headmaster, Mr R.O.Bishop, and four other masters to teach Latin, French, Science and Maths. The boys were frightened of the Headmaster but he made them work and taught them English. He was a first-class cricketer, a fast bowler, and encouraged the boys in their games, soccer in winter and cricket in summer. Gordon was much better at games than Tom. Tom was better at work and received many prizes at school for English including Macaulay's *Essays and Lays*; Carlyle's *French Revolution* and Milton's *Poetical Works*.

Marjorie, the eldest child, was born in 1891. She was fair with blue eyes like her mother. She married an army officer, John E. Haynes, and had four daughters. Commenting on her brother Tom, Marjorie said that he had inherited his mother's ability, power of concentration and capacity for hard work. On retirement Marjorie and her husband returned to live in Whitchurch at 'The Hermitage', the small house which Reg had bought for his father and mother to live in during their later years. Denning described the house as follows:

It is probably the oldest house in the place. It is very pretty. It is built of oak timbers sloping upwards from ground level to the roof. 14th century. With later additions. And gabled roof. Father and mother lived there – in peace after so much distress – until father died in 1941 aged 81 and mother in 1947 aged 83.[13]

Jack, the eldest brother, was born in 1892, and was baptised John Edward Newdigate Poyntz, in accordance with family tradition. He was good looking, with features like his mother's, and a good games player. Immediately the First World War was declared he was called up and served as a gunner. Commissioned in the 3rd Lincolnshire Regiment, he saw active service in France and was twice wounded. On 24 September 1916 orders were given to attack the next day. Jack was in command of a company and had to lead the attack. He had a premonition of death as he wrote to his parents: 'This may or may not be my last letter to you, as we are for it I think tomorrow.' Denning has recorded the sad end to his life:

Jack was one of those wounded – with a piece of shrapnel through his stomach – bleeding his life away. He lay there for about three hours. Then he was found. They carried him on a stretcher a long way. To the Field Ambulance. Then by motor ambulance to the Casualty Clearing Station. They got him there by 10 p.m. As he was taken in he said to a comrade next to him, 'I'm done for'. The nurses did all they could to relieve the pain. He was wandering all night, murmuring of home. He died in the morning of the 26th. The Chaplain wrote home to father and mother saying, 'I prayed with him ... He was very grateful for my ministrations and died a good soldier of Jesus Christ.' They buried him in the war cemetery at Heilly-sur-Somme. They stamped out his name on a piece of tin and tacked it on a rough wooden cross.[14]

Tom greatly admired Jack and thought that he was born to be a soldier, as he had all the right qualities, a splendid brain, was a brilliant leader of men and had great determination.

Reg, the second brother, was born in 1894 and joined up as a private in the Queen's Westminsters on the outbreak of the First World War. He went to France in the winter of 1914–15 and served on the Ypres salient. Later, in 1915, he was commissioned in the Bedfordshire Regiment and on 15 July 1915 he was severely wounded. He served as a regular soldier between the two wars and was on the staff when the Second World War broke out. He helped to prepare the expeditionary force for France and was Brigadier on the staff of 11th Corps. By 1943 he had been promoted to Major-General and dealt with the advance planning for the Normandy invasion. Within a few days of D Day he was posted to Lord Mountbatten's headquarters in South East Asia. He became the Principal Administration Officer for the whole of the Allied Forces in South East Asia under Lieutenant-General Browning, the Chief of Staff. In 1947 he was appointed Chief of Staff, Eastern Command, and in 1949 General Officer Commanding in Northern Ireland with the rank of Lieutenant-General. Reg was a highly professional soldier and a very brave man. He proved himself to be an outstanding administrator.

The third brother, Gordon, was nearly two years older than Tom but they were particularly close as all their schooling was done together. In 1913 at the age of fifteen he was accepted for training as a Master Mariner by General Steam Navigation Company. He was appointed to the steamship *Stork*, which sailed with cargo to and fro to Genoa from London Bridge, with the pay of £1 a month. On 31 December 1914 he was appointed a midshipman in the Royal Naval Reserve. In March 1915 he joined HMS *Hampshire*, one of the latest cruisers (which was to sink with Kitchener aboard). Six months later he joined the destroyer *Morris*. He played a distinguished part in the Battle of Jutland and was promoted Sub-Lieutenant RN. The citation in *The London Gazette* of 15 September 1916 read: 'For the cool and skilful way in which he, as officer of the quarters, while continuously under heavy fire, controlled the foremast 4 inch gun, the primary control having broken down.' The harsh conditions of life at sea in wartime brought on tuberculosis which was diagnosed in November 1916. He was discharged as unfit for further service and placed on the retired list at the age of nineteen. He lived for another eighteen months and died at home at Whitchurch in May 1918. Tom was in France when he died and was very deeply distressed at the loss of his brother.

Norman was only fourteen when the First World War ended. He had bad eyesight but was accepted by the Paymaster Branch of the Royal Navy. He became an expert in naval intelligence. He took part in pre-war planning and wartime control of surface ship intelligence. In the early thirties he was stationed for two years in Singapore and wrote in a report that the Japanese were in a position to advance on Singapore by land. This report was dismissed. 'This young officer is over-exercising his imagination. The Japanese have no seaborne assault force. It is ridiculous to imagine any army advancing hundreds of miles through jungle territory.'[15] In 1937 Norman was called back to the Admiralty for naval intelligence and during the Second World War he spent his time in the Citadel, by the Admiralty in Whitehall. He had a genius for intelligence work. In 1961 he became Director of Naval Intelligence and was promoted Vice-Admiral. Lord Mountbatten said that he was one of the finest Directors of Naval Intelligence the Navy had ever had and when there was a reorganisation of the armed forces Lord Mountbatten chose him for the new appointment of Deputy Chief of Defence Staff (Intelligence). He had two sons and one daughter and died in 1979.

The Dennings were a very close family. Those who survived to retirement went to live in Whitchurch or in the surrounding country and kept in touch with each other. They all achieved distinction, were good administrators with a mathematical bent, and were very brave men who succeeded in their chosen professions.

At the outbreak of the First World War Denning was aged fifteen and working hard for a University scholarship in mathematics. The masters at Andover Grammar School joined up and their places were taken by women. None of them knew enough to teach advanced mathematics and so Denning had to study on his own. He went to the Castle in Winchester for an examination to qualify for University College, Southampton. He did well and came top in English and mathematics. The Headmaster advised him to stay on at school and try for Oxford or Cambridge. He did as advised and sat for the Oxford and Cambridge examination at the age of sixteen. Magdalen College, Oxford, offered him an exhibition of £30 a year. This he accepted although it was not enough to live on and his father could not help.

Denning went up to Magdalen in October 1916 at the age of 17¾. The President of Magdalen at the time was Sir Herbert Warren; he proved a very good friend to the young man. He arranged for the exhibition of £30 to become a demyship of £80 and persuaded the Goldsmith's Company to grant him an exhibition of £30 a year. Denning could just manage on £120 a year but had to watch every penny. The College was full of army officers in training. There were a few men under age awaiting call-up and some who were medically unfit. Denning's rooms were in Chaplain's Quad on the first floor of the Tower. Every morning those who were fit had to go to drill in anticipation of their call-up. In the afternoon there was again military training with route marches and sometimes night operations. Writing to Reg on 24 November 1916 he said:

Yesterday we went for a route march of 12 miles with rifles etc. First long march. Today I have been doing bayonet fighting which I think is very interesting. This evening we dined in Hall for the first time. Formerly we dined in the Junior Common Room as we were so few.[16]

Despite all the military training Denning worked hard at his mathematics and now had proper teaching from A.L.Pedder. Writing to his first wife, Mary, he said: 'A.L.Pedder gave me tutorials smoking his pipe and throwing spent matches over his shoulder into the fireplace.'[17] In June 1917 he obtained a first class in Mathematical Moderations and in August 1917 he was called up for war service. The age of call-up was eighteen and a half but no one went to France before the age of nineteen.

By the time that Denning joined up military service was compulsory; he joined the Royal Engineers. Writing to Reg on 15 November 1916 he said that Jack had advised him not to go into the infantry but to try for the gunners or the engineers where his mathematics would be an advantage.[18] He went to an Officers Training Corps near Newark and was commissioned as a Second Lieutenant in the Royal Engineers at Aldershot. Each officer had a horse and horses pulled the Engineers' wagons, with pontoons and bridging equipment. In March 1918 the Germans had advanced to within striking distance of Amiens and Paris; young soldiers were rushed out to help defend the line. On 12 April 1918 Lord Haig issued an order that every position was to be held to the last man and there was to be no retreat. Denning sailed from Southampton and went on to a transit camp at Rouen. From there he joined his unit, the 151st Field Company of the Royal Engineers. The unit was attached to the 38th Welsh Division in a sector not far from Albert – Denning proudly wore the Red Dragon of Wales as an arm flash. The unit dug in every night under continuous shell fire.

For the next three months the Division held the line. Each night reconnaisances were made into enemy territory. The River Ancre was flooded to a width of two to three hundred yards and there were no bridges. On 15 August Denning and six other ranks got an infantry patrol across the river with the help of light bridges. The infantry made the crossing of the Ancre at night followed by the sappers, busy making foot-bridges across the river and the swamp and repairing them under continuous fire. Getting the main body over the river with guns and equipment was a formidable task but this was done between 21 and 24 August. The sappers had to make a roadway across the marshes with logs and sleepers and had to erect trestles and road-decks to cross the river. An enemy aeroplane dropped a bomb on the bridge and they had to start all over again. Another bridge was built and the guns and wagons went over by day and night. Denning and his unit were two days and nights without sleep. There is an entry in *The History of the Welsh Division* recording the night of 23/24 August 1918:

Meanwhile two battalions of the 115th Brigade crossed the Ancre at Aveley over a bridge made by 151st Field Company RE under the supervision of Lieutenants Denning and Butler and formed up on a one battalion frontage on the left of the 113th Brigade ... At 1 a.m. the attack was launched and the 114th Brigade stormed the heights and took Thiepval ... By 4 p.m. the Division had captured in the day's operation 634 prisoners and 143 machine guns.

On 1 September Denning wrote to his parents that he had ridden some distance on horseback to visit his brother Jack's grave at Heilly Station Cemetery, five miles south west of Albert:

Today I had a day free so rode over some distance to see Jack's grave. I enclose the only two small flowers on it. . . . On the cross was printed Captain M.P.Denning, 1st Lincolnshire Regt 26 September 1916. So I printed the correct name as well as I could on a board and stuck it in the ground. The grave maintenance people will probably erect a new cross. I have written my name and the date I visited on the board there.[19]

After the crossing of the River Ancre the troops came to the Canal du Nord. All the bridges had been destroyed and the enemy was holding the further bank in strength and using gas. The job of the sappers was to bridge the canal and the work was made harder as they had to wear gas masks. When they went into action the officers always took off their insignia of rank and dressed as private soldiers. There were other crossings to be made over the Rivers Selle and Sambra with heavy fighting all the way. At the time of the armistice Denning had been struck down by the virulent influenza prevalent at the end of the First War. On 8 November he was taken in an ambulance train to the base hospital at Rouen crowded with the sick and dying. The men were too ill to rejoice when the Armistice was signed at 11 a.m. on 11 November but there was weary relief that it was all over.

Denning was demobilised on Thursday 6 February 1919 and on Monday 10 February he was back at Magdalen. He had lodgings in the High Street, opposite the College. He toyed with the idea of taking Natural Sciences and went to the Physics Laboratory to make enquiries. He was given a test and this, in his own words, was the result:

I was told to tie a piece of cotton on to a lead weight. It took me two hours before the demonstrator was satisfied. That decided me. Not Applied Mathematics for me. Only Pure Mathematics. That depends on reasoning, not on mechanical aptitude. I was never anything of a mechanic. If the car breaks down – even if a wheel has to be changed – I am no good at it.[20]

Denning remembers the summer term of 1919 as one of the happiest of his life:

One of the finest summers on record. Oxford at its best. Magdalen at its most beautiful. About 60 of us at the College back from the war. No examinations ahead for any of us. In the mornings attend lectures or work. Afterwards take canoe or punt on the river, play tennis or cricket on the playing field. On Sundays, out for the day leisurely on the river with picnic lunch and tea. Magdalen the head of the river – with a crew of the very first quality – all blues.[21]

Denning moved to rooms in Cloisters on the next staircase to Edward Bridges. Each morning they used to run round Adders (Addison's Walk) and have a swim in the swimming pool. He played soccer for the Magdalen 2nd Eleven. He was a member of the Union but, unlike many of his friends, took no part in the debates nor did he aspire to be President. He was diffident about having been to a grammar school when every one else had been to a public school. Questions about where he had been at school he tended to avoid. Social class was considered far more important in those days than it is now. When Jack applied for a commission in the Army his Commanding Officer advised him to put 'Gentleman' as his father's occupation and when Denning applied for membership of Lincoln's Inn he again described his father as 'Gentleman'. Magdalen, at that time, had the reputation of being a rich man's college where the undergraduates were fairly idle and where no student had been awarded a first class degree for years.

Denning took a first class in the Mathematical Final School of 1920; the problem then was what to do for a living. The Headmaster of Winchester College offered him a job teaching mathematics. The Headmaster's report of 1920 says:

Mr Aris will leave at Christmas. He will retire at the age of fifty-one to the life of a country gentleman. This causes a vacancy in our mathematics staff. After prolonged search in England and America I have secured a young man of good ability, Mr A.T.Denning, who comes with an excellent mathematical record.[22]

Even in those days there was difficulty in finding teachers for science and mathematics. The salary was £350 a year, which was good for the time, and he would not be far from home. The appointment accepted, he taught mathematics to all levels and geology to some classes. He did not enjoy teaching boys; writing to Mary (later to become his wife) on 26 November 1920 he said: 'I feel that I don't want to settle down here doing the same thing day after day, a very mediocre schoolmaster with no ambition and no hope.'[23] In July 1921 he sought the advice of Sir Herbert Warren on his future career. He was ambitious and wanted to get on in the world. He saw the law as an avenue for advancement in life.

While at Winchester he visited the Assizes and, as a result, felt that the law was a profession that would suit him. Sir Herbert Warren said that he would be willing to take him back at Magdalen to study law. Before returning to Oxford he had a walking holiday with his brother, Reg, in Chamonix. In September he bought a copy of Anson on contract and so began his study of the law. In October 1921 he returned to Magdalen to read for the Final Honours School of Jurisprudence. The Headmaster's report from Winchester for 1921 said: 'Mr Denning has left us to resume study at Oxford. He has been a useful teacher.'[24] Denning had lodgings in Iffley Road and worked very hard. His law tutor was Robert Segar of whom he later wrote: 'He knew no law except the Statute of Frauds on which he had once had a case. I learned nothing from him.'[25] He went to lectures by other dons and took notes. He had such a good verbal memory that when questions were asked in the examination papers he was often able to repeat the notes word for word.

Denning's main problem was money and Sir Herbert Warren again came to the rescue. He went up to London to recommend Denning for the Eldon Scholarship founded in memory of Lord Eldon, the famous Lord Chancellor of the early nineteenth century. The scholarship was awarded to 'a Protestant of the Church of England who had obtained a first.' The first did not need to be in law so Denning qualified with his first in mathematics and in being a communicant member of the Church of England. The scholarship was worth £100 a year and lasted for three years. The trustees met annually in the Lord Chancellor's room in the House of Lords and when Sir Herbert returned to Magdalen with the good news of Denning's election he sent a note from the High Table telling him that he had been successful and adding: 'You are a marked man. Perhaps you will be a Lord of Appeal some day.'[26] On 12 November 1921 *The Times* recorded that Denning had been appointed Eldon Scholar.

Denning took his final examination in June 1922. At the *viva voce* examination the examiner was Geoffrey Cheshire, later Vinerian Professor at Oxford, who became a personal friend. Cheshire asked questions on the new Law of Property Act which only received the Royal assent on 29 June 1922. Denning had read up all about the Act and with his good memory was able to make a good impression on the examiner. He was placed in the first class in this examination, Roman Law being a compulsory subject.[27] Subsequently Cheshire showed Denning his marks, a wide range of alphas but one gamma for jurisprudence. He was not fond of jurisprudence and once wrote:

> Jurisprudence was too abstract a subject for my liking. All about ideologies, legal norms and basic norms, 'ought' and 'is', realism and behaviourism: and goodness knows what else. The jargon of the philosophers has always been beyond me. I like to get down to the practical problems which come up for decision. Contracts, torts, crime and the like.[28]

In 1948 Denning was made an Honorary Fellow of Magdalen; many years later his son, Robert, also became a Fellow in inorganic chemistry and was Dean and Tutor in the College.

Denning did not return to Oxford to take his BCL but did go back to try for a fellowship at All Souls in the autumn of 1923. He had to answer legal questions and read Latin aloud. He wrote: 'My pronunciation was mixed between the old and the new. That did not suit that stronghold of classicists. So I joined the distinguished company of "Failed All Souls".'[29] He does not seem to have any bitterness about his lack of success. From the point of view of his career it was a godsend that he failed as he might have spent time at All Souls which would have been better spent preparing for his legal career. Denning did not have the makings of an academic lawyer. His bent is practical, in the world of affairs. He has a very quick mind but was never an intellectual.

It was on 25 October 1914 that Denning first met Mary Harvey. He was fifteen and she was just fourteen. She was the daughter of the Vicar of Whitchurch, the Rev Frank Harvey, and they were both being confirmed by the Bishop of Winchester. She was a smiling girl with dark brown eyes and long black hair. During the First World War they seldom met as Mary was away at school and later studying agriculture at Reading University. When Denning was at Oxford they occasionally met during the vacations. The course of true love did not run smoothly as Mary was attached to a man much older than herself and her parents were against her marriage to him. In 1923 Mary's father left Whitchurch and was appointed Rector of Fawley. As a result of this move Denning rarely met Mary for some years.

On 29 September 1929 Mary invited Denning to a dance at Beaulieu and soon afterwards they became engaged. Denning spent every weekend at Fawley and the couple planned to get married in August 1930. He wrote:

The living was one of the best in the diocese. The Rectory was a large rambling house of the period of Queen Anne. No modern conveniences. Oil lamps in the living-room. Candles up to bed. Two or three maids in the kitchen. A spacious drawing-room opening up three large French windows on to a wide expanse of lawn – and beyond, the flower-garden and the kitchen-garden. It was there that Mary and I happily planned our future together. We would be married in August – during the long vacation.[30]

It was in June 1930 that disaster struck:

It was in June that Mary fell ill. She had pains in her shoulder. The doctor did not know what it was. Perhaps it was rheumatism. She started to run a temperature. The good kind doctor had her taken to a nursing home in Southampton. Then she was taken up to London to Guy's Hospital to see a specialist. It was when I was on circuit at Exeter – with a brief of some kind. I was not staying at the Bar hotel – The Royal Clarence. That would be expensive. Mary had arranged for me to stay with her cousin – Dr Blackley and his dear wife Mary – in their lovely house and garden high on the hill.

Then in the evening there was a ring on the telephone. It was for me – from Mary's mother. 'It is worse than we thought. The doctors have diagnosed it as TB.' I fell to the floor in a faint – for the first time in my life. It was the shock. I knew what it meant. I remembered my brother Gordon. When I came to, the doctor and his wife were there. They helped me upstairs. I did not sleep much. But next morning I went down to the Castle and did my case ...[31]

The wedding was only six weeks away. It had to be put off. The invitations had to be cancelled. Some day, we hoped, we would get married. But how long? No one could tell. Mary was under the care of Dr Geoffrey Marshall (afterwards Sir Geoffrey Marshall, Royal Physician) of Guy's Hospital. He became a close friend of ours. We trusted him completely. He recommended that she go to a sanitorium at Mundesley in Norfolk. She was there for several weeks. A strict routine, keeping to a rigid timetable. Then she was back at home at Fawley. She had a hut in the garden. Set in the middle of the lovely lawn. She had her bed there. We took her out her meals. Whilst there she went to London every three weeks or so for treatment.[32]

Two and a half years after Mary was taken ill the wedding took place on 28 December 1932 at the norman church in Fawley. Dr

Boutflower, Bishop of Southampton, officiated, assisted by the bride's father, the Rev Frank Harvey. The bride wore a cream satin frock and had a ringlet of orange blossom with the family veil. The bridesmaids were cousins of the bride – Misses H.B. and K.Blackley – and were dressed in green. The bride was given away by her brother Major F.Barrington Harvey. Mary had four brothers, two of whom were in the Indian Political Service and two in the Army. The best man was a barrister friend from his chambers, Mr A.Grattan-Bellew. There was no reception and the honeymoon was spent in Devon.

The newly married couple went to live in the top floor flat of No. 1 Brick Court, Temple, overlooking Middle Temple Hall. Dr Marshall went to look at the flat and was well satisfied with it. He thought that they should have the big room overlooking the trees in the court as their bedroom as it was the most airy. He advised against having a spare bedroom as visitors entail so much extra effort.[33] The rent of the flat was £187 10s a year. No heating except coal fires. No lift but sixty stairs to climb. Cooking was by gas. Looking back Denning felt that living in London was a mistake. In the 1930s, before the clean air legislation, London was dirty and foggy and soot filtered through the windows and covered everything with a layer of dirt. This was too much for Mary's health and after eight or nine months living in London she was admitted to Guy's Hospital. The treatment at Guy's was not successful and she was transferred to Brompton Hospital for surgery. She had one lung removed and had a long stay in hospital. Eventually she recovered but they had to give up their flat in the Temple. Mary's father had now retired and her parents had gone to live in a small house in Southampton, near the cricket ground. Mary went to stay with them and Denning went down every weekend.

Two years later in 1935 Mary had fully recovered and they found a house of their own at Cuckfield called 'Fair Close' in Tylers Green. Denning walked to the station every morning and came back in the evening by bus, price one penny. They also had help in the house, a Welsh girl called Rose who came to them at the age of fifteen and became a firm friend of the family. Sometimes they played a game of golf together and there were long walks in the countryside. In 1937 Dr Marshall advised that it was now safe for Mary to have a child and on 3 August 1938 their son, Robert, was born at Nuffield House, Guy's Hospital. This happy time was all too short as a year later on 3 September 1939 war broke out. Early in 1940 they moved to another house in Copyhold Lane, Cuckfield which they again called 'Fair Close'. The village was vulnerable to attack from enemy bombers and on one occasion the front door was forced open by blast but no damage was done. Mary, Rose and the baby were often there alone as Denning was either away on war work or could not get home because of air raids.

Two

THE BAR
1924–44

*All good wishes for an income which, I cannot help feeling, in view of
your clear headed capacity for getting to the point and sticking to it,
is in no manner of doubt.*[1]

Mr Justice Clauson

Denning is a tall man, 6' 1½", slim and clean shaven. Baldness runs
in the family and he became bald at a fairly early age in life. His
approach is diffident and his manner unassuming. He is unfailingly
courteous and has a good sense of humour. His face is round and
rosy and his eyes bright and kindly. He talks and moves quickly,
and is always quick to take up the point. He has a photographic
memory, is very thorough and worked hard throughout his career.
He has never drunk or smoked nor, since 1945, has he driven a car.
He is no good with his hands. He always gives credit when credit
is due and appreciates the efforts of others. He likes simple English
food, his habits are frugal and he is always careful with money.

He has a great love of English literature, in particular the Bible
and Shakespeare and has built up a fine library of the classics and
the law. Although he has travelled widely throughout the rest of
the world, he has visited few European countries and, apart from
reading French, cannot speak any foreign language. Having led a
very busy life he has had little time for interests like music or the
arts that lie outside the law. He once said that he only read on holiday
and that his favourite bedside reading was *The Oxford Book of English
Verse*. This was a matter of concern to some of his friends. In a
letter to Mary on 1 October 1930 he wrote: 'Henn Collins dragged
me off to walk home with him this evening – he preached me a little
homily about the necessity of a hobby etc.'[2] Henn Collins himself
was an expert on violins and had made several with his own hands.
Above all else family life was important to Denning.

Having decided to make his career at the Bar Denning was admitted
as a member of Lincoln's Inn on 4 November 1921. He tried for

Lincoln's Inn in particular because the Under Treasurer at the time was a Magdalen man. The problem then, as now, was to find a seat in chambers. Denning himself had no influence but his brother, Reg, had an army friend, Frank Merriman (later Lord Merriman, President of the Probate, Divorce and Admiralty Division), who was a silk; he suggested that Denning should seek a pupillage with Henry O'Hagan, a junior with a good commercial practice. O'Hagan agreed to take him and in September 1922 he started as a pupil at 4 Brick Court, Middle Temple Lane. It was a small set with only two juniors, Henry O'Hagan and Stephen Henn Collins (later Mr Justice Henn Collins). Each had a fine room overlooking Brick Court and each had his own library. The only other rooms were a small dark room jutting over Middle Temple Lane, used as a pupil room, and a cubby hole for the clerks, a senior and a junior clerk and a typist. O'Hagan did commercial work and some libel and Henn Collins did railway work and copyright. Denning had little in common with O'Hagan although he respected his knowledge as a lawyer. He became very friendly with Henn Collins and they frequently walked home together. Denning lived at 145 Beaufort Street, Chelsea, in bachelor apartments kept by a talkative but good hearted lady, Mrs Cross. Henn Collins had a house nearby, in Beaufort Gardens.

As a pupil of O'Hagan he saw all the paperwork in the chambers but did not attend conferences with solicitors except when specially invited. He went into court with his pupil master. Denning started his pupillage before he had taken his final Bar examination, which he took in May 1923. He had no money except the Eldon Scholarship and he aimed at the Prize Studentship of the Bar. He studied in Lincoln's Inn Library for his examinations while keeping up his practical work in chambers. He kept six dinners in Hall each term. He came out top in the Bar examination and was placed in the first class. He was awarded the Studentship and a Certificate of Honour which was worth 100 guineas a year for three years.

Denning was called to the Bar by Lincoln's Inn on 13 June 1923. After his call he went down to dinner and, as he was the junior called, he had to make a speech. Denning was offered and accepted a seat in the chambers of his pupil master. His name was painted on the door and he was ready to accept briefs. Like every new barrister he was briefless for a time and occupied himself in 'devilling' for members of his chambers and for busy juniors in the other chambers.

A 'devil' did not always get paid but Denning was given work by Mr D.N.Pritt who did pay him for his work. Pritt had a very large commercial and Privy Council practice. He was also the very left-wing MP for Hammersmith. When Pritt was a silk he gave Denning his 'red bag' as a mark of his appreciation of Denning's work in a case they had done together. Normally a barrister carries a blue bag, but, if he does particularly well, a silk may give him a red bag. In his letter to Mary of 23 October 1930 he wrote: 'I am pleased today because Pritt has given me a red bag – and written me a charming note which I will show you – the only sad thing is that I shall not be using the blue bag on which you sewed my initials.'[3] A few years later, in 1934, Stuart Bevan had returned a brief and Denning was asked to recommend a leader. He was glad to recommend Pritt as he said that he could not think of anyone else available who could do it better.

During Denning's first year, 1923, his expenses of practice were £69 10s and receipts nil. The expenses consisted of Robes £12, Pupillage £52 10s and Clerk's fee £5.[4] For the second year, 1924, briefs were £94 10s and expenses £35 10s leaving a net income of £59.

He joined the Western Circuit in February 1924. One of his first cases was in the Greenwich County Court but he got on the wrong train at Charing Cross Station which did not stop at Greenwich. He pulled the communication cord, walked half a mile along the track and got to the court in time. In 1924 he got some work from Mary's uncle, Mr T.H.Woodham, who was the Clerk to the Peace for the City of Winchester. He gave Denning small prosecution briefs for £2 2s. He attended quarter sessions and received occasional dock briefs of £1 3s 6d. He received instructions from Nicholas Graham & Jones, Syrett & Sons, and from Theodore Goddard & Co – his largest brief in 1924 was £6 6s.

In 1925 Denning was receiving small briefs in the police courts and the county courts but the breakthrough came when Stephen Henn Collins recommended him to the solicitor for the Southern Railway, Mr W.Bishop. He prosecuted people for travelling without paying their fare, went to county courts on small claims for possession and learnt his way round the Rent Acts. He wrote a railway police manual giving guidance to the railway police and re-drafted the railway by-laws, for which he was paid £15 15s. Later on he was entrusted with more important work such as assessing compensation in personal injury cases. In 1925 he more than doubled his 1924 earnings, making £315.

His earnings increased steadily until he took silk in 1938.[5] His fees were: 1926 – £360; 1927 – £470; 1928 – £860; 1929 – £1,130; 1930 – £1,410; 1931 – £1,670; 1932 – £1,960; 1933 – £2,230; 1934 – £2,630; 1935 – £2,530; 1936 – £3,307; 1937 – £3,240. In 1925 he received a brief from the Secretary of the Law Society, Mr E.R.Cook, on an appeal from the Disciplinary Committee of the Law Society. In 1926 he got his first brief from Soames, Edwards & Jones, the solicitors for *The Times*, and he had more work from this firm than from any other. He was instructed by Nicholson and Graham Jones for the *Illustrated London News* and H.A.Phillips for the Small Property Owners' Association. He had briefs from Charles Russell & Co; Field Roscoe; Potter, Crundwell & Bridge; Church Adams & Co; Laurence Jones & Co; Park Nelson & Co; Collyer Bristow; Blythe Dutton; McKenna & Co; Stibbard Gibson; Piesse & Sons; Montagu's Cox & Cardale; Pothecary & Barratt and other well known firms.

In the 1930s the work began to change. There was far more High Court work, settling pleadings, attending before the judges and masters in chambers and more unusual work; viewing at Winchester and Peckham Rye; attending at *The Times* and the Foreign Office; attending a conference with Sir William Jowitt; instructions to settle a case stated; drafting an apology; drafting a petition for leave to appeal to the House of Lords in *forma pauperis*; and in 1933 the first brief of 50 guineas. In 1932 his clerk was advising that he ought not to be seen going about in the county courts and that he should leave this class of work for other members of the chambers. In 1934 there was a brief on an enquiry for damages, a number of briefs at 50 guineas and a brief on an appeal of 90 guineas. In 1936 there were briefs of 125, 135, and 235 guineas, the latter being the highest fee that he obtained as a junior.

Denning found the work at the Bar to be one of joys and disappointments. He thought that this made life interesting but rather precarious. When he was pressed the constant clash of cases was a great trial but he does not seem to have got rattled. When business was slack and there were no more papers to read he would say that his practice was at an end. In his letter to Mary of 27 February 1930 he wrote: 'All this winning and losing cases is rather exciting isn't it?'[6] He much preferred being in court to drafting papers in chambers. When he was very busy he found difficulty in finding time to go to the barber or have a fitting with his tailor. Nevertheless he wrote to Mary every day that they were apart; her poor health forced frequent separations.

Business came in different ways. In 1931 Pritt recommended Denning to the Canadian Government and he was briefed with Pritt as his leader. In the same year Lady Dilkes had written to the Attorney-General telling him about Denning and he had received his first brief from the Crown at the Exeter Assizes. This proved a frustrating experience as the case was continually postponed and he lost work in London as a result. Anthony Moir, who lived in the same lodgings in Chelsea as Denning, worked for Fladgate & Co and introduced him to that firm in 1929. Moir subsequently became the senior partner and Sir Winston Churchill's personal solicitor. Reputation is very important for a barrister. Mr Bishop, the solicitor for the Southern Railway, thought very highly of Denning and no doubt mentioned him to other solicitors. He was also getting work on the Western Circuit.

By the mid-thirties Denning was getting very busy. In his letter to Mary of 12 March 1934 he wrote: 'I have had people to see me continuously today – seven conferences one after the other all day – and it is now 6.10 p.m.'[7] There was always the worry about cases clashing. About this time he had three cases in court on the same day, one of his own after a part heard, one being led by Samuels and the last in the Court of Appeal, led by Henn Collins, second in the list. As it turned out his own case was settled, Samuels was ill so his case was adjourned, and Henn Collins' case was never reached. Denning was liable to overwork and Henn Collins often pressed him to walk home with him to Chelsea. On 5 February 1934 Denning wrote to Mary: 'I have made up my mind at all events not to work too late in the evenings because it affects my work next day if I do.'[8] It was not always so busy however and in May 1935 he wrote: 'General depression reigns over chambers owing to lack of work.'[9] This was only a temporary hiccup – according to the fee books fees did go down a little in 1935 but were well up again in 1936. Sometimes when work was slack Henn Collins, O'Hagan and Denning would hold a moot for their pupils.

Among Denning's papers are some notes on the art of advocacy which throw light on his own practice:

1 Be brief in re-examination.
2 Open clearly, but not at too great length.

3 Never call unnecessary witnesses.
4 Never interrupt opponent or object to questions unless it is flagrant.
5 Do not labour points of law.
6 Do not speak too loud.
7 'Take this from me, that what grief soever a man hath, ill words work no good and learned counsel never use them.' Coke
8 Treat every court with the utmost respect: express what you have to say, if justified, firmly but with patience.
9 Brevity, clarity and fairness: slow in speech.
10 In summing up, even to a judge, state briefly the law before proceeding to the facts.
11 Accept the word of counsel absolutely.
12 If you have one good point and other doubtful technical points, do not take the technical points but rely on the good point, for the weakness of one may influence the tribunal in regard to the others by way of creating a suspicion of unsoundness.
13 Always prepare the first few sentences of a speech – it is highly important to start off slowly, clearly, with confidence without fumbling for words.[10]

He thought that you win more cases with oil than with vinegar; and that there had been a change in the style of advocacy in his day. No longer was oratory and declamation the fashion but the quiet reasoned representation of the case.

One of the ways that a barrister hopes to get known is to write or edit a book. In Denning's case he was asked to assist in editing *Smith's Leading Cases*. In 1837 John William Smith collected together the leading cases of his time on all aspects of the law with a commentary on each of them. New editions were brought out from time to time and Sir Thomas Willes Chitty was editing the 13th Edition. He asked Cyril Harvey and Denning to help him and Denning's section related to commercial cases. Denning's urge to restate the law can be found in the notes to this edition. He re-wrote the notes on three leading cases: on *Lamplugh* v *Braithwaite* (23 pages on consideration), on *Cutter* v *Powell* (48 pages on part performance), and *Taylor* v *Caldwell* (25 pages on impossibility of performance). He subsequently had the satisfaction of knowing that these notes came to be accepted by later judges as the law without recognition of their origin. The 13th Edition was published by Sweet & Maxwell in two volumes in 1929, each volume containing over 900 pages. Denning found that being one of the editors of *Smith's Leading Cases* was very hard work but he said that it taught him a great deal of law. When he became a judge he was asked to edit another edition but he did not have the time. The 13th was the last edition of that famous work.

In February 1932 Denning was asked by the publishers to act as supervising editor of Bullen & Leake's *Precedents for Pleadings in the King's Bench Division*, 9th edition. Arthur Grattan Bellew of his chambers was asked to do the spade work. This was a practitioner's book of precedents of pleading in the King's Bench Division. This was good experience for junior counsel whose duties included drawing pleadings in common law actions. Henn Collins thought that Denning was unwise to undertake this as he did not have sufficient time. He was quite right as Denning had the greatest difficulty in finding the time to do the work and the 9th edition was not published until May 1935. He was paid a fee of £250 and allowed Bellew the sum of £180. Bellew had done most of the work and had even prepared the table of cases himself. Denning and Bellew presented O'Hagan with a signed copy of the book inscribed 'To our master in the law'.

As Denning worked in the Middle Temple he was called *ad eundum* to the Middle Temple which in those days cost £25. As well as being a member of Lincoln's Inn he needed to be a member of Middle Temple to enable him to take over the tenancy of a new set of chambers and also to lunch in Middle Temple Hall. His success at the Bar meant that he needed chambers of his own. Early in 1932 he was negotiating for a set of chambers in Brick Court at £187 10s per annum. His clerk bought a second-hand roll top desk, and a chair and a typewriter, all for £5 4s. A set of Law Reports was bought for £120 and he moved into the new set of chambers on 5 April 1932. He lunched daily in Hall when in London and often shared a table with Theobald Matthew. Matthew wrote a book – *Forensic Fables* – in which one fable, entitled 'The double first and the old hand', dealt with a real case where Martin O'Connor and Denning were the respective counsel. The first class – Denning – had a good case and was confident of success but he was no match for the old hand who won hands down. Denning was clearly getting noticed as, writing to Mary in October 1932, he said: 'Henn Collins said that my performance (in the Court of Appeal) was admirable, and apparently one of the Lord Justices at lunch told Henn Collins that I had a pleasing manner.'[11]

In 1934 the case of *L'Estrange* v *Graucob Ltd*[12] brought him a lot of work. A lady with a tobacconist's shop in North Wales entered into a contract in writing to purchase an automatic slot machine. The machine was delivered but it did not work. She refused to pay the instalments under the contract. There was in the contract in very small print an exemption clause 'excluding any express or implied condition or warranty, statutory or otherwise'. The lady won in the County Court and the defendant company appealed to the Court of Appeal. The Court of Appeal consisted of Scrutton and Maughan, and Denning submitted that the lady had signed the contract and that in the absence of fraud or misrepresentation she was bound. The Court of Appeal held that that was the law at the time and reversed the County Court judge. The Company was very pleased and had the judgment privately printed and circulated. After this Denning went round the County Courts, often winning cases for his clients. In those days Denning was most concerned to win his cases and to make his living. When he became a judge, however, he did all in his power to minimise the effects of exemption clauses. As he once said: 'If you are an advocate you want your client to win, you want to do well for him, and for your career and so on. When you are a judge you don't care who wins exactly. All you are concerned with is justice.'[13]

A pupil of Denning, who started his pupillage in 1936, remembers that he paid 100 guineas for the privilege and that Denning, as a junior, was earning as much as the Permanent Secretary to the Lord Chancellor: over £3,000 a year. In the 1930s a barrister thought that his duty to his pupils was done if he permitted the pupils to read his papers and go into court with him. Denning had not attended conferences with solicitors and clients when he was a pupil and did not invite his pupils to attend conferences. If a pupil drafted a pleading he did not correct it nor did the pupil see the pleading subsequently drafted by Denning. If, however, a pupil asked for an explanation of a particular point he would willingly give it. He would send a pupil into the Library to look up all the cases on a certain subject which might have a bearing on the case in hand.

All the pupils of Henn Collins and O'Hagan shared a pupil room and at tea-time all the members of chambers would meet for tea and biscuits. Sometimes Denning would come into the room and say: 'I am very worried. I cannot find the case I want.' He would then go to the shelves and find it immediately. Lord Havers tells a similar story of when he was a judge's marshal. Denning, Byrne and Henn Collins were on Assize together and one of their customs was to lunch together in the Library of the Assize Court. Inevitably they talked about their cases. On one occasion Denning said: 'I think the case of *McManus* v *Bowes* covers this problem.' The marshal went to the shelves where the Law Reports were kept to find the case. Denning went on: 'You will find it in 1938 1 KB in the judgment of Lord Justice Slesser on page 123 at, I think, the paragraph which starts "I would add a few words." ' That Denning was a good pupil master is indicated by a letter he wrote to Mary on 1 July 1935: 'Sir Sidney Rowlatt (retired judge) said he had made inquiries in two very distinguished quarters for advice about a pupil and both said that Denning was the best person for him to come to. This new pupil is John Clifford who was at Eton and Merton.'[14]

Denning acted as Chancellor of the Diocese of Southwark from 1937 until his appointment as a judge in 1944 and was Chancellor of the Diocese of London from 1942–44. In the Diocese of London the official title was 'Vicar-General in Spiritualities and Official Principal and also Commissary and Sequestrator General'. On 5 January 1943 *The Times* reported that Denning and Wigglesworth acted for the Archbishop of Canterbury in a case where certiorari was sought to have a decision of the Bishop of Bath and Wells reversed. The application was refused. Certiorari is a writ directed to an inferior tribunal requiring the proceedings to be transferred to the High Court to be dealt with there. In 1944 he wrote an article in the *Law Quarterly Review* entitled 'Meaning of Ecclesiastical Law'.[15] In this article he explained that ecclesiastical law meant the law administered by ecclesiastical courts and persons. This was the discipline of the clergy in matters of doctrine and ritual, the grant of faculties, the grant of marriage licences and matters relating to consecration, sequestration of livings, dilapidations, monuments, parsonage houses and repairs. On all these subjects the Chancellor has to adjudicate. A Chancellor is usually an experienced practising barrister who is a communicant member of the Church of England.

Denning's last case as a junior was one in which he was led by

Sir William Jowitt before Mr Justice Swift and a special jury.[16] Major Richardson had insured his life for £80,000. The policy would expire unless he could find the premium by 3 p.m. on a June afternoon. At 2.30 p.m. on that afternoon he went to see his solicitor in Chancery Lane. At 2.45 p.m. he took a taxi back to his flat in Albermarle Street and said to the taxi driver: 'As you pass St James's Palace look at the time shown on the clock and note it.' As the driver passed St James's Palace it was three minutes to three. Driving up St James's Street the driver heard a loud bang, stopped the taxi and got out. It was then two minutes to three. The major was dead. Denning was instructed by the personal representatives who claimed the money from the insurance company. The company argued that suicide was a crime and the estate could not claim the money even though there was a contract to pay. The jury found in favour of the estate but said that the major was of sound mind. On appeal the Court of Appeal had no difficulty in reversing the judge on the ground that the estate could not benefit from the crime of the deceased. The personal representatives appealed to the House of Lords and Sir William Jowitt had to leave early so that the case was left in Denning's hands. It was to no avail as the House of Lords held that it was contrary to public policy to permit policy moneys to be paid out on account of a crime. Nowadays the personal representatives would have been successful as by the Suicide Act 1961 suicide is no longer a crime.

Denning had a very wide experience at the Junior Bar. He started in the magistrates' courts and the county courts. He appeared before King's Bench judges both in civil and criminal cases and made many appearances in chambers before judges and masters. He made the occasional foray into the Chancery Division. He was a specialist in ecclesiastical law. His practice took him to the Court of Appeal and the House of Lords but his particular strength was in commercial law. He had taken sale of goods and charterparties as special subjects in the Bar examination. He was the pupil of a commercial specialist and being one of the editors of *Smith's Leading Cases* gave him a good grounding in commercial law. He had a good all round common law experience.

Denning had been a junior for fifteen years when he applied for silk on 15 January 1938. In those days a junior had to notify all those senior to him on his own circuit. If he were refused this was a bad mark against him. Denning took the plunge and wrote a short letter of application to the Lord Chancellor. Today there are ten times as many applications and very few are successful on the first application. Only about a quarter of the applications are granted. Each applicant has to fill in a form giving, among other things, details of his earnings. The announcement that Denning was successful was made on 1 April 1938 and he was sworn in before the Lord Chancellor, Lord Maughan, on 7 April. On 3 August his son, Robert, was born. In 1938 Denning was one of only fifteen chosen. No longer was he permitted to draft pleadings and his work was limited to appearing in court and giving opinions. Among the congratulations received was a letter from Rayner Goddard (later Lord Chief Justice Goddard) saying that to be a silk was rather like travelling first class; it also meant that you had more room for your papers.[17] His mentor, D.N.Pritt, wrote: 'A silk and a lawyer, a rare and precious combination'. The solicitor for the Southern Railway wrote: 'I'm impressed by your great ability. Ready at short notice to speedily assist me. You have certainly made your mark at the Bar. I predict a great future.' John Whitford (later Mr Justice Whitford) said: 'I understand you have succeeded in a very crowded field.'

His earnings did not go down as sometimes happens when a man first takes silk but remained on a plateau. It must be remembered that most of the time that he was a silk was during the war. His earnings as a silk were as follows: 1938 – £3,310; 1939 – £3,274; 1940 – £3,230; 1941 – £2,350; 1942 – £3,825; 1943 – £3,500. There were many briefs at 100 guineas and 150 guineas and the largest brief received was 300 guineas in 1940.[18] Despite his success at the Bar Denning was not a fashionable silk, nor did he earn large fees. Norman Birkett was earning £30,000 while Denning was earning £3000. He was a good advocate but did not have the verbal fluency of the top flight advocate. He was too hesitant. He was not an orator in the same way that Edward Marshall Hall or Birkett were; nor would he have been described as 'silver tongued' as was Lord Mansfield. He did not have the great skill in cross-examination enjoyed by the greatest advocates. His great skill was as a judge. Although Birkett was appointed a judge before Denning, Denning was the better judge and was appointed to the Court of Appeal before Birkett. The greatest advocates seldom feel at home in the Court of Appeal or the House of Lords as they miss the excitement of the court-room struggle.

Just over a year after taking silk the war came and changed everything. He was forty and too old for active service. He volunteered to do anything needed and was invited to go and see Sir Alexander Maxwell, Permanent Secretary at the Home Office. Sir Alexander said that England was to be divided into self-governing regions so that if one region was cut off the others could function independently. Each region was to have its own Regional Commissioner and a Legal Adviser. Denning was asked to act as Legal Adviser for the North East Region, with no pay except travelling expenses, and he accepted the appointment. Hartley Shawcross (later Lord Shawcross) became the Legal Adviser for the South East and Charles Romer (later Lord Justice Romer) for the North Midlands.

Leeds was the headquarters for the North East Region and Denning frequently travelled there, always by train. The wartime journeys took seven or eight hours owing to air raids, bombs and alerts. Most of the work at Leeds was to detain people under Regulation 18B. The military collected information about individuals who were suspected and laid it before Denning. If an investigation was required he saw the person and asked questions. The suspect could be represented by lawyers. In one case there was a parson known as the 'Nazi Parson' in a village in Yorkshire. He was a Nazi sympathiser and spent his holidays in Germany. The military were afraid that German parachutists might land on his lonely vicarage. Although there was no proof against him Denning detained him under Regulation 18B. The Bishop of Ripon protested, but in vain. The power to detain was discretionary and could not be questioned in the courts.

It was in 1941 that Denning was involved in a case which went to the House of Lords.[19] The case was heard during the evacuation from Dunkirk. The case itself was complex and of no particular interest. Denning was apprehensive in opening the appeal as the plaintiff had failed in all the lower courts. Lord Atkin encouraged him and asked a few questions. Denning was under the impression that Atkin asked the questions with the object of bringing his colleagues round to his point of view.[20] The simple point was whether, if the action had not been started in the right form, judgment could be given in the plaintiff's favour. The plaintiff was successful and in Atkin's judgment appears the famous sentence: 'When the ghosts of the past stand in the path of justice, clanking their medieval chains, the proper course for the judge is to pass through them undeterred.' Denning was so sure that the Court of Appeal decision was wrong that he had offered to conduct the case in the House of Lords for no fee as the plaintiff could not afford the costs of an appeal and there was no legal aid at that time.

The year 1941 was the worst one of the war for the Denning family: Denning's father, Charles, died in February; their friend and helper, Rose, left them to join the WRNS; Denning caught meningitis travelling on dirty trains to Leeds and would have died if he had not been dosed with the recently discovered M&B; Mary fell ill with gallstones and was admitted to the Brompton Hospital. At home Mary's old nanny came to the rescue to look after Robert and Mr Parker tended the garden.

Mary's operation was successful and she was allowed home for three or four weeks. One evening Denning, working in his study, heard a knock on the ceiling. He rushed upstairs to Mary who said: 'I've had a haemorrhage' and had coughed up blood. Dr Marshall came down to Cuckfield to see her and administered oxygen. He believed there to be just a hope if he could get her to Brompton Hospital. She was taken by ambulance to the hospital where she had a very distressed night. Denning remained all night by her side. Early in the morning of 22 November 1941 she died peacefully. The Dennings had lived at Cuckfield for seven years and Mary had been an active member of the Church. She was buried in the churchyard and each Sunday Denning took Robert to the children's service and then tended her grave.

It is not surprising that as a result of his war work in Leeds Denning's practice at the Bar suffered and his earnings fell from £3,230 in 1940 to £2,350 in 1941. In 1942 he did another appeal without charge but this time it was in the Court of Appeal and not in the House of Lords.[21] It was a case of professional negligence. A child had warts on her face and was admitted to Essex County Hospital for treatment. The radiologist was negligent and as a result the child was badly burned and disfigured. There was an earlier decision that a hospital was not liable for the negligence of its professional staff and the judge of the lower court felt bound to follow the previous decision and decided against the child. The reason for the earlier decision was probably one of policy. The court had felt that it was too much to burden charitable hospitals with actions for damages – this was before the advent of the National Health Service. Denning, building on the arguments of Professor Arthur Goodhart in the *Law Quarterly Review*, persuaded the Court of Appeal to overrule the earlier case and award damages. The clients were so pleased that they presented Denning with a table lamp for his chambers.

Denning continued to go on circuit during the war and in July 1942 was instructed by the Attorney-General to defend a young sailor charged with murder for strangling a girl on Southampton Common. Denning went to see the sailor the night before the trial in the cells at Winchester prison. He found him dirty and unkempt and told him to clean himself up before the trial which was to be held in the Great Hall at Winchester. The defence was that the girl had slapped his face and that he had put his hands round her throat and she had died. The only hope was to reduce the offence from murder to manslaughter on the grounds of provocation. The next morning the young sailor appeared clean and spruced up for the trial. The judge, Mr Justice Charles, thought very little of the defence. When Denning was about to put forward the defence of provocation to the jury the judge intervened: there was not enough evidence of provocation for the charge to be reduced to manslaughter. Denning insisted that he should put the defence of provocation to the jury and did so.

The judge, in summing up, told the jury that there was no defence of provocation here and that it was a clear case of murder. It was a Hampshire jury and Denning thought that it helped that he was a Hampshire man. In the event the jury found the accused guilty of manslaughter only. In those days a man was hanged for murder and the jury did not want this to happen. The judge was very angry and said to the jury: 'Get out of the box. You've been false to your oaths. You are not fit to be there.' In sentencing the sailor the judge said that he had to accept the verdict but sentenced him to thirteen years imprisonment. Denning considered the sentence too long for manslaughter and told the sailor that he could appeal. He also informed him, however, that the Court of Criminal Appeal could increase the sentence if they so wished. Afterwards he received a note from the sailor in prison saying that in view of the chance of an increase in sentence he had decided not to appeal. He said: 'the possibility of my sentence being at all increased is too much for me to consider.' He added the thanks of his mother and father and ended: 'No one could have possibly done more than you did.'[22] Speaking on the radio in the 1960s Denning said: 'In all serious criminal cases I would be wholeheartedly in favour of trial by jury and indeed it is a most useful corrective against any technicalities of the lawyers, or indeed against harsh laws.'[23]

In December 1943 Mr Justice Wrottesley was taken ill on circuit at Manchester and the Lord Chancellor, Lord Simon, asked Denning to go to Manchester as a Commissioner of Assize to take his place.[24] In those days being made a Commissioner was regarded as a trial run for a judgship and Denning was only forty-four years old. He sat at Manchester for three weeks. The leader of the circuit was Mr George Lynskey KC (later Mr Justice Lynskey) who told Denning afterwards that he had won 'golden opinions' for his work as a Commissioner.

On 26 Feburary 1944 Denning was appointed Recorder of Plymouth in the place of Mr J.C.Trapnell KC who had been appointed an Official Referee. He had previously acted as Deputy Recorder at Southampton when there had been an interregnum between two recorders in 1941. On 6 March 1944 when arguing a case in the House of Lords[25] the Lord Chancellor, Lord Simon, asked Denning to come to his room. He said that he would like Denning to become a judge and, if he agreed, he wished to appoint him to the Probate, Admiralty and Divorce Division. Another judge was needed to cope with the great increase in divorce petitions. Denning had some reservations about being a divorce judge but agreed. At Lord Simon's express request the announcement of the appointment was made before Denning's case in the House of Lords was finished.[26]

Three

HIGH COURT JUDGE
1944–48

*The social service which the judge renders to the community is the
removal of a sense of injustice.*[1]

Lord Devlin

Denning was appointed a High Court judge on 7 March 1944 at
a salary of £5,000 and went to Buckingham Palace to receive the
customary knighthood on 15 March 1944. He was assigned to the
Probate, Admiralty and Divorce Division and although he may have
known something of Probate and Admiralty law he had no practical
experience of divorce law. The general opinion in the 1930s was that
divorce law was unpleasant and inferior and this opinion was shared
by Denning: 'The best juniors did not touch it. No one in our
chambers did any. The fashionable silks might now and again, if
paid enough. But not us.'[2] There was at the time a great need for
more divorce judges because of the increase of divorce work caused
by wartime separation. Denning said that he never refused any
appointment except when Lord Gardiner asked him to return to the
House of Lords in 1968.[3] Divorce work did not present any legal
difficulties and although Denning had no previous experience this
was no bar to his appointment. On becoming a judge Denning was
elected a Bencher of his Inn, Lincoln's Inn, and subsequently became
Treasurer of the Inn in 1964.

Many have commented on the fact that he was appointed a judge
at such a young age. Patrick Devlin (later Lord Devlin) wrote: 'Of
course a seat on the bench was your inevitable destiny, but it is nice
that you should have got there so young.'[4] Others were glad that
a sound and learned lawyer had been appointed. Guy Aldous said:
'It can only be for the benefit of the law generally that the greatest
lawyers be appointed to the Bench.' Henn Collins' daughter, Pamela,
wrote: 'I remember when you first became a pupil of my father his
saying: "That young man will go far".' An old pupil, M.F.V.Swan,

said: 'Besides your thoroughness (how well I remember it) there can be nobody before whom it would be pleasanter to appear.' Harry Vaisey looked at the appointment from another point of view: 'I am delighted except for the sake of the Church of England which is now deprived of one of its few remaining buttresses.' The general opinion was, however, that it was a waste of Denning's abilities to make him a divorce judge and that he should be transferred to the King's Bench Division as soon as possible as there he would have more scope. From the point of view of his own career the appointment was the best thing that could have happened to him. It widened his experience in an important field of law unknown to him and proved invaluable when he became a judge in the Court of Appeal. In writing to congratulate him Mr Justice Luxmore said that the Athenaeum Club usually invited newly appointed judges to be members without paying the entrance fee and that he would be happy to propose him. Denning was not a club man but he did join the Athenaeum.

Denning disliked divorce work. In those days everything depended on proof of a matrimonial offence and private enquiry agents gave evidence of unpleasant snooping. Cases could go on for days to find out who was to blame for the breakdown of the marriage. For the first few months of his service as a judge he sat in London. It was during the war and the time of the flying bombs. On one occasion, when he arrived at the courts for work, he found the windows of his room shattered and broken glass everywhere. Denning recollects that he did go out on circuit with Mr Justice Cassels; the latter dealt with eighty-three undefended divorce cases in one day while the less experienced Denning did fifty-two. Although Denning did not like divorce work he immediately set out to master the law and procedure. A solicitor's legal executive once found Denning at Somerset House obtaining a copy of a decree nisi. Denning said that he had been appointed a judge and wanted to find out what went on before the case came into court for hearing. The legal executive explained to him the procedure from the time of filing the petition until the case came into court.[5]

For the first year of his service on the Bench he always gave an extempore judgment. His first reserved judgment was not given until 28 March 1945.[6] He said that this was good advice for a new judge.[7] This practice was first pioneered by Lord Mansfield in 1756 as he felt that when judgment was clear and obvious it was for the benefit of the parties and the judge himself that judgment should be delivered forthwith and without more ado. Denning was clearly of this opinion and also thought that it was good practice for a new judge to accustom himself to giving immediate judgment. The fact that he was in the Divorce Division perhaps made it easier to carry out this resolve. This is a difficult art and requires great skill and practice to perfect it.

In giving judgment Denning tried to make himself clear so that he could easily be understood by the parties. He called the parties by their names and did not speak of plaintiff and defendant. In telling the story he set out the merits as the merits show where justice lies. He used short sentences and tried to cultivate a style which commanded attention. A judge speaks to give judgment and he attempts to persuade all his hearers, lawyers and laymen alike, that his judgment is right. His reasons are given to persuade and justify but if his judgment is dull or difficult to follow his hearers may fail to pay attention. If the judgment is lively and interesting people will attend and take notice. He thought that style was the dress of thought and that the first few sentences set the tone.

Denning was an excellent storyteller and his distinctive style was to record the facts in the form of a story. He wrote:

I try to make my judgment live – so that it can be readily understood. ... I start my judgment, as it were, with a prologue – to introduce the story. Then I go on from act to act as Shakespeare does – each with its scenes – drawn from real life .... I draw the characters as they truly are – using their real names – .... I avoid long sentences like the plague: because they lead to obscurity. It is no good if the hearers cannot follow them. I strive to be clear at all costs. Not ambiguous or prevaricating. I refer sometimes to previous authorities – I have to do so – because I know that people are prone not to accept my views unless they have support from the books. But never at much length. Only a sentence or two. I avoid all reference to pleadings and orders – They are mere lawyer's stuff. They are unintelligible to anyone else. I finish with a conclusion – an epilogue – again as the chorus does in Shakespeare. In it I gather the threads together and give the result.[8]

Suffice it to give here two classic examples of his style in giving judgment. In *Lloyds Bank Ltd* v *Bundy* he said:

Broadchalke is one of the most pleasing villages in England. Old Herbert Bundy, the defendant, was a farmer there. His home was Yew Tree Farm.

It went back 300 years. His family had been there for generations. It was his only asset. But he did a very foolish thing. He mortgaged it to the Bank. Up to the hilt. Not to borrow money for himself, but for the sake of his son. Now the Bank has come down on him. They have foreclosed. They want to get him out of Yew Tree Farm and sell it. They have brought this action against him for possession. Going out means ruin for him. He was granted legal aid. His lawyers put in a defence. They said that, when he executed the charge to the bank, he did not know what he was doing: or at any rate that the circumstances were such that he ought not to be bound by it. At the trial his plight was plain. The judge was sorry for him. He said he was a 'poor old gentleman'. He was so obviously incapacitated that the judge admitted his proof in evidence. He had a heart attack in the witness box. Yet the judge felt he could do nothing for him. 'There is nothing' he said, 'which takes this case out of the vast range of commercial transactions'. He ordered Herbert Bundy to give up possession of Yew Tree Farm to the bank. Now there is an appeal to this court. The ground is that the circumstances were so exceptional that Herbert Bundy should not be held bound. ... Gathering all together, I would suggest that through all these instances there runs a single thread. They rest on 'inequality of bargaining power'. By virtue of it, the English law gives relief to one who, without independent advice, enters into a contract upon terms which are very unfair or transfers property for a consideration which is grossly inadequate, when his bargaining power is grievously impaired by reason of his own needs or desires, or by his own ignorance or infirmity, coupled with undue influence or pressures brought to bear on him by or for the benefit of others.[9]

The Court of Appeal rejected the bank's claim and were upheld in the House of Lords. The House, however, based its judgment on undue influence.

The other example is *Beswick* v *Beswick*:[10]

Old Peter Beswick was a coal merchant in Eccles, Lancashire. He had no business premises. All he had was a lorry, scales and weights. He used to take the lorry to the yard of the National Coal Board, where he bagged coal and took it round to his customers in the neighbourhood. His nephew, John Joseph Beswick, helped him in the business.

In March 1962, old Peter Beswick and his wife were both over 70. He had had his leg amputated and was not in good health. The nephew was anxious to get hold of the business before the old man died. So they went to a solicitor, Mr Ashcroft, who drew up an agreement for them. The business was to be transferred to the nephew: old Peter Beswick was to be employed in it as a consultant for the rest of his life at £6-10-0 a week. After his death the nephew was to pay to his widow an annuity of £5 a week, which was to come out of the business . . .

After the agreement was signed, the nephew took over the business and ran it. The old man seems to have found it difficult at first to adjust to the new situation, but he settled down. The nephew paid him £6-10-0 a week. But, as expected, he did not live long. He died on 3 Nov 1963, leaving his widow, who is 74 years of age in failing health. The nephew paid her the first £5. But then stopped paying her and has refused to pay her any more . . . .

The action came for hearing before the Vice-Chancellor of the County Palatine of Lancaster, who held that she had no right to enforce the agreement. He dismissed the action.

If the decision of the Vice-Chancellor truly represents the law of England, it would be deplorable. It would mean that the nephew could keep the business to himself, and at the same time repudiate his promise to pay the widow. Nothing could be more unjust. . . .

The general rule undoubtedly is that 'no third person can sue, or be sued, on a contract to which he is not a party': but at bottom that is only a rule of procedure. It goes to the form of the remedy, not to the underlying right. Where a contract is made for the benefit of a third person who has a legitimate interest to enforce it, it can be enforced by the third person in the name of the contracting party or jointly with him or, if he refuses to join, by adding him as a defendant. In that sense, and it is a very real sense, the third person has a right arising by way of contract. . . . The widow is entitled to an order for specific performance of the agreement, by ordering the defendant to pay the arrears of £175, and the instalments of £5 a week as they fall due.

Sometimes, while waiting for judgment to be pronounced, counsel would amuse themselves with a competition as to who could get closest to the first line of Denning's judgment.

Denning seems to have been reversed only once as a divorce judge and this was a case involving connivance.[11] Early in 1945 three of his judgments were reported.[12] In a case heard on 6 July 1945[13] he had to consider the subject of presumptions and burdens of proof in the law of evidence and wrote an article in the *Law Quarterly Review* on the subject.[14] This was an attempt to clarify a difficult branch of the law and he ended the article: 'I am concerned here, not with particular branches of the law, but with a new set of distinctions running through the whole law, in an attempt to remove the confusions produced by the old.' This was in line with his urge to straighten out the law on the basis of old principles.

With the end of the war and the election of a Labour Government, Lord Jowitt became the Lord Chancellor. He did not think that Denning was in the right place in the Divorce Division and transferred him to the King's Bench Division on 24 October 1945. This move met with general approval from the Bar and the Bench.[15] David Scott Cairns (later Lord Justice Cairns) wrote: 'Everybody will be delighted that you are coming back where you belong. ... I am afraid you will not remain long in the King's Bench Division.' H.Glyn-Jones KC (later Mr Justice Glyn-Jones) remarked: 'Welcome home'. Mr Justice Charles wrote: 'You are wasted in the Divorce Division and will add strength to our brotherhood of the King's Bench.' A rather more mundane note was received from Mr Justice Cassels: 'What are you doing about robes? They are very expensive now and Lynskey had to pay an enormous sum. Why not negotiate with James Tucker?' Immediately he was transferred to the King's Bench Division he had to go out as Judge of Assize on the Midland Circuit from October to December 1945.

After Mary's death in November 1941 Denning had sought refuge in work and caring for Robert in the evenings and at weekends. It was a sad and lonely time. On his return from circuit in December 1945 he married again, to Joan, daughter of J.V.Elliott Taylor and widow of J.M.B.Stuart. She had four children, one of whom had died in infancy, two girls, Pauline and Hazel and a boy, John. Denning and Joan had first met at a party given by the Headmaster of Parkfield Preparatory School for parents and prospective parents in September 1945. Joan's son was a pupil at the school and Denning was planning to send Robert there. They discovered that Joan had known Mary when she was a member of a Wives Group at Haywards Heath run by Joan. Owing to the rigidity of the Mothers' Union on the subject of divorce Lady Barton had started a Wives Group at the Church in Haywards Heath and Joan had taken over from her. The Group catered not only for Haywards Heath but for the surrounding area and Mary had come over from Cuckfield.

Joan's first husband had been a civil engineer and she had met him on a visit to her sister in Burma. He was engaged on large engineering work relating to the supply of water and drainage in Burma. Joan spent some time in Burma until her husband came back to

England and joined a firm of civil engineers in London. He often went abroad on his business but they made their home at Haywards Heath where Joan's parents had a house. There she brought up her three children. The eldest, Pauline, married and was engaged in social work. The second, Hazel, went from Roedean to Somerville College, Oxford, to read modern languages. She changed to law and obtained a first class degree is jurisprudence. In 1954 she married Michael Fox, subsequently a Lord Justice of Appeal, and in 1982 became the Director of the British Institute of International and Comparative Law of which Denning had been for many years the President. After school at Repton, John, the third child, joined ICI and, after taking early retirement, enjoyed buying old houses, improving and selling them.

Denning followed up his meeting with Joan by inviting her to lunch at the Savoy Hotel. They were married quietly in the Parish Church at Cuckfield on 27 December 1945. Denning's son and Joan's children were all present. The marriage proved one of great happiness for both of them. Giving an interview to a newspaper in 1982 Joan said:

> His job and all the travelling he has done has meant that I have had to make sacrifices. I haven't always been able to see my family when I would like to have done. ... Life is a funny business. If you don't have a little courage and jump in at the deep end now and again you miss out a lot in life. It's a mistake to be over cautious. We have been very happy. It has worked out very well for our respective families.[16]

After their marriage Joan gave up her house at Haywards Heath and joined Denning at 'Fair Close', Copyhold Lane, Cuckfield.

> The house was built in 1933. Good to look at and to live in. The Arch-deacon of Lewes had designed it himself. He had bought an old Sussex barn – and used the oak timbers and tiles to build it. It was just the right size. Three large bedrooms and two smaller ones. We turned a room down-stairs into my library. We put in shelves and bookcases and housed all the Law Reports – and the English Reports. The house was set in two acres. We bought the adjoining two acres – so as to save it being built upon. We bought another 12 acres of the field – towards the village. The farmer put his cows there. Afterwards we planted trees.[17]

The house was one and a half miles from Haywards Heath station and Denning commuted to London every day in term time. He caught the morning train at 7.55 a.m. or 8.25 a.m. and tried to catch the 4.45 p.m. train back from Victoria. He used to spend the time in the train working. He walked to the station in the morning but was often met by Joan, with the car, in the evening. This he did for seventeen years until he became Master of the Rolls in 1962. In those days he seldom stayed late in London as he was anxious to get home to Joan and the family. He enjoyed felling trees, mowing the grass, extending the tennis court, walking on the Downs or going down to the sea to swim. On Sunday morning they would go to the 8 o'clock service at the church. They took their holidays in Cornwall, sometimes in Ireland and once in Scotland, surfing, sailing or walking on the cliffs and shore.

Immediately after his marriage Denning went on circuit:

Then I exercised the privilege always accorded to a new judge. I chose to go my own circuit, the Western. My wife drove in her old car DGP 745 (we called it 'Dogpie') with my son of 7 and stepdaughter of 17. I do not drive. I always say: 'If anyone is to be convicted of careless driving, it is not this judge.' All the way round the Western Circuit. Those lovely places – Salisbury, Dorchester, Wells, Bodmin and on to Exeter, 'the ever faithful city'.[18]

Although Denning did not drive, Joan was a skilled and keen driver, still driving in her nineties. Her father held the first driving licence in London. Denning was looking forward to going on to Bristol and Winchester. His mother was still alive and it would be an opportunity to visit her. This, however, was not to be as the Lord Chancellor, Lord Jowitt, recalled him from Exeter to chair a committee on the procedure in divorce cases.

The object of this committee was to seek ways of speeding up the hearing of divorce cases. The committee was a strong one including Terence Donovan (later Lord Donovan), Sir Edwin Herbert (later Lord Tangley), and John Foster (later Sir John Foster). The secretary was Tom Skyrme (later Sir Thomas Skyrme) of the Lord Chancellor's Department. Denning took no time off from his work as a judge and the committee sat in a Committee Room in the House of Lords from 4.30 p.m. until 7 p.m. John Foster was successful in listening to the evidence and writing letters at the same time. The committee was appointed on 26 June 1946 and worked swiftly.[19] In July 1946, the first interim report was published, price one penny, which recommended the reduction of the time between decree nisi and decree absolute from six months to six weeks.[20] This was implemented at once. A second interim report was published in November 1946, price sixpence, recommending that County Court judges should be appointed as commissioners to try cases and suggesting procedural reforms relating to the contents of the petition, affidavits, service, evidence and fixed dates for trial.[21]

The final report, published in February 1947, price ninepence, recommended the establishment of a Marriage Welfare Service.[22] Denning was impressed by the methods used in the Chancery Division when dealing with wards of court. In many cases the infant was made a party and could put forward his or her point of view through the official solicitor who was appointed guardian for the purposes of the suit. The Government was not anxious to set up a Marriage Welfare Service on account of the cost. The Lord Chancellor did not propose to take any speedy action although divorce cases were running at about 50,000 per annum at that time. He hoped that the figures would come down to 10,000 a year and did not want to take any hasty action. He thought that voluntary organisations could fill the gap. This was wishful thinking. Eventually the committee's recommendations were adopted and a Court Welfare Service was set up staffed by professional social workers paid by the State. Their service soon proved of such value that their help was sought by the Chancery Division as well as by the Divorce Division.

The President of the Probate, Admiralty and Divorce Division, Lord Merriman, had given evidence to the committee and had proposed a scheme for the reform of practice and a commission of conciliation which would work in tribunals. The committee did not follow these recommendations but Denning failed to consult Lord Merriman before the report was published as he should have done. Denning subsequently admitted that this was a mistake on his part but Lord Merriman never forgave him.[23] Meeting Denning later he said: 'You are a blackguard, you ought to have consulted me.'[24] After the report was published the committee held a dinner to which the Lord Chancellor was invited. He presented Denning with a copy of the report bound in leather in which he wrote:

> To Mr Justice Denning
> With all my thanks

for the great work he has done
23rd April 1947   Jowitt C.

All the members of the committee signed the copy report.

In paragraph 19 of the report the committee had considered the history and work of the Marriage Guidance Council. This was a voluntary organisation, registered as a charity, formed in 1938. The work was brought to a standstill by the war in 1939 but was reconstituted in 1943 and had grown rapidly. It had opened Marriage Guidance Centres in London and several in the provinces. The work at the Centres was done by carefully selected counsellors. They were trained to recognise the nature of the matrimonial disharmony and deal with the case in the most appropriate way. Sometimes they would themselves try to reconcile husband and wife. Often they would refer the parties to specialists. People came to the Centres from every section of society. Sometimes magistrates, after a court hearing, would suggest to couples that they should seek expert advice at the Centres.

The committee had recommended in paragraph 29 of the report that it should be recognised as a function of the State to give encouragement and financial help to marriage guidance as a form of social service. In 1949 Denning was approached to become President of the National Marriage Guidance Council. He accepted and took an active part for many years, taking the chair at the Annual General Meeting and attending annual conferences. There were many problems of finance, staffing and individual differences. In 1950 he addressed the Council concluding his address by saying: 'The only basis for a sound family life is Christian marriage – the personal union of one man with one woman, to the exclusion of all others on either side, for better or worse, so long as both shall live.'[25] The work of the Council continued to grow and in the Foreword to the Marriage and Family Trust brochure of 1979 Denning wrote that the movement had become one of the most valuable of the social services.

Denning frequently remarked that adultery was no bar to advancement in any office of the State, high or low, while any other form of stealing would mean the end of a career. He said: 'Adultery is not the concern of the parties alone. It is the concern of the whole community because it strikes at the foundation of marriage and marriage is the basis of that family life on which the moral strength of the country depends.' Speaking in Australia in 1967 he said: 'We should do everything of course to maintain the marriage if we can, but if it has irretrievably broken down let the empty shell be buried and done away with with as much quietness and lack of bitterness and lack of humiliation as possible.'[26] He was not sure that the Church was right to set its face against re-marriage in church after divorce. One party might be quite innocent and wish to re-marry. He thought that marrying in church would give a better start in life and that the Church should show mercy and permit the marriage.

When Denning had been transferred to the King's Bench Division he had been nominated by the Lord Chancellor to hear Pension Appeals. He thought that the Minister and Pensions Tribunals had been applying the wrong principles and took steps to put them right. The Minister had put upon the applicant the burden of proving that his injury or illness was due to war service. Denning changed the burden of proof. He held that if a man or woman were fit when he or she joined up and unfit when discharged the burden was on the Minister to prove that the injury or illness was not due to war service. The slogan was: 'Fit for service, fit for pension.'[27] In the leading case of *Starr* v *Ministry of Pensions* he said that prior to 1943 the claimant was not entitled to a pension unless there was good and sufficient evidence that his disability was due to war service.[28] But by Article 4(2) of the Royal Warrant of December 1943 it was stated: 'In no case shall there be an onus on any claimant to prove the fulfilment of the prescribed conditions and the benefit of any reasonable doubt shall be given to the claimant.' Denning used this article as the justification for interpreting the regulations in favour of claimants. This was to tip the scales in favour of the claimant instead of in favour of the Crown.

This ruling did not affect past cases where pensions had been refused and the claimants were out of time for appeal. In the case of *James* v *Minister of Pensions*, heard on 28 July 1947, Denning held that where an application is made out of time to a Pensions Appeal Tribunal for leave to appeal, and the tribunal refuses to grant an extension of time, the nominated judge for Pensions Appeals has jurisdiction to give leave to appeal and to extend the time.[29] Denning, throughout his career, always maintained that a judge had an inherent jurisdiction to extend time when the demands of justice require it. The Rules of the Supreme Court provide that time for compliance with the rules may always be extended if deemed necessary by the court.

These two cases made a profound difference to applicants for pensions. Many just cases had been turned down as the claimant could not provide the evidence needed. The Minister stated that all those whose claims had been rejected by tribunals up to 31 July 1946 should have the right to have their cases reviewed by the Minister with appeal to a special tribunal. Counsel for the British Legion informed Denning that this system worked well and that many people whose claims had previously been rejected had been awarded pensions under the Royal Warrant. There was no appeal from the judge for Pensions Appeals and Denning enjoyed the freedom of being able to do justice without having to be constantly looking over his shoulder to satisfy a higher court. These decisions were popular with the public and in the climate of public opinion at the time the Minister would not want to oppose them too vigorously. Mr Paget paid tribute to Denning's work in the House of Commons and the Norbury branch of the British Legion wrote to him to indicate their deep appreciation of his work saying: 'by his penetrating investigation and clear exposition he had won their entire confidence.'[30]

In the long vacation of 1947 Denning tried a case at the Old Bailey which lasted six weeks.[31] Six men were charged with black market offences during the war. There were many witnesses and many documents. The summing up took three hours; five were convicted and one acquitted. The five appealed and their conviction was quashed, not on the ground of any fault in the summing up, but because the indictment did not contain separate counts of what was alleged against each of the accused. The Court of Criminal Appeal held that if the law of criminal conspiracy was to be invoked, as it had in this case, then each count of the indictment should be so framed so as to enable the jury to put their finger on any specific part of the conspiracy. This was not just a technicality but raised the important question of a fair trial. The accused were entitled to know the exact crimes that each had committed, as the length of sentence might be affected if convicted of some and acquitted of others. Denning was concerned with the merits of the case and had no doubt the jury was entitled to its view. Denning was always keen to nail the rogue and this had a higher priority with him than the procedural question of a fair trial. He thought that this case might imperil his chances of promotion to the Court of Appeal, but it did not.

This case does indicate Denning's propensity to give priority to the merits of the action over procedural matters such as a fair trial. There has been another instance of this where he has been much criticised. This was the case of *Ward* v *Bradford Corporation* where a young girl, Gillian Ward, was expelled from a teachers' training college after being found with a man in her room at night.[32] The two rules of natural justice are that no man should be judge in his own cause and that each side be heard. An assistant education officer had been present throughout the hearing and had advised the board on the policy they ought to adopt in the particular case. This was technically a breach of the first rule of natural justice. Denning said:

I do not think she has been treated unfairly or unjustly. She has broken the rules most flagrantly. I say nothing about her morals. She claims that they are her own affair ... But instead of going into lodgings, she had this man with her night after night. That is a fine example to set to others! And she is a girl training to be a teacher! She would never make a teacher. No parent would knowingly entrust their child to her care.

Two other Court of Appeal judges, Phillimore and Orr, agreed with him.

Denning always maintained that when a judge sits he too is on trial.[33] He must be dignified and earn the respect of all who appear before him. He must be understanding and merciful. He strongly supported the retention of trial by jury in serious criminal cases. In civil cases he followed the tide of current opinion which was to eliminate juries altogether except in cases of libel and slander. He felt that there should be no civil juries unless there were exceptional circumstances, and no juries in running down cases. He held strong views on summing up. He deplored cases where the judge recited all the evidence or thought that all that was necessary was to give the jury a short outline of the evidence. The jury had heard all the evidence and to 'sum up' meant just that. The jury brought common sense into the law and could, perhaps, assist in changing it. This is precisely what happened in 1770 in *R* v *Miller* when John Miller, the printer of the *London Evening Post* was tried for seditious libel.[34] Lord Mansfield directed the jury that the question of libel or no libel was a matter for the judge as this was the law at the time. The jury refused to accept this and a verdict of 'not guilty' was entered. As a result of this verdict and pressure in Parliament, the law was changed by

Parliament in Fox's Libel Act of 1792. Lord Maugham, writing about juries, said: 'The law ought not to be too logical if it is to command human sympathy. There are cases in which juries refuse to convict the guilty person in spite of the exhortation of the judge, and most sensible people will think it is well that it should be so.'[35] Denning thought that, by sitting as jurors, the English people had taken an active part in the administration of justice and that this participation in justice had done more than anything to establish the English habit of obedience to the law.

When Denning was a King's Bench judge flogging and hanging were permitted punishments. In one case on circuit, a young man of eighteen had come up behind a woman of eighty, hit her over the head, injuring her badly, and stolen her savings of £20. Denning ordered twenty-five strokes of the birch. In 1947, at the Gloucester Assizes an army captain was charged with murdering his wife. He had climbed up through the ranks of an infantry regiment and had been commissioned. He had a spendthrift wife who, on two previous occasions, had almost had her husband cashiered by passing dud cheques. He found that she had again passed a dud cheque and in sudden desperate anger had shot her with his service revolver. Denning directed that the jury should find him guilty of murder but the jury brought in a verdict of manslaughter. Denning said that he did not intend to add to the man's distress any further and sentenced him to two years imprisonment. If there had been no capital punishment the jury would probably have given the true verdict of murder. Capital punishment has always had a tendency to distort the law as judges and juries bend over backwards not to bring in a sentence of murder in cases where hanging did not seem an appropriate sentence.

What are Denning's views on capital punishment? In giving evidence to the Royal Commission on Capital Punishment he was in favour of retaining it for murder. He said: 'The death penalty is a farce if one can see in one's mind an obvious case for reprieve. Death sentences should be passed only in cases which really deserved it and when the sentence was likely to be carried out.' He proposed that there should be different degrees of murder. He subsequently changed his mind saying that it was a question of policy and an ethical question. He asked the hypothetical question: 'Is it right that we, as a Society should do a thing, hang a man, which none of us would be prepared to do, or even witness?'[36] Nevertheless, as a judge it was his duty, from time to time, to put on the black cap and pronounce the death sentence.

Denning enjoyed going on circuit, especially his own circuit, the Western Circuit. He upheld the trappings and the ceremony. In those days the judge had his own establishment, his butler, cook, clerk and marshal. The marshal was a young barrister, chosen by the judge, to go with him on circuit and was paid £2 2s a day. It was good experience for the young man to see how things were done on circuit and his duties were mainly social. At the Assize Town the judge was greeted by the High Sheriff and was guarded by the javelin men. It was a very hard winter in 1947 and Denning, accompanied by his wife, went on the Welsh Circuit. They started at Brecon and were housed in the North Canonry. There was no heating in the bedroom and Joan was reduced to sleeping in her fur coat. At Carmarthen the judge's large car could not get through the snow and the judge walked to the Assize Court in borrowed Wellington boots. His clerk managed to find a small car in which to transport a pile of documents. The trumpeters were all ready and when the clerk got out of the car he was greeted by a fanfare of trumpets, while the judge walked in a few minutes later quite unnoticed.[37]

There was a convention that a junior judge could not take his wife on circuit unless she were invited by the senior judge. This rule was first broken by Mr Justice Byrne and Joan frequently accompanied her husband. If the list collapsed and they had a free afternoon the Dennings were able to motor out into the countryside and play golf. Denning greatly missed all these pleasures when he was promoted to the Court of Appeal as he enjoyed listening to witnesses, summing up to juries and talking to the local people. He also greatly regretted the passing of the old Assize traditions:

Nowadays, since the reforms embodied in the Courts Act 1971 all has changed. No longer does a High Court Judge go on assize. He has been shorn of much of his trappings – and with it, I regret to say, some of the esteem in which Judges of the past were held. More's the pity of it.[38]

Four

DESERTED WIVES

Equality is the order of the day. In both directions. For both sexes.
What is sauce for the goose is sauce for the gander.[1]

Denning

As long ago as 1919 that great judge, Lord Atkin, said that the family was 'a domain into which the King's writ does not run' and 'The common law does not regulate the form of agreements between spouses. Their promises are not sealed with seals and sealing wax.'[2] Legal principles cannot be used to deal with transactions between husband and wife. The family is the unit and not the individual. Property rights are not considered unless there is a marriage settlement and all property is considered to be family property. The House of Lords attempted to bring in legal principles but failed.

In November 1947 Denning was sitting as King's Bench judge in chambers hearing an appeal from a master and gave judgment in open court so that it could be reported.[3] The matrimonial home was in the husband's name. He had lived there before the war with his wife and invalid son. During the war the husband left his wife and went to live with another woman. The wife had obtained a maintenance order against her husband on the basis that she would go on living in the matrimonial home with the son. The husband wanted the wife to divorce him and said: 'I'll give you the house if you will give me my freedom.' The wife refused and the husband took proceedings for possession of the house. The master made the order as he could see no answer to the husband's claim at law. The house belonged to the husband, the wife was not a tenant and had no right to remain in the house.

Denning was always astute in finding the way round a problem in order to do justice. In this case he invoked the provisions of s 17 of the Married Women's Property Act 1882. That section provided that in case of any question between husband and wife as to the title to or possession of property the judge might make such order with respect to the property in dispute as he thinks fit. Denning said:

> He [the husband] has no right in law to claim possession from her except such as may be given to him by s17 of the Married Women's Property Act 1882. But that section does not, in my opinion, give him the right which he now claims. It enacts that the judge before whom the applicant comes may make such order as he thinks fit. The intention is that in the innumerable and infinitely various disputes as to property which may occur between husband and wife the judge may have a free hand to do what is just. The discretion is in no way fettered, though it must be exercised judicially ... Applying the discretion vested in me in that section I am satisfied that it would be unjust to turn the respondent and the son out, and I decline to make the order for which the husband asks.

As between husband and wife the 1882 Act worked well but difficulties arose when the interests of third parties were affected. In 1952 in the case of *Bendall* v *McWhirter* the husband was the owner of the house where he lived with his wife and children.[4] He deserted his wife but before he left he said: 'You can have the house and furniture.' Later he went bankrupt and his trustee in bankruptcy wanted to sell the house and divide the proceeds of sale among his creditors. To get the best price he wanted to sell with vacant possession. The wife refused to leave the house and the trustee in bankruptcy brought an action for possession against her. The County Court judge made the order for possession and she appealed to the Court of Appeal. The Court of Appeal, consisting of Somervell, Denning and Romer, held that a deserted wife in occupation of the matrimonial home had a personal licence, revocable only upon the husband obtaining an order under s17 of the 1882 Act. They refused to make the order for possession. Denning said:

> The result of the whole case is that the wife's right to stay in the matrimonial home does not come to an end automatically on the husband's bankruptcy. The trustee in bankruptcy takes subject to equities. He takes therefore subject to her right, for it is an equity. The trustee must apply to the court for possession, and the judge who hears the case will take into account the various competing interests. In my opinion the appeal should succeed and judgment be entered for the wife.

For the next thirteen years Denning tirelessly tried to develop this

50

equity and it must be emphasised that he was supported by the other judges in the Court of Appeal at that time.

This decision produced an outcry from practitioners at the Chancery Bar and Robert Megarry (later the Vice-Chancellor of the Chancery Division) wrote an article in protest in the *Law Quarterly Review* in which he said:

It may well be that justice requires that the wife's occupation of the house should be protected in some special way: and modern ideas of sex equality may require that the right should not be exclusively feminine in gender. Yet with all respect it may be suggested that legislation and not litigation is the only satisfactory way of delimiting the bounds of so complex a subject. Any protection for the wife should, it is suggested be provided by statutory amendments of the matrimonial law operating on the recognised rights of property, rather than by what (in effect, at all events) the judicial intervention of a new proprietary right. ... Few would suggest that the law as to the new found right of the wife is at present in a satisfactory state, and some indeed, may express the hope that the House of Lords will blow away the whole uncertain structure.[5]

Prior to the war it had been established that where the husband owned the matrimonial home and was living there with his wife he could not turn her out. Denning argued that if he deserted his wife he could not put himself in a better position than if they were living together. He could not take advantage of his own wrong – desertion. The husband's duty was to provide the wife with a roof over her head, and by providing a matrimonial home he gives her authority to be there. In law a deserted wife always had an irrevocable authority to pledge a husband's credit for necessaries, so in modern times she has an irrevocable authority to remain in the matrimonial home. Such authority is only revocable by the court. In 1956 the Royal Commission on Marriage and Divorce[6] said:

We think it has been right to afford this protection to a deserted wife, to allow her to keep a roof over her head; it would be shocking to contemplate that a husband could put his wife and children into the street, so that he could himself return to live in the house, perhaps with another woman.

Denning's efforts to establish 'the deserted wife's equity' were finally defeated by the House of Lords in the case of *National Provincial Bank Ltd* v *Ainsworth* in 1965.[7] A husband deserted his wife, leaving her with four children, in occupation of the matrimonial home. The husband charged the house to the bank to secure business debts but failed to repay the debt. The High Court judge made an order for possession against the wife. The Court of Appeal – Denning and Donovan with Russell dissenting – reversed the judge and the House of Lords restored the order for possession. The House unanimously rejected Denning's views and decided that a deserted wife had no equity to occupy the matrimonial home. To allow this would put her in a better position against her husband's creditors than when husband and wife were living together. The House held that the rights of a deserted wife were of a personal nature only against her husband and property rights were not affected. Lord Hodson said: 'The court has power to restrain parties or postpone the enforcement of legal rights but not to vary agreed or established rights to property in an endeavour to achieve a kind of palm tree justice.' Academic lawyers were not the only people who objected to Denning's efforts on behalf of deserted wives. A correspondent wrote:

Dear Sir

   You are a disgrace to all mankind to let these women break up homes and expect us chaps to keep them while they rob us of what we have worked for and put us out on the street. I only hope you have the same trouble as us. So do us all a favour and take a Rolls and run off Beachy Head and don't come back.[8]

The decision in *National Provincial Bank Ltd* v *Ainsworth* was very unpopular in the country and there was pressure on Parliament to introduce legislation. Denning said that this decision had blown the deserted wife's equity to smithereens. Provided the courts were able to give some protection to deserted wives Parliament had not intervened but now it could not leave them without some legal remedy. On 4 May 1966 the Baroness Summerskill introduced a bill 'To amend the law of England and Wales as to the right of a husband and wife to occupy the matrimonial home'. Parliament accepted that the wife had an equitable right to remain in the matrimonial home provided she registered that right as a land charge at the Land Charges Registry. The object of this was to give notice of this right to purchasers and others before they dealt with the property. Denning protested about this and spoke against it in a debate in the House of Lords. He said:

Is the poor wife who has not resorted to lawyers, and remains in the house, hoping that her deserting husband will return, likely to go to a solicitor and say 'Please register this as a land charge on the Land Register'? Unless she does this she has no protection.[9]

The bill was enacted on 27 July 1967 as the Matrimonial Homes Act 1967 with the clause about registration included. Wives now have to register their rights under the Land Charges Act 1925 as a Class F land charge. Despite Denning's fears, the Act has proved a success in giving wives some protection. Denning's efforts in aid of deserted wives proved unsuccessful in the long run but they gave some relief over a period of thirteen years until Parliament at last intervened to regularise the law.

The other main issue in matrimonial law in Denning's time was how to share the proceeds of the matrimonial home. The home may stand in the husband's name but the resources of both are mingled. When they break up how is the property to be divided? A case came up for decision in 1953.[10] The husband was a sailor in the Merchant Navy and the wife went out to work. He allowed her £4 a week for housekeeping and she paid the instalments under the Building Society mortgage. Later he deserted her. As the house was in his name he turned her out and sold the house with vacant possession. The wife claimed a share. Before the war the husband would have been entitled to it all as it was his property, and the wife had no contract giving her any part of it. Denning invoked the provisions of the Married Women's Property Act 1882, saying:

In 1882, when Parliament declared that a wife was entitled to have property of her own, it enacted that in any question between husband and wife as to the title to or possession of property, the court was to decide the matter as it thought fit. Parliament laid down no principles for the guidance of the courts, but left them to work out the principles themselves. That is being done. In cases when it is clear that the beneficial interest in the matrimonial home, or in the furniture, belongs to one or the other absolutely, or it is clear that they intended to hold it in definite shares, the court will give effect to their intentions; but when it is not clear to whom the beneficial interest belongs, or in what proportions, then in this matter, as in others equality is equity. ... It seems to me that when the parties, by their joint efforts, save to buy a house, which is intended as a continuing provision for both, then the proper presumption is that the beneficial interest belongs to them both jointly.

The 1882 Act was used by Denning and many other judges with good effect until 1970. Then in the case of *Pettitt* v *Pettitt* the House of Lords unanimously held that s 17 of the 1882 Act was procedural only and does not permit questions of title to be decided except in accordance with the strict legal and equitable rights of husband and wife.[11] By s 19 of the 1882 Act it is stated that nothing in the Act shall interfere with the rights of the parties under any marriage settlement. It is clear that Parliament felt that when the rights of husband and wife had been formally established by a deed, after proper advice, the Act was not needed. It was only to operate when the parties had not considered their legal rights. It was in this case that Denning first coined the expression 'family assets'. In the House of Lords Lord Upjohn said that the expression 'family assets' was devoid of legal meaning and its use could define no legal rights or obligations. Nevertheless the expression has proved a useful shorthand which has been used by the Law Commission.

Although the House of Lords destroyed the efficacy of the 1882 Act in *Pettitt* v *Pettitt* Lord Diplock attempted to put in its place in another case, the law of trusts, saying: 'The legal principles applicable to the claim are those of the English law of trusts and in particular, in the kind of dispute between spouses that come before the courts, the law relating to the creation and operation of resulting, implied or constructive trusts.'[12] Denning latched on to this and was able to use the equitable doctrine of trusts in later cases. A good example of his use of the trust principle occurred in 1971. In the case of *Heseltine* v *Heseltine* the husband said that his wife had full confidence in him and readily fell in with all the suggestions he had made about the wife's own property.[13] The bulk of the wife's fortune stood in the husband's name. It was held that the court could impute a trust for the matrimonial home and the wife should have a 75% share and the husband a 25% share. A commentator has remarked that if Denning had really decided the case on the principles of resulting trusts the wife would have got 80% of the proceeds and not 75%.[14]

At this time the Law Commission and the Government were working hard on the subject of matrimonial property and in 1970 the Matrimonial Proceedings and Property Act was passed. By s 4 of this Act, the court was empowered on or after divorce, to make an order transferring assets from husband to wife and vice versa. This was a return to the idea of the 1882 Act but took effect on or after divorce, while the 1882 Act could be used at any time during the subsistence of the marriage. In 1870, prior to the passing of the first Married Women's Property Act, Lord Cairns, the Lord Chancellor, in supporting the bill said that the main object of the bill was to meet the case of married women in the humbler classes of life, especially those who were in the habit of working for wages or acquiring earnings for the support of themselves and their families. The object of the Act was to protect women from having their wages pounced on by idle, intemperate and dissolute husbands. He said that the Court of Chancery had modified the doctrine of the common law even when there was no settlement, so that whenever property devolved on a husband in right of his wife an adequate portion should be settled on the wife and children.[15] The rich could always apply to the Court of Chancery for relief but the new Act was meant to help those of modest means. The Matrimonial Proceedings and Property Act 1970 sets out in detail all the considerations which the court should bear in mind when exercising its discretion. Experienced judges do not require guidelines on how to exercise their discretion to act fairly between the parties. Counsel feel compelled to go through each item set out in the Act to protect their client and the hearing is unduly lengthened. The Matrimonial Causes Act 1973 in s 24 repeats s 4 of the 1970 Act. Perhaps all the flurry of Parliamentary activity could have been avoided if the House of Lords had been prepared to use the powers given by the 1882 Act.

In 1973 the Court of Appeal had to decide what was meant by some of the provisions of the new Act. In *Wachtel* v *Wachtel* the court consisting of Denning, Phillimore and Roskill gave a reserved judgment fully considered by all the judges.[16] Phillimore was a particularly experienced divorce judge. The Act said, among other things, that the court had to consider the contributions made by each of the parties to the welfare of the family, including any contributions made by looking after the home or caring for the family. The court said:

> If the court comes to the conclusion that the home has been acquired and maintained by the joint efforts of both, then, when the marriage breaks down, it should be regarded as the joint property of both of them, no matter in whose name it stands. Just as the wife who makes substantial money contributions usually gets a share, so should the wife who looks after the home and cares for the family for 20 years or more.

The Act stated that conduct was a relevant factor to take into account but the court said that this was only to be considered when it was obvious and gross. It also held that no order should be made for a lump sum unless the husband had capital assets out of which to pay it, but where he had the means to pay, such an order could properly be made as this helped to remove the bitterness so often felt with periodical payments.

Denning tried to treat a man and woman who were co-habiting in the same way as husband and wife and a good example of his methods is given in the case of *Bernard* v *Josephs* in 1982.[17] A house was acquired in their joint names by an unmarried couple – Bernard and Josephs. Bernard put in £200 of her own money. Josephs put in £250 of his own and borrowed £400. The balance was found by a mortgage from a building society. Both went out to work and part of the house was let. In such cases the shares of each party are ascertained according to the circumstances and the contributions of each party. It was held that they held the property in equal shares. The interesting feature of this case is the practical way in which the court dealt with it. Josephs was living in the house with another woman and wanted to stay. All the tedious details of valuation, interest on capital and other necessary calculations were made by the court there and then. The court found that the sum of £6,000 was due from Josephs and the sale was postponed to give him time to find the money. It is not often that judges will take the trouble to make all the calculations themselves but it is a great benefit to a litigant to have a final judgment. Most family business is dealt with in private, in chambers, and is not reported. A solicitor recalled that on one occasion when Denning was sitting in chambers, a man complained through his counsel, that his wife was a slut. Denning said: 'I see no reason why she should not be a slut if she wishes to be. He should have made sure that he never married a slut.'[18]

Denning's actions in family litigation are one aspect of his concern for justice. His use of s17 of the Married Women's Property Act 1882 was justified and lawful. Parliament fully understood that as between husband and wife property rights, unless formalised in a marriage settlement, were vague and shifting. The only possible solution was to leave it to the court to apply the principles of fairness. In 1970 Parliament said in essence what it had said in 1882. The attempt by the House of Lords to bring in legal principles to transactions between husband and wife was doomed to fail as by their very nature such dealings are incapable of legal treatment. Applying the principles of fairness is not palm tree justice. It is not capricious but is fully understood by all those concerned.

Over a large area of law this principle of fairness is applied. Equity means evenness, fairness and justice. The High Court of Justice is a court of equity as well as a court of law. The Judicature Act 1873 provided that in matters not specifically provided for, or in the event of conflict, equitable rules should prevail. Here is some legal authority for the deserted wife's equity and Denning's determination to do justice in the individual case. One of the maxims of equity is: 'Equity will not suffer a wrong to be without a remedy.' Denning tried to apply this maxim when dealing with the problems of husband and wife and the matrimonial home. His efforts were not successful but they did give relief to litigants until Parliament intervened with legislation. Professor Freeman has summed up his contribution to family law as follows: 'Without Lord Denning family law today would have been more rigid and less sensitive: it would be oriented to rights more than to needs and welfare. ... He has been both a harbinger of, and a catalyst for, reform.'[19]

Five

CONSTRUCTION

In all cases the object is to see what is the intention expressed by the words used.[1]

Lord Blackburn

Judges spend most of their time construing statutes, contracts, wills and other documents and there is a great deal of law about how this should be done. Lord Wensleydale laid down the golden rule of statutory construction, namely that a judge is to apply statutory words and phrases according to their natural and ordinary meaning without addition or substitution, unless that meaning produces injustice, absurdity, anomaly or contradiction in which case you can modify the natural and ordinary meaning so as to obviate such injustice but no further. When Denning was called to the Bar in 1923 the Public General Statutes contained 481 pages but by 1981 just before his retirement there were 2876 pages.

For Denning the task of the judge in the construction of statutes was to find out the intention of Parliament.[2] You must, of course start with the wording of the statute but not end there. The prevalent theory in the nineteenth century was that a judge must look at the words and no more. For Denning this was wrong in principle. A judge is entitled to inquire into the mischief which gave rise to the statute to see the evil which it sought to remedy. For this purpose he can look at the reports of royal commissions, departmental inquiries, law reform committees and the like but there is a rule of practice that he must not look at *Hansard*, the reports of Parliamentary debates. Denning fought long but unsuccessfully to change this rule. As this is a rule of practice it is not a likely subject for legislation and can only be changed by the House of Lords. Parliament would be reluctant to interfere with the court's power to regulate its own practice.

There is no doubt that *Hansard* can be a very useful tool to enable a judge to find out what Parliament really meant. In an unreported case about the powers of the Ombudsman Parliament had given the Ombudsman power to investigate complaints of maladministration but did not define what this meant in the Act. Richard Crossman, the Minister in charge of the bill in Parliament gave illustrations of what maladministration meant and his examples became guidelines for the Ombudsman. They were known as 'Crossman's catalogue'. It was only because they had been quoted in full in a public address given by the Ombudsman that they could be used in court.[3]

Denning always set his face against artificial fetters which the law seeks to impose on judges which prevent them from reaching the right decision. In 1979 the House of Lords reaffirmed that *Hansard* should not be referred to in court. Lord Scarman said that the rule was maintained by Parliament and was not the creation of the judges.[4] The clerks in the House of Commons can find no authority for this. The rule originated with a dictum of Willes J. in 1769.[5] He said: 'The sense and meaning of an Act of Parliament must be collected from what it says when passed into law and not from the history of changes it underwent in the House where it took its rise. That history is not known to the other House or to the Sovereign.' In 1879 two appeal judges allowed a speech of the Lord Chancellor in the House of Lords to be cited as an authority for the construction of a statute.[6] In 1880 another appeal judge thought himself to be at liberty to refer to the circumstances under which an Act had been passed as a means of solving a particular difficulty.[7] This is a rule of practice which is enforced by the House of Lords on the grounds of public policy to ensure that trials are not unduly prolonged by reference to material that is not strictly relevant. On the other hand the truth of the case may be illuminated by reading the debates and what the proposer of the bill said.

Denning expressed his views on the interpretation of statutes as early as 1949. In the case of *Seaford Court Estates Ltd* v *Asher* he was a very junior Lord Justice of Appeal sitting with Greene and Asquith.[8] It was a reserved judgment backed by both the other judges. This was a case where the rent of a flat had been increased from £175 a year to £250 a year. The increase arose as the landlord agreed to provide hot water. The tenant agreed to pay £250 but later changed his mind and refused to pay more than the original rent of £175. The problem arose by reason of the wording of the Rent Acts which governed the property. The court reserved judgment for four weeks. Denning wrote the judgment which had the backing of Lord Greene, the Master of the Rolls, and Lord Justice Asquith. Denning said:

Whenever a statute comes up for consideration it must be remembered that it is not within human powers to foresee the manifold sets of facts which may arise, and, even if it were, it is not possible to provide them in terms free from all ambiguity. The English language is not an instrument of mathematical precision. Our literature would be much poorer if it were. This is where the draftsmen of Acts of Parliament have often been unfairly criticized. A judge, believing himself to be fettered by the supposed rule that he should look to the language and nothing else, laments that the draftsmen have not provided for this or that, or have been guilty of some or other ambiguity. It would certainly save the judges trouble if Acts of Parliament were drafted with divine prescience and perfect clarity. In the absence of it, when a defect appears a judge cannot simply fold his hands and blame the draftsman. He must set to work on the constructive task of finding the intention of Parliament, and he must do this not only from the language of the statute, but also from consideration of the social conditions which gave rise to it, and of the mischief which it was passed to remedy, and then he must supplement the written word so as to give 'force and life' to the intention of the legislature. . . . A judge should ask himself the question: If the makers of the Act had themselves come across this ruck in the texture of it, how would they have straightened it out? He must then do as they would have done. A judge must not alter the material of which it is woven, but he can and should iron out the creases.

This case went to the House of Lords and the decision of the Court of Appeal was upheld by a majority; Lord MacDermott, dissenting, thought that the Court of Appeal had stated the principles 'rather widely'.

Denning has always been concerned to fill the gaps in legislation and believed this to be a job for the judge. He once said:

The one point at which we get stuck is when there is a gap. The words are clear enough. But they do not cover the matter in hand. Something has taken place which the draftsman has not foreseen. Nor have the members of Parliament. . . . So they have not provided for it. Or else by some mistake they have overlooked it.[9]

But with the return of a Conservative Government in 1951 Lord Simonds became Lord Chancellor and there was a change of emphasis in the House of Lords. He was only Lord Chancellor for three years but a period of rigidity set in. Very soon after Simonds' appointment the case of *Magor and St Mellors Rural District Councils* v *Newport Corporation* was heard. Newport Corporation had expanded its boundaries by taking in parts of the two Rural District Councils – Magors and St Mellors. The Act provided for reasonable compensation to be paid to the two district councils. The Minister then made an order amalgamating the two district councils into one. On that account Newport Corporation sought to reduce the compensation to nothing, relying on the literal meaning of the order. Newport Corporation succeeded in all the courts, Denning only dissenting in the Court of Appeal.

Denning's views began to find favour with the House of Lords in the 1960s and the 1970s and in 1971 Lord Diplock drew a clear distinction between the literal approach and the purposive approach and used the latter to solve the problems confronting the court.[11] Denning also received support from the Renton Report on statutory interpretation:

> The courts should, in our view, approach legislation determined, above all, to give effect to the intention of Parliament. We see promising signs that this consideration is uppermost in the minds of the highest tribunal in the country.[12]

The strict constructionists are not easily defeated; and as late as 1978 the Employment Appeal Tribunal stated:

> We are bound to apply the provisions of an Act of Parliament however absurd, out of date and unfair they may appear to be. The duty of making or altering the law is the function of Parliament and is not, as many mistaken persons seem to imagine, the privilege of judges or the judicial tribunals.

In response to an appeal to the Court of Appeal Denning said:

> In all cases now in the interpretation of statutes we adopt such a construction as will promote the general legislative purpose underlying the provision. It is no longer necessary for the judges to wring their hands and say 'There is nothing we can do about it'. Whenever the strict interpretation of a statute gives rise to an absurd and unjust situation, the judges can and should use their good sense to remedy it – by reading in words, if necessary, so as to do what Parliament would have done, had they had the situation in mind.[13]

Denning was merely returning to an older tradition of the common law. In the seventeenth century Sir Edward Coke said that it was the task of the judiciary in interpreting an Act to seek to interpret it 'according to the intent of them that made it'.[14] The common law itself followed the Christian tradition. Jeremy Taylor wrote:

> In obedience to human laws we must observe the letter of the law where we can, without doing violence to the reason of the law and the intention of the lawgiver: but where they cross each other, the charity of the law is to be preferred before its discipline, and the reason before the letter.[15]

The interpretation of statutes has become an increasingly important part of a judge's task. In 1989 over 90% of the reported cases in the Court of Appeal related to the interpretation of statutes. If the administration of justice is not to grind to a halt judges must take a more positive role in the construction of statutes and Denning showed the way. This method of interpreting statutes has been given added point by the advent of the European Community as it is in line with the methods used by the European Court of Justice. European statutes lay down general principles and the details are filled in by regulations and directives of the Commission. By Article 190 of the Treaty, regulations have to give the reasons on which they are based. The regulations start off with recitals explaining the purpose and intent of the regulations. Words and phrases are used without defining their import. The details are left to be filled in by the judges. The judges must look at the purpose and intent of the Treaty and must deduce from the wording and spirit of the Treaty the meaning of the community rules.

Owing to the vast increase in the number of statutes the methods used in the nineteenth century are no longer appropriate. On account of the pressure under which legislation is passed it is not always clear what was intended and the judges need to have the power to fill the gaps if justice is to be done. The judge needs all the help he can get if he is to know what Parliament intended and he may need *Hansard* to help him find out the purpose of the Act. For the hard-pressed Parliamentarian Denning's attitude was a relief. Lord Renton said:

> It is said that Lord Denning usurps the functions of the legislature. Well I venture to say that I have been a democratically elected legislator for almost as long as Denning has been a judicial one, and I don't mind a

bit. He saves a lot of time in Parliament where we always pass too many laws.[16]

Denning also brought a new approach to the interpretation of wills. The general principle was that the court must ascertain the intention of the testator but the rule was fettered by a rule of construction that the intention could only be ascertained from the words used. There were hundreds of decided cases on the meaning of individual words such as 'children', 'relatives' or 'money'. Denning agreed that the court must discover the testator's intention from the words used but he thought that the court must put upon the testator's words the meaning that they bore for him. He thought that the court should place itself, so far as possible, in the position of the testator and then say what he meant by the words. For this proposition he had the authority of a House of Lords decision twenty years earlier.[17] Lord Simon, a very conservative lawyer, had said: 'The fundamental rule in construing the language of a will is to put on the words used the meaning which, having regard to the terms of the will, the testator intended.' Lord Atkin hopefully added: 'I anticipate with satisfaction that henceforth the group of ghosts of dissatisfied testators who, according to a late Chancery judge, wait on the banks of the Styx to receive the judicial personages who have misconstrued their wills, may be considerably diminished.'

In 1963 Denning gave a strong dissenting judgment in the case of *Re Rowland decd.*[18] Dr Rowland made his will himself on a printed form. He gave all his estate to his wife, but in the event of her death preceding or coinciding with his own, to his brother and nephews. His wife made a similar will with a gift to her niece. Both were lost at sea, near the Solomon Islands, in a ship which sank without survivors. Nobody knew exactly what had happened. The Chancery judge and the other two judges in the Court of Appeal had no difficulty in deciding the case. By s 184 of the Law of Property Act 1925 there is a presumption of law that: 'When two or more persons died in circumstances rendering it uncertain which survived the other, the younger shall be deemed to have survived.' It was clear that in the circumstances nobody knew for certain who had survived the other and therefore the presumption took effect. The wife was the younger and therefore her niece took the estate of both husband and wife. The logic of the majority view was impeccable but Denning turned the argument on its head by saying that the fallacy of the argument was that it started in the wrong place. He said: 'For in point of principle the whole object of construing a will is to find out the testator's intention so as to see that his property is disposed of in the way he wished.' Denning applied this principle and it was clear that Dr and Mrs Rowland intended to cover just what had happened. If they both died together his estate would go to his family and his wife's estate would go to hers. This was the reality of the matter which was frustrated by the majority decision.

Denning did not give up and was more successful in 1966 when sitting in the Court of Appeal with Winn and Danckwerts. In *Re Jebb decd* a testator, by his will, gave his estate to the children of his daughter and his grandson.[19] The daughter, aged forty-seven, had an adopted child. The question was whether the daughter's adopted child could be regarded as her child and therefore take her share. By s 5(2) of the Adoption of Children Act 1926 'the expression children used in a will shall not, unless the contrary intention appears, include an adopted child.' The Chancery judge held that there was no contrary intention in the will and the adopted child was cut out. Denning discussed the facts of the case. The testator knew about the adoption and knew the child before he made his will. It seemed clear to him that when the testator spoke of the child or children of his daughter he intended to include the adopted child or any further adopted children as his daughter had passed the age for child bearing. All three judges allowed the adopted child to take. The interesting feature of the case was that it was the unanimous decision of all the judges in the Court of Appeal. Winn was a very sound common lawyer and Danckwerts was a Chancery judge who had previously been Treasury counsel for Chancery business. Danckwerts had been one of the counsel in the House of Lords case in 1943 and may have taken particular note of the dicta of Lord Simon and Lord Atkin in that case. Danckwerts was a strong supporter of Denning's approach and on one occasion when counsel appeared before him with an armful of authorities he said: 'What are those for? This is only a construction summons [for the interpretation of a will].'

This case was more than the academic stomach could stand and Dr John Morris of Magdalen College, Oxford, wrote an article entitled 'Palm Tree Justice in the Court of Appeal' published in the *Law Quarterly Review*.[20] He wrote:

By departing from the established rules of law the Court of Appeal seems to have usurped the functions of the legislature. The decision will require the re-writing of the whole of the chapters on gifts to children in the text-books on wills, unless the editor has the courage to say that it is manifestly wrong. . . . If this new addition to the construction of wills comes to prevail, it will not be sufficient just to re-write the chapter on gifts to children in the text-books on wills. The text-books themselves will have to be scrapped and construction reduced to the level of guesswork. It is submitted that the rules of law binding on the court cannot be evaded merely by calling them technical.

From a conveyancer's point of view it is necessary to have terms of art which are understood by all professionals but a will is a document which the law permits a man to make without professional help. Terms of art are out of place in a home-made will. By sticking to the intention of the testator the Court of Appeal refused to be bound by the terms of art used by conveyancers. What are these terms of art? They are often the *obiter dicta* of judges which have hardened into rules of construction. In fact these rules of construction are the most difficult forms of law to alter. In the eighteenth century Lord Mansfield caused a furore with Charles Fearne and the conveyancers by trying to change the rule of construction known as the 'Rule in Shelley's case'. He was unsuccessful and it was not until 1925 that the rule was abolished by the Law of Property Act 1925.

It comes as no surprise that Denning was defeated only one year after his success in *Re Jebb decd*. In 1967 in *Sydall* v *Castings Ltd* an Insurance Group scheme was drawn up for the benefit of relations and a county court judge held that an illegitimate child was included in the term 'descendant'.[21] In the Court of Appeal Diplock and Russell held that in a legal document which conferred property rights 'descendants' must be construed as a term of art and they construed it to mean blood relatives in the legitimate line. They relied on the text-book *Jarman on Wills* which says that a gift to children imports only legitimate children and relatives mean legitimate kindred. Denning dissented saying that the word 'descendant' had not been construed in any leading authorities to make it a term of art. The word should be given its ordinary meaning and an illegitimate child was a descendant of her father. He said:

If the contention [in *Jarman on Wills*] be correct, it means that because Yvette is illegitimate, she is to be excluded from any benefit. She is on this view no 'relation' of her father: nor is she 'descended' from him. In the eye of the law she is the daughter of nobody. She is related to nobody. She is an outcast and is to be shut out from any part of her father's insurance benefit ... Even Victorian fathers thought they were doing right when they turned their erring daughters out of the house. They visited the sins of the fathers upon the children – with a vengeance. I think we should throw over these harsh rules of the past. They are not rules of law. They are only guides to the construction of documents. They are quite out of date. We no longer penalise the illegitimate child. We should replace these old rules by a more rational approach.

Denning was on weaker ground than when dealing with the interpretation of wills, often prepared by laymen. This was a legal document intended to confer property rights where there is a stronger argument in favour of a strict interpretation. The majority could without stretching the law at all have come down on Denning's side as the term 'descendant' had never been construed as a term of art. Denning was looking at the reality of the transaction. Was it really intended to exclude illegitimate children and was it just?

Six

COMMON LAW

When a man, by his words or conduct, has led another to believe that he may safely act on the faith of them, and the other does act on them, he will not be allowed to go back on what he has said or done when it would be unjust or inequitable for him to do so.[1]

Denning

Professor Atiyah has written:

In every significant area of the common law Lord Denning's judgments can be found to illustrate modern trends and ideas. Further, a survey of these judgments will dispel any belief that, in this area at least, Lord Denning's views have been constantly rejected by his colleagues or over-ridden on appeal. Certainly this has occurred in some instances; but what is most striking about his contribution to the common law is the number of times in which his views, while originally being received with doubt or rejection, have ultimately been vindicated. This vindication has sometimes come through the judicial process, while in other cases it has come from legislation; in some of the latter cases it is, of course, arguable whether the process truly amounts to vindication. In some instances legislative support for Lord Denning's views may have amounted to a repudiation of his views of the proper extent of judicial power, although it may have represented a confirmation of his views on the appropriate policy to be adopted; but there are other instances in which it seems quite clear, in retro-spect, that Lord Denning has been conducting a temporary staying operation, pending statutory intervention, and a respectable case can be made for saying that such operations are perfectly acceptable uses of judicial power. In yet other instances, it seems clear in hindsight, that Lord Denning's approach to the permissible extent of judicial development of the common law was more sensible and realistic than that of his colleagues.

One other common illusion ought to be dispelled by a study of Lord Denning's common law cases, especially his contract cases. A widespread criticism of his technique is based on the belief that Lord Denning's stress on doing justice in the circumstances of individual cases has destroyed what certainty the law possessed, especially in commercial matters. In fact, Lord Denning has almost always distinguished, in his contract judgments, between commercial and consumer transactions, and he has not infrequently adopted a fairly tough, freedom of contract stand in commercial transactions which contrasts markedly with his approach to consumer cases. Where he has departed from this approach, it will often be found that his views accord closer with those of the mercantile community than do those of his colleagues.[2]

In July 1946 Denning had only been a judge of the King's Bench for six months and had been out on circuit. During his first spell in London he heard the 'High Trees' case.[3] During the war many people went out of London because of the bombing and flats were left empty. In one block, let on 99 year leases at £2500 a year, the landlord agreed to reduce the rent to £1250 a year. When the war was over and the tenants came back the landlord sought to recover the full £2500 a year. Denning held that he could not recover the full rent for the time when they were empty. Under the common law a lease under seal could not be varied by agreement whether in writing or not, but only by deed. When Denning was at the Bar and working on a new edition of *Smith's Leading Cases in the Common Law* he had unearthed a decision of Lord Cairns in 1877[4] and another by Lord Justice Bowen in 1888.[5] In 1877 Lord Cairns said that it was a first principle upon which the Courts of Equity proceed that if parties have entered into a legal contract and afterwards one party leads the other to suppose that the strict rights under the contract will be varied, he will not be permitted to enforce his legal rights where it would be inequitable to do so. They were both Chancery judges applying equitable principles. Denning found justification for his decision in these equitable principles and also found support in the Report of the Law Revision Committee on the doctrine of consideration (1937) which had recommended 'That a promise which the promisor knows, or reasonably should know, will be relied on by the promisee, should be enforceable if the promisee has altered his position to his detriment in reliance on the promise.' In his judgment Denning said that in his opinion the time had come for the validity of such a promise to be recognised. He based his judgment on this principle and there was no appeal.

The principle of 'High Trees' was extended in another case in 1950.[6] Mr Oppenheim ordered a body to be built on the chassis of his Rolls Royce Silver Wraith. In July 1947 the coachbuilders promised to deliver it within six or, at the most, seven months. They did not deliver on time and Mr Oppenheim still pressed them to deliver. Denning held that Mr Oppenheim promised not to insist on his legal rights and that the promise was intended to be acted on and was in fact acted on. He was not permitted to go back on it. In the 'High Trees' case there was an actual promise but in Mr Oppenheim's case it was conduct on his behalf. Denning said:

> Previously it would have been said that there was no consideration; or if the contract was for the sale of goods, that there was nothing in writing to support the variation ... all these difficulties are swept away now. If the defendant, as he did, led the plaintiffs to believe that he would not insist on the stipulation as to time, and that, if they carried out the work, he would accept it, and they did, he could not afterwards set up the stipulation as to time against them. .... It is a kind of estoppel. By his conduct he evinced an intention to affect their legal relations. He made, in effect a promise not to insist on his strict legal rights. That promise was intended to be acted on, and was in fact acted on. He cannot afterwards go back on it.

Denning modified his stance a little in 1951 in the case of *Combe* v *Combe* by saying that the 'High Trees' principle did not create a new cause of action where none existed before.[7] It only prevented a party from insisting upon his strict legal rights when it would be unjust to enforce them, having regard to the dealings which have taken place between the parties. Denning was afraid that if the principle was stretched too far it might be endangered.

What is striking about 'High Trees' is that Denning, as a young judge, was prepared to strike out in a new direction rather than reach the same result by manipulating the old authorities. As Lord Devlin has said: 'Denning, a very recent puisne, prepared to cut a new channel from the main stream.'[8] 'High Trees' merely provided the opportunity for Denning to put in a judgment ideas which had been simmering in his mind since the 1920s when he was one of the editors of *Smith's Leading Cases*. It meant ignoring a House of Lords case of 1854.[9] Not that the idea was new in the law. In the eighteenth century Lord Mansfield had tried to introduce the idea of moral obligation and the power of the court to enforce such an obligation, but he was unsuccessful. Many academics have accepted the principle but would have preferred to have rested it on the idea that a person who has let another act to his prejudice on a promise or other conduct should not be able to go back on his word or conduct. The American Law Institute in Restatement of Contracts s90 provides that in some circumstances subsequent reliance on a promise could justify enforcement. For Denning the promisor is bound because he has promised, not because the promisee has been prejudiced by the promise. 'High Trees' is a good example of the lottery of litigation and the system of precedent. That the principle of promissory estoppel is now firmly established results from the fact that there was no appeal. If there had been an appeal the judgment would probably have been reversed.

Denning was always a champion of the consumer and his name will long be associated with the fight against the small print of exemption clauses. He adopted the technique of strict construction of the contract to avoid these clauses and two cases illustrate how he worked. In *Olley* v *Marlborough Court Ltd* Mr and Mrs Olley lived in a residential hotel for nearly two years.[10] One day they left their room locked up and deposited the key at the reception desk in the usual way. On their return they found that the key was no longer on the hook. When they entered their room they found that jewellery worth £50 and clothing had been stolen. There was a notice in the room that the proprietors would not hold themselves responsible for any loss unless valuables were deposited with the manageress for safe keeping. The judge found the hotel guilty of negligence and awarded the Olleys damages of £329. On appeal Denning said that the common law made the hotel liable for loss unless they could prove that they had taken reasonable care of the key. This they had not proved. People who rely on a contract to exempt themselves from the common law liability must prove that contract strictly. The best way of proving it is by a written document signed by the party. Another way is by handing him, before he signs, or at the time of the contract, a written notice specifying its terms and making clear what those terms are. A third method is a prominent public notice when he makes the contract or an express oral stipulation would have the same effect. A notice put up in a bedroom does not make a contract. As a rule a guest does not see it until he has been accepted as a guest. The appeal was dismissed.

The other case was *Adler* v *Dickson*.[11] The sailing ticket for a Mediterranean cruise contained the following condition: 'Passengers are carried at passengers' entire risk'. Adler was injured when mounting the gangway of the ship in port and brought an action for negligence against the employees of the shipping company. The Court of Appeal, which consisted of Denning, Jenkins and Morris, stated: 'The law permits a carrier to stipulate for exemption from liability of those whom he engages to carry out the contract, even though they are not parties, provided that the injured party assents expressly or by necessary implication to the exemption.' This the company had not proved. Parliament eventually stepped in to pass the Unfair Contract Terms Act 1977 which outlaws unreasonable indemnity clauses.

Denning's last case in 1982 related to exemption clauses.[12] Some farmers ordered 30 lb of cabbage seed at a cost of £192. On a printed clause the suppliers' liability was limited to £192. It turned out that what came up was not cabbage and the loss to the farmers was over £61,000. Denning held that the buyers had no opportunity of knowing whether the seed was cabbage or not while the sellers could and should have known that they were selling the wrong seed. The sellers could have insured but the buyers could not gain that protection. The sellers were held liable despite the exemption clause and the Court of Appeal was upheld by the House of Lords. In 1978 in a commercial case Denning tried to spirit away an exemption clause but was reversed by the House of Lords who said that in commercial cases where there was no inequality of bargaining power such clauses should be strictly construed.[13]

Inequality of bargaining power was a principle which Denning tried to establish as a principle of law without success. The leading case was *Lloyds Bank Ltd* v *Bundy*.[14] Herbert Bundy was an elderly farmer who had been a customer of Lloyds Bank for many years. His son formed a company to run his business and the father guaranteed the overdraft and mortgaged his farm to the bank. The son went bankrupt and the County Court judge made an order for possession in favour of the bank. Bundy appealed to the Court of Appeal who allowed his appeal. Denning based his judgment on the American policy of inequality of bargaining power but, in the event of this being wrong, on the equitable doctrine of undue influence. He said:

Gathering all together, I would suggest that through all these instances there runs a single thread. They rest on 'inequality of bargaining power'. By virtue of it, the English law gives relief to one who, without independent advice, enters into a contract on terms which are very unfair or transfers property for a consideration which is grossly inadequate, when his bargaining power is grievously impaired by reason of his own needs or desires, or by his own ignorance or infancy, coupled with undue influence or pressures brought to bear on him by or for the benefit of others.

The other two judges were more cautious and based their judgments on undue influence. In a case ten years later the House of Lords considered the question of inequality of bargaining power and said that in some cases of undue influence an unequal bargain would be a relevant factor. Lord Scarman said: 'I question whether there is any need in the modern law to erect a principle of relief against inequality of bargaining power.'[15]

One of the problems in contract law is what to do when new circumstances have arisen which make it inequitable to enforce a contract. In 1978 a case was heard which was not considered important enough to be included in the main series of law reports: *Staffordshire Area Health Authority* v *South Staffordshire Water Co.*[16] In 1929 the Water Authority agreed to supply the Hospital at all times thereafter with 5000 gallons of water a day free and, if any more were needed, at 7d per thousand gallons. Inflation had made the agreement an absurdity. Nobody in 1929 had considered inflation. The case came on for trial in the Chancery Division and the judge felt bound to follow precedent, whatever his personal feelings might be, and dismissed the action. On appeal Denning said that when a contract, which made no provision for determination, constituted an agreement to supply goods and services over an unlimited period, it could be determined by reasonable notice. He said that the court shrank from holding such an agreement to be an agreement in perpetuity. The parties in 1929 never directed their minds to the future and never envisaged the inflation which took place. If they had done so they would, as reasonable persons, have made the agreement determinable on reasonable notice. He said:

> But I think that the rule of strict construction is now quite out of date. It has been supplanted by the rule that written instruments are to be construed in relation to the circumstances as they are known to or contemplated by the parties: and that even the plainest words may fall to be modified if events occur which the parties never had in mind and which they cannot have intended to operate.

Denning attempted to bring in a principle which he called 'presumed intent' to the construction of contracts.[17] He wanted the court to accept the fact that the parties had never agreed at all because they had never envisaged that such a situation would arise. Some remedy was clearly needed to deal with a situation that was not all that uncommon. Denning wanted the court to find their 'presumed intent'; that is what they presumably would have agreed if they had envisaged the situation. It presumes that the parties would have agreed upon a fair and reasonable solution and the court makes a declaration in those terms. The Court of Appeal unanimously took that view in *British Movietonews* v *London District Cinemas* (see page 161). Denning thought that in the case of an unforeseen turn of events the court was justified in asking itself: 'What is the fair and just solution of the problem?'

In the law of negligence Denning was swimming with the tide of legal thinking and received support from the House of Lords. The old law was that there was a difference between a negligent act and a negligent statement. Denning's dissenting judgment in *Candler* v *Crane, Christmas & Co* in 1951 set the ball rolling for change.[18] Accountants prepared company accounts knowing that Candler was thinking of investing money in the company. On the strength of the accounts Candler invested £2000 and lost the lot. The judge found that the accountants had been careless but dismissed the action because, in the absence of fraud, there was no duty of care owed by the accountants to Candler. He was upheld by the majority of the Court of Appeal, which consisted of Cohen and Asquith. Denning dissented saying:

Did the accountants owe a duty of care to the plaintiff? If the matter were free from authority I should have said that they clearly did owe a duty of care to him. They were professional accountants who prepared and put before him these accounts, knowing that he was going to be guided by them in making an investment in the company. On the faith of these accounts he did make the investment, whereas if the accounts had been carefully prepared he would not have made the investment at all. The result is that he has lost his money.

He held that the accountants owed a duty of care not only to their clients but to any third person to whom they showed the accounts and who acted on them to his detriment – in this case Candler. Twelve years later in the great case of *Hedley Byrne & Co* v *Hellar & Partners Ltd* Denning's reasoning was adopted by the House of Lords and the earlier cases overruled.[19] This is a very good example of Denning's technique of dissenting with good arguments in the hope that the House of Lords would come round to his point of view in a later case.

In *Arenson* v *Arenson* the question of negligent misstatement arose again.[20] Shares were sold to the plaintiff at their fair value, as determined by auditors for the company. The question at issue was whether the auditors were acting as experts or arbitrators. The accountants made a negligent valuation and the plaintiff suffered a substantial loss. The majority held that the accountants were acting as arbitrators and were therefore not liable for damages. Denning held that they were acting as experts and therefore liable. This was another dissenting judgment subsequently upheld by the House of Lords. The majority could, without stretching the law in any way, come down on Denning's side.

Denning played a great part in changing the law relating to professional negligence. After the advent of the National Health Service an important case came before the Court of Appeal.[21] The year was 1951. A man went to Walton Hospital in Liverpool to be treated for two stiff fingers. His hand was put in splints. When the splints were removed his hand was useless. The trial judge found for the hospital saying that the plaintiff had failed to prove negligence on the part of any particular individual on the staff. The Court of Appeal reversed the judge and Denning said that the hospital authorities accepted Cassidy as the patient for treatment and it was their duty to treat him with reasonable care. They selected the surgeon to attend him. If he was not treated with proper care and skill then the hospital must answer for it. The hospital cannot do the job itself. It must do it by the staff it employs and if the staff are negligent the hospital is liable for that negligence in the same way as any employer who employs others to do his duties for him.

The medical profession was alarmed by this decision as it foresaw many groundless claims for negligence which it would have to defend. Denning sought to allay their fears in a case in 1954.[22] In that case the doctors concerned were not found to be negligent and Denning said:

We should be doing a disservice to the community at large if we were to impose liability on hospitals and doctors for everything that happens to go wrong. Doctors would be led to think more of their own safety than the good of the patients. ... A proper sense of proportion requires us to have regard to the conditions in which hospitals and doctors have to work. We must insist on due care for the patient at every point, but we must not condemn as negligence that which is only misadventure.

The House of Lords case of *Hedley Byrne & Co* v *Hellar & Partners Ltd* is important not only because it upheld the Denning dissent in the Candler case but it opened the door to actions against professional advisers. Hedley Byrne was an advertising agency which was about to enter into a contract with a customer and wanted a banker's reference. A firm of merchant bankers gave a reference that the customer was good for ordinary business arrangements. The agents gave the customer credit. The customer was very unsound and the agents lost their money. The House of Lords held that a professional man was liable for negligent statements when he knew that they were going to be acted on and they were acted upon.

This case encouraged a client to sue a barrister for negligence. The law has always been that a member of the Bar could not be sued. In *Rondel* v *Worsley* Rondel was charged with causing grievous bodily harm.[23] He was defended by a barrister, convicted and sentenced. He complained that the barrister had not cross-examined sufficiently and had not called the witnesses he wanted. In every court the action was struck out. Denning based his judgment on public policy that so far as hearings in court were concerned a barrister had a duty to the court as well as to his client and to enable him to do this duty fearlessly and independently he ought not to be subject to the risk of vexatious actions. He said: 'Every convicted person who blamed his counsel could at once bring an action for negligence. Rather than open the door I would bolt it.' This is known as the 'floodgates' argument. Eleven years later Denning accepted that barristers should be liable for negligence for 'pure paperwork'.[24] This brought them into line with solicitors and other professional men.

Reasons of policy were given for decisions involving damages for economic loss, that is loss of business or earnings arising from the actions of the wrongdoer. In 1973 some contractors, when digging up a road, damaged an electric cable which supplied several factories. Power was cut off for fourteen and a half hours. It was held that the plaintiffs were entitled to loss of profits for the work actually spoilt by the stoppage but not for the loss of profits that they would have received if they had been able to work continuously.[25] Denning said that statutory undertakers had never been liable for economic loss and it would seem right for the common law to follow the legislature and to adopt the same policy for contractors. Cutting off electricity was a normal hazard of life and was usually restored in a few hours. The loss was suffered by the whole community. There would be no end to the claims if economic loss was permitted. Here again the 'floodgates' argument was used that the legal process could not cope with the flood of claims. The policy arguments used, however, do not relate to liability but only to the measure of damages.

A case in 1972 was regarded by Denning as one of the first importance as it brought together all the problems of negligent statement, economic loss, public authorities and previous decisions. It was *Dutton* v *Bognor Regis UDC*.[26] Some builders in Bognor Regis built a house on a former rubbish dump. They did not build on proper concrete foundations. The council's surveyor made his inspection and either did not notice the defects or turned a blind eye. He was undoubtedly negligent. The builders sold to Mrs Dutton. After she went into possession cracks appeared which cost her £2,240 to repair. The builders paid £625 to settle the claim against them and Mrs Dutton sued the Council for the balance saying that their surveyor had been negligent. The case was entirely novel. Never before had a council been sued on the grounds of the negligence of its surveyor. Denning considered the policy considerations which he thought should be borne in mind. Firstly the builders were responsible. Secondly the Council's surveyor was responsible. Thirdly the Council was entrusted by Parliament with the task of seeing that houses were properly built. They received public funds for this purpose. The object of the inspection was to protect purchasers and occupiers of houses. The Council had failed in their task and their shoulders were broad enough to bear the loss. He considered the 'floodgates' argument but thought that cases of this kind would be rare as claimants would normally claim against the builders alone. The court held that the Council was in breach of its duty to Mrs Dutton and awarded her damages.

In the Dorset yacht case, policy arguments were again used.[27] Borstal boys had escaped from a working party and caused considerable damage to yachts moored in the vicinity. The three officers in charge had gone to bed and left the boys unattended. Denning remembered that the Court of Appeal had great difficulty with the case. On whom should the risk of negligence fall? On balance he felt that the officers of the Borstal should be liable for negligence because of the people who lived in the neighbourhood. Those living nearby should be entitled to expect that reasonable care be taken to protect them. He made it clear that action would only lie on proof of negligence. An error of judgment would not be sufficient but something that was genuinely blameworthy. For negligence at the operational level a government department or public authority should certainly be liable. The Home Office was held liable and this decision was upheld by the House of Lords.

Denning was always anxious to restate the law and provide solutions for knotty problems. Sometimes he went too far. In *Launchbury* v *Morgan* Mrs Morgan owned a motor car which her husband used to go to work on most days.[28] Having been to a public house he had too much to drink and asked Cawfield to drive him home. Cawfield collided with a bus and both he and Mr Morgan were killed. The other passengers in the car sued Mrs Morgan claiming that Cawfield was her agent in driving the car. Denning stressed that increased liability had been placed on the car owner both by the State and by the courts because he was the person insured. He argued that this principle should be adopted since the owner puts his car on the road and should shoulder the responsibility for it whoever he permits to drive. He also introduced the concept of 'the family car' whereby the car should be considered as the property of the whole family. The House of Lords was not impressed and unanimously rejected the proposed basis for the law on vicarious liability. Some law lords pointed out that any new scheme would be complex involving policy choices. Any new arrangements would best be decided by Parliament who could take into account all policy considerations. The House felt that the system of insurance and liability had become so interconnected that they would need to be properly briefed on the consequences for insurance before any new rule of liability was introduced. They felt that although the proposals of the Court of Appeal had merit their effect on insurance was so great that changes should not be made by judicial action but were a matter for Parliament and for public discussion.

It is probably in the field of contract and tort that Denning had the greatest legal influence. This is essentially common law where statute is not so ubiquitous. It has been said that his greatest contribution to the law of the Commonwealth has been in this area.[29] 'High Trees' was a decision of very great importance: that promises should be kept when the other party has relied on the promise to his detriment. The dissenting judgment in *Candler* v *Crane, Christmas & Co* widened the scope of negligence and was the start of a new era.

Seven

APPEAL JUDGE
1948–62

*I feel you will bring great strength to the top courts, and have even
more opportunity to bring fresh air into the law.*[1]

D.N.Pritt QC

On 12 October 1948 Denning was appointed to the Court of Appeal
after only four and a half years as a trial judge. The Lord Chancellor,
Lord Simon, wrote: 'My dear Denning, I am delighted that my choice
is so soon a winner. How absurdly ill informed the newspapers are
– a 'divorce expert' no doubt, but what about the common law?
Yours very sincerely, Simon.' Denning himself explains what it
meant:

It did not mean any increase in pay. It only meant that I was a Privy
Councillor – to be addressed as 'Right Honourable' instead of 'Honourable'
– and to have the privilege of the entrée – of entering Buckingham Palace
by the side-door instead of the front. But it meant a very different kind
of work – to sit on appeals from others – not trying cases myself.[2]

He was sworn in as a Privy Councillor on the 25 October 1948.

The letters of congratulation received on his appointment include
praise for his work as a King's Bench judge.[3] F.W.Beney KC wrote:
'The Bar thinks that your work was outstanding in its aspects of
quick understanding, patience and courtesy.' P.J.Nelly wrote: 'The
work you have performed in dealing with pension appeals will be
regarded as an outstanding achievement in your judicial life.' Professor Percy Winfield, of Cambridge University, said: 'The reports
of your judgments have given me the greatest pleasure and helpful
instruction in all branches of the law.' Again from Cambridge Professor Jack Hamson wrote: 'Academic lawyers will be especially glad
of the news; for I think, as a puisne, you have delivered as interesting
a series of judgments as I can recall, and that in a very short period
of time.' Even the dons at Oxford were happy about the appointment

according to Cecil Fifoot. Looking ahead Henn Collins wrote: 'I think this job will suit your temperament and talents better than the rough and tumble of the King's Bench Division.' Others were appreciative that someone had been appointed who knew something of their speciality. R.E.Megarry wrote: 'I feel sure that all who are condemned to deal with the Rent Acts will particularly applaud the percipience of the Prime Minister, if I may say so.' William Latey said: 'Perhaps you will sometimes be hearing divorce appeals and I may have the opportunity of arguing before a Lord Justice who knows his stuff.'

The work of a judge in the Court of Appeal is quite different from the work of a trial judge. A trial judge has to keep his eye on the witnesses and also on counsel and take notes of the evidence. At the conclusion of submissions by counsel he may have to sum up to a jury or give judgment straightaway. In the Court of Appeal the evidence is on paper and the decisions are usually taken by three judges. The work is unremitting and without the respite that a trial judge may get when a case collapses and it is too late to put another case in the list. A Lord Justice of Appeal works in London and may miss the stimulus of going on circuit and meeting people in the country. The work is, however, very varied and interesting and the judge is able to spend more time at home with his family. When Denning was appointed there were only six judges in the Court of Appeal, one division of three judges took common law appeals and another division of three took chancery appeals. Denning was a judge of the Court of Appeal for nine years from 1948–57 and for another twenty years when Master of the Rolls between 1962 and 1982.

Denning always thought that the best method of reaching the right decision was by word of mouth, the method used by Socrates. A good barrister can reduce a complicated case to its essence in a comparatively short space of time. To read the papers prior to the hearing may take a great deal of time and much that is read is unnecessary to gain a grasp of the issues. The oral method means that longer time must be spent in court while the case is opened but, on the other hand, the judges can get through more work in the time available. The Bar helps the court get to the pith of the case quickly without having to wade through a mass of irrelevant papers. For the oral method to work there must be a supply of good specialist advocates who can provide this service to the court. From the cost point of view the time spent in court is the most expensive and the more the judge knows about the case beforehand the better.

There are two schools of thought about whether judges should read the evidence beforehand. Denning was against this. As a judge he feared that if the papers were read before the hearing the judge might come to a conclusion before hearing counsel and that was not fair to counsel. Counsel should be able to put his case in his own way and persuade the judge without any predisposition on the part of the judge. He was critical of Lord Atkin who read the papers carefully beforehand and was ready to ask searching questions right from the start. He thought that litigants felt that their case had been prejudged before counsel had been heard. He felt that a judge should not ask questions too soon, nor too many, nor interrupt counsel until a convenient moment arrives. The other school of thought is that an experienced judge will not make up his mind before hearing counsel and it is a great saving of time if the judge has read the papers and knows what the case is all about. In practice Denning did look at the papers beforehand if he had the time.

Denning approved of Sir Francis Bacon's advice in his 'Essay on Judicature':

Patience and gravity of hearing is an essential part of justice; and an over-speaking judge is no well tuned cymbal. It is no grace to a judge first to find that which he might have heard in due time from the Bar or to show quickness of conceit in cutting off evidence or counsel too short; or to prevent information by questions, even though pertinent.

But how does a judge stop counsel who goes on too long? Denning thought that the best method was to sit quiet and say nothing. Show no interest in what he is saying and let him run down. Denning was particularly good with litigants in person who came to make their applications to the Court of Appeal on a Monday morning. He listened to them courteously and tried to explain any decision made by the court. A litigant in person will often go away satisfied, even if the decision is against him if it is explained to him in a polite and considerate manner. His particular skill was to send them away satisfied in a short space of time. Lord Scarman has written:

His way with that bête noir of lawyers, the litigant in person, can only be characterised as genius. He discovers by a series of unerring questions what, if any, is his case, upholds or dismisses it with all due speed – and sends him away with fond memories of the judge, even when he sorrows in defeat.[4]

It was not always plain sailing. One Monday morning Miss Stone, a regular client, came in to make her application which was dismissed. She flung a book at the judges and missed. She threw another book which went wide. As she was hustled out of court by the usher she was heard to say 'I am running out of ammunition.' Then a parting shot: 'I congratulate your Lordships on your coolness under fire.'

What was Denning's attitude to the other judges in the Court of Appeal? He did not try to persuade his colleagues to agree with him. He felt that each judge should reach his own conclusions. If all were agreed, so much the better, but if they did not, the majority should settle the matter. It had been the practice of some judges in the House of Lords and the Court of Appeal to try and persuade their brethren to come round to their point of view but this was not Denning's way. In his experience his colleagues seldom changed their minds in discussion after the hearing. Sometimes he appeared to be pleased that his brother judges were against him. This then gave him the opportunity of giving a dissenting judgment which might well be approved by the House of Lords at a later time.

In 1949 Denning gave the first Hamlyn Lecture (see Chapter 16) and thereafter he was in constant demand as a lecturer. He lectured to universities, colleges and other institutions in London, Birmingham, Oxford, Dublin and Newcastle. The following examples show the range of his activities in the 1950s. In 1951 he addressed the Association of Municipal Corporations Conference at Southport and argued that local government should be the focal point of public opinion, ready to rally its forces in defence of individual freedom. He maintained that the real function of a local authority is to represent the people and that this can only be done by elected representatives. He deplored the loss of local hospitals and fire services and, while admitting that large scale organisations could be more efficient, thought that if they disregarded the spirit of man they could lead to the totalitarian state. He thought that the unit of local government should be the community unit.[5] This was going against the conventional wisdom of the time – the bigger the better.

At that time Denning was very much concerned about the encroachment of the State on the rights of the individual and on 18 March

1953 he delivered the 12th Haldane Memorial Lecture at Birkbeck College, London, entitled 'The Rule of Law in the Welfare State'. He had just been elected as the President of Birkbeck College and a month later, on 28 April 1953, a new building at the College was opened by the Queen Mother. In the lecture he emphasised the great value of the Crown Proceedings Act 1947 which enabled government departments to be sued. This lecture gave rise to a leading article in *The Times* on 19 March 1953.

On 27 May 1953 Denning delivered the 33rd Earl Grey Lecture at King's College, Newcastle-upon-Tyne, and chose as his subject 'The influence of religion on law'. He showed that many of the fundamental principles of our law had been derived from the Christian religion. He said: 'I cannot help thinking that the literal interpretation of contracts and statutes is a departure from real truth. It makes words the master of men instead of their servants.' He went on: 'The law proceeds, I suggest, on Christian principles; if you love your neighbour, you will take care not to injure him. And if, perchance, you should by your negligence do him any damage, you will wish to compensate him.' He quoted with approval the words of William Temple who said: 'The person is primary, not the society; the State exists for the citizen, not the citizen for the State.' He ended by saying: 'Religion concerns the spirit in man whereby he is able to recognise what is truth and what is justice; whereas the law is only the application, however imperfectly, of truth and justice in our everyday affairs.'

This lecture repeated some of the ideas set out in an article in the Church of England Newspaper on 6 April 1948 entitled 'What we owe to the Church' in which he wrote:

The teaching of the Church has been in favour of rejecting formalities and insisting on good faith. The just man is 'He that sweareth unto his neighbour and disappointeth him not though it were to his own hindrance'. More and more the courts are insisting that men should honour their promises without requiring formalities.[6]

This was the basis of the 'High Trees' case described earlier. The doctrine of consideration for a contract is a formality and in 1937 the Law Reform Committee recommended its abolition. Nevertheless formality is still firmly established and will not go away.

Asking the question 'Who is my neighbour?' Denning said: 'The answer seems to be the persons who are so closely and directly affected by my act that I ought reasonably to have had them in contemplation as being so affected when I am directing my mind to the acts or omissions which are called in question.' Giving an interview in 1979 he said:

I use the little aphorism: 'without religion there can be no morality and without morality there can be no law'. ... So many of the Christian precepts have given origin to the precepts of law. ... The Church has exercised a tremendous influence over the centuries on men and affairs. It still has an important part to play. It has a teaching function as much as anything, a guiding function.[7]

Denning was President of the Lawyers Christian Fellowship which held a service for lawyers at the Temple Church in October every year. He often attended and was fond of telling the story of a bishop who came to preach at the Temple Church, where the acoustics are bad. The verger gave the following advice to the bishop: 'Pray, my Lord, speak very clearly and distinctly because the agnostics here are terrible.'

In November 1954 he gave the address at this service and quoted William Temple: 'I can't say that I know much about the law, having been more interested in justice.'[8] Denning went on to ask the question: 'Why do people obey the law?' and answered it:

The people of England do not obey the law because they are commanded to do so; nor because they are afraid of sanctions or being punished. They obey the law because they know it is the thing they ought to do. ... For this reason it is most important that the law should be just. People will respect rules which are intrinsically right and just, and will expect their neighbours to obey them, as well as obeying them themselves: but they will not feel the same about rules which are unrighteous or unjust. If people are to feel a sense of obligation to the law, then the law must correspond, as near as may be, to justice.

Not only did Denning give many lectures but he also took part in such charitable activities as the Marriage Guidance Council, The Cheshire Homes and Cumberland Lodge, Windsor. In 1952 he became Chairman of the Trustees of The Cheshire Homes which involved him in a great deal of work. The inspiration behind the venture was Group Captain Leonard Cheshire VC, the son of Denning's old friend Professor Geoffrey Cheshire. Professor Cheshire wrote: 'We approached Lord Justice Denning and, always ready to help a lame duck over a style, he consented without hesitation. This was an act of faith and courage.'[9] Denning remained as Chairman for ten years until his appointment as Master of the Rolls in 1962. Part of the success of the Homes was due to his enthusiasm and to the energetic way in which he nursed its development. He travelled up and down the country, sometimes to iron out a tangled situation and at other times to persuade hesitant promoters to establish a new home. By patience and forbearance as Chairman he promoted harmony and settled differences. The driving force behind the homes was Leonard Cheshire but Denning played an important part in getting the organisation off the ground.

The other voluntary organisation to which Denning gave a great deal of time was Cumberland Lodge. In 1947 King George VI and Queen Elizabeth established a Foundation which was an educational trust based on Christian principles. It was established at Cumberland Lodge, Windsor Great Park, an old house built for the first Duke of Cumberland. The first Principal was Sir Walter Moberly and in 1950 he invited Denning to become Chairman of the Trustees. Students from the four Inns of Court spent weekends there with Benchers and barristers of their Inn. The Dennings often attended these weekends but the Chairman of the Trustees had many administrative duties. Raising money and staff problems caused many headaches. Denning remained as Chairman for nineteen years until December 1969 and thereafter kept his connection with Cumberland Lodge as the Visitor.

Denning found it difficult to refuse when approached by a friend for help. His friend, the sculptress Josephine Banner, who made the portrait bust of Denning which now stands in the Hall at Magdalen College, Oxford, asked for his support in connection with a charity founded by her in 1967 called 'Outpost Emmaus'. The object of the charity was to help disabled children and young people. A trawler – 'Harriet' – beached off Millom, Cumbria was repaired and adapted as a holiday home for the children. Denning helped to raise funds for 'The Harriet Trust' and took a close interest in the affairs of the charity.

When Denning had been a Lord Justice of Appeal for nine years the opportunity arose for promotion to the House of Lords as a Lord of Appeal in Ordinary. In England there is a two-tier system of appeals, first to the Court of Appeal and then to the House of Lords. The second appeal is the result of the vicissitudes of politics. Lord Selborne was the architect of the Supreme Court of Judicature Act 1873. He intended that there should be only one Court of Appeal and the Act was passed in this form. Lord Selborne was Lord Chancellor in Gladstone's administration which fell in 1874 and he was succeeded by Lord Cairns. Lord Cairns had to deal with the problem of appeals from Ireland and Scotland. He introduced a bill to provide for Irish and Scottish appeals to go to the new English Court of Appeal to be styled 'The Imperial Court of Appeal'. This was too much for the national feelings in Ireland and Scotland and the bill was dropped. In 1876 a bill was introduced establishing a final court of appeal for England, Scotland and Ireland, consisting of the Lord Chancellor and a number of professional law lords to be called Lords of Appeal in Ordinary. This bill was enacted as the Appellate Jurisdiction Act 1876.

Early in 1957 Lord Oaksey retired as a law lord and Denning was offered the appointment. He wondered whether acceptance would prejudice his chances of becoming either Lord Chief Justice or Master of the Rolls but after consulting Lord Justice Parker decided to accept.[10] On 5 April 1957 the Prime Minister's secretary wrote to him: 'At the Prime Minister's request I write to let you know that the Queen has been pleased to approve that you be appointed a Lord of Appeal in Ordinary. Garter King of Arms has been instructed to communicate with you with a view to settling your title.' When Denning applied to the College of Arms for his coat of arms he suggested that the supporters to the coat should be palm trees to represent 'Palm Tree' justice. The College of Arms was not amused and would not agree. Eventually Lord Mansfield and Sir Edward Coke appeared as supporters to the coat. The appointment of Lord of Appeal in Ordinary took effect on 24 April 1957 when Denning was 58 years old.

The Bar approved of the appointment but many were sorry that it would mean fewer opportunities of appearing before him. There seems to have been great dissatisfaction with the performance of the House of Lords at that time. Professor C.J.Hamson, of Cambridge University, wrote: 'You may know that I take a gloomy view of the damage which the House of Lords have collectively done to the law of England over the past 50 years and more – indeed ever since their reprieve in 1874 ... But I do think that you, more than any other single person can, will help to improve the situation.[11] Another comment was: 'I hope you will not find the House of Lords too much of a cold storage place.' The barrister Leonard O'Malley wrote: 'The judgments of the House of Lords have appeared for about five or six years to have been arid and unpredictable.' He gave the warning, however, that Denning must go slowly, not too fast for the men with him. There were some signs of the trouble that lay ahead. One law lord wrote: 'You will have, I suspect, some tussles with Gavin Simonds behind the scenes. He has a powerful intellect but a narrow outlook and I think that Scott Reid is first rate, and so, of course is Cyril Radcliffe when he has time to sit.' Judge Gerald Hurst wrote: 'We need a man of your vision in the House of Lords,' while the Oxford University Law Society were delighted that a judge, whom they regarded as the most progressive on the bench, should be promoted to the House of Lords where they thought (wrongly) that he could have a greater effect on the law than in the Court of Appeal.

There was another dimension to the congratulations. Lawyers from overseas wrote welcoming the appointment. Mr Justice Oliver Schreiner from South Africa wrote: 'That should give you more scope than you have had in the past. Just recognition of what you have done for the development of the English law, and indirectly for all systems of law.' Another comment was: 'For my point of view I feel that the hearing of Privy Council Appeals from Africa will greatly benefit from this accession of strength.' Rodger Winn (later Lord Justice Winn) said that he had: 'Great pleasure that such outstanding early recognition had been given to the very special qualities of intellect and integrity that I have known since we met at the Bar.' Professor C.K. Allen wrote: 'We are all so much indebted to you for trying to bring the law into its proper relationship with real justice.' Miss Mavis Hill, the law reporter, wrote that she appreciated the chance 'to be able to make available to a wider public than lawyers the wisdom, generosity and humanity of your decisions.'

The pace of life became easier and, as the House did not sit on a Friday, he was able to get down to his house in Sussex for long weekends. Occasionally he would play golf on the hilly downland course at Pyecombe. There was also more time to cultivate friendships. Lord Reid, the Scottish Lord of Appeal, visited the Dennings at Cuckfield and they went to Wales to stay with Lord Morris of Borth-ys-Gest. As an antidote to his work in the House of Lords he acted

Second Lieutenant Tom Denning, Royal Engineers, 1917.

Mary Harvey, Denning's first wife, with her family.

Denning marries Mary on 28 December 1932.

Denning as a young barrister.

1944 – Denning is made a judge, seen here with his son, Robert.

Denning's second marriage to Joan Stuart in December 1945.

Denning on holiday at Brighton with his son, 1946.

On the beach at Hove with Joan, John and Robert (foreground), 1946.

'Fair Close', Cuckfield, Denning's home from 1941 to 1963.

Denning's coat of arms.

EX LIBRIS

ALFRED THOMPSON, BARON DENNING
of Whitchurch, co. Southampton, One of Her Majesty's Most Honourable
Privy Council, a Knight Bachelor
The Master of the Rolls

On the way to the Lord Chancellor's Breakfast, the Lord Justices of Appeal process from Westminster Abbey to the House of Lords, 1955. Denning is second in the procession.

Norman Hepple R.A. painting a portrait of the Law Lords. Denning stands on the right of the photograph.

'The Lawn', Whitchurch, the Dennings' present home.

as Chairman of the Quarter Sessions for East Sussex. The sittings were not arduous, five days in the long vacation and two or three days in the other vacations. This enabled him to keep in touch with the criminal law, sum up to juries and keep abreast of sentencing policy. He acted as Chairman of the Quarter Sessions for seven years and did not resign until 30 March 1964 after he had become Master of the Rolls and after he had left Cuckfield to live in Hampshire. What he enjoyed most was sitting with the magistrates and talking with them afterwards over lunch. Denning was always ready to help magistrates and seldom turned down an invitation to speak to them. He recognised the importance of their work and tried to encourage them.

One of his first cases in the House of Lords was a Privy Council case of constitutional importance.[12] On the 8 February 1957 Mr Strauss MP wrote a letter on House of Commons notepaper to Reginald Maudling, the Paymaster-General, complaining about the behaviour of the London Electricity Board. He alleged that the Board was disposing of scrap cables at knock-down prices and that their conduct was a scandal. Mr Maudling replied that he was passing on the complaint to the Board. The Board maintained that the complaint was unfounded and asked Mr Strauss to withdraw his remarks. He refused and the Board threatened legal proceedings. Mr Strauss said that the letter was a breach of the privileges of Parliament and that the Board should be punished by the House. The Board replied that they were entitled to have recourse to the courts and could not be stopped.

The Board did not issue a writ. Nevertheless Mr Strauss would not let the matter rest. He thought that it was his privilege to write to a Minister without hindrance and that the threat of a writ infringed his privilege as a member of Parliament. He relied on s9 of the Bill of Rights 1688 which stated: 'that the freedom of speech and debates or proceedings in Parliament ought not to be impeached or questioned in any court or place out of Parliament.' The case was submitted to the Committee of Privileges which referred one issue to the Privy Council for its opinion. The issue was whether the House would be acting contrary to the Parliamentary Privilege Act 1770 if it treated the issue of a writ against a Member of Parliament in respect of a speech or proceeding by him in Parliament as a breach of its privileges. Section 1 of the 1770 Act provided that any person may at any time commence any action against any Member of Parliament and no action shall be stayed by any privilege of Parliament. The fact that the Committee referred the issue to the Privy Council showed that relations between the House and the judiciary were better than in the nineteenth century when such a reference would never have been made.

The Judicial Committee of the Privy Council hearing the issue consisted of seven law lords: Simonds, Goddard, Morton, Reid, Radcliffe, Somervell and Denning. The judgment of the Privy Council was that the words of the statute of 1770 applied only to proceedings against Members of Parliament as individuals and not in respect of their conduct in Parliament as Members of Parliament. This was a delphic judgment but was clearly based on grounds of public policy that disputes between Parliament and the judiciary should be avoided. It was wrong in principle that in the case of a dispute between the subject and Parliament one of the parties, Parliament, should be a judge in its own cause. It was an affront to natural justice. Denning thought that it was for the courts to interpret statutes and not for the Houses of Parliament. He said that all the Queen's subjects had a right to seek redress in the courts without interference from the House of Commons. It was for the judge hearing the case to decide whether Mr Strauss had any defence by way of Parliamentary privilege and Parliament had no right to prevent the courts from inquiring into it. Denning took the greatest of pains with his dissenting judgment and made out a good case at law.

In those days a dissenting opinion in the Privy Council was not permitted and only one opinion could be given. Denning argued that his dissenting opinion should be published but all the other judges were against any change of the existing practice at that time. The rule against the disclosure of dissenting opinions was laid down in 1627 and, at an Imperial conference in 1911, several delegates from the Dominions proposed that dissenting opinions should be published but Australia was against the proposal and it was dropped. The matter was again raised in 1966 when there were discussions about the constitution of the Privy Council. On that occasion Australia said that it would not come into the Privy Council unless dissenting opinions could be expressed. Since 1966 dissenting opinions have been permitted. Denning's dissenting opinion in the Strauss case has now been published as Annexe to an article by Mr Geoffrey Lock in the journal *Public Law*.[13]

In 1960 Denning joined the other law lords in one of the most controversial criminal judgments of that decade. This was *DPP* v *Smith.*[14] Smith had stolen goods in the back of his car. He was stopped by a policeman but Smith, fearing discovery, drove off. The policeman jumped on the bonnet of the car and called on Smith to stop. Smith drove the car right into the oncoming traffic. The policeman was knocked off and killed by an approaching car. Smith was charged with murder, convicted and sentenced to death. The Court of Criminal Appeal reversed the verdict and substituted a sentence of manslaughter, and ten years imprisonment.

On 28 July 1960 the House of Lords – the Lord Chancellor, Lord Kilmuir, Goddard, Tucker, Parker and Denning – unanimously restored the conviction of murder. The Lord Chancellor, in the course of his judgment said: 'If, in doing what he did, he must as a reasonable man have contemplated that serious harm was likely to occur, then he was guilty of murder.' The critics fastened on these words to argue that the House had made a fundamental change in the criminal law and that by using the words 'reasonable man' the House had introduced an objective test whereas in the criminal law the test had always been subjective. The critics included academics, practitioners and Sir Owen Dixon, Chief Justice of Australia. Smith was reprieved but some years later Parliament took account of the criticism by passing s8 of the Criminal Justice Act 1967. Denning had no doubt that on the facts of the case it was rightly decided but that some expressions in the judgment may have misled the critics. In January 1961 he went to Jerusalem to give the Lionel Cohen Lecture at the Hebrew University; it was entitled 'Responsibility before the Law'.[15] He tried to explain what he thought was a misunderstanding about the judgment in the House of Lords. No one had suggested that Smith had intended to kill the policeman. By his actions in driving his car into the oncoming traffic with the policeman clinging on he intended to do him grievous bodily harm. Denning concluded: 'Did he [Smith] intend to cause death or grievous bodily harm? If he intended grievous bodily harm and death resulted, that was murder.'

Denning did not enjoy his time in the House of Lords. He once said: 'To most lawyers on the Bench the House of Lords is like heaven – you want to get there some day – but not while there is any life in you.' Lord Simonds was Lord Chancellor to begin with and the emphasis was on maintaining the status quo and the integrity of the existing law. Personal relations between Simonds and Denning were cool. Denning thought that Simonds was too dogmatic and emphatic. He felt that Simonds looked down on him because of his social origins, although Simonds himself came from a family of brewers. In later years the Dennings showed many kindnesses to Gavin and Mary Simonds and he came to fish in the Test at Denning's home. He was verbally 'beheaded' by Lord Simonds on at least three reported occasions. A long time after he had left the House of Lords, in 1978, he told an interviewer:

It wasn't as much fun as I had thought it would be as fifth member. Not much good dissenting. As Master of the Rolls I have more say. I pick the cases. I can choose more or less. And then in the House of Lords they don't often put the right people on the right cases. It is very badly selected. Or you may be in the Privy Council which is not nearly so interesting. ... You only have about 30 cases a year and you may only sit on about half of them because you may be in the Privy Council. And then I didn't like it much, you don't have much influence. I have a good deal more influence now and I'm doing more than I would have done as a Lord.[16]

Denning dissented in one of his first cases: *Rahimtoola* v *Nizam of Hyderabad* in which he restated the law relating to sovereign immunity (see Chapter 14). As I have already mentioned he also dissented in the Privy Council case of Mr Strauss. Nevertheless he only dissented in 16% of the cases heard by him. He sat in the House of Lords on eighty occasions between 1957 and 1966 and wrote seventy-six judgments, dissenting on ten occasions. Lord Keith dissented on more occasions: in 22% of the cases on which he sat.[17] But by 1962 this period of his life was about to end.

Eight

PRECEDENT

> *For I observe that, in the past, when the lawyer's precedents have been*
> *found to work injustice, they have been corrected, as often as not, by*
> *the actions of juries; or by the Lords of Parliament who were, for the*
> *most part, not lawyers. It is these ordinary folk who have broadened*
> *the basis of freedom, not by sticking to bad old precedents, but by*
> *making good new ones.*[1]
>
> Denning

A binding precedent is the enunciation of the reason or principle upon which a question before the court has been decided. This must take place as an adjudication in open court. A precedent is a judicial decision and not a rule of construction or a rule of practice although these are often labelled as precedents. A precedent established by a lower court can be overruled by a higher court in the legal hierarchy. A lot of confusion is caused by treating statements made by judges in an earlier case as precedents which must be followed. A rule of practice can be changed by the court which established the practice. A rule of construction is the most difficult to alter as there is no established means to do this except legislation. If the courts make the attempt the conveyancers are up in arms.

Talking about precedent Denning said:

> If lawyers hold to their precedents too closely, forgetful of the fundamental principles of truth and justice which they should serve, they may find the whole edifice comes tumbling down about them. They will be lost in 'The codeless myriad of precedent. That wilderness of single instances.' The common law will cease to grow. Like a coral reef it will become a structure of fossils.[2]

This is the nub of the problem. There are many ways that judges try to get round awkward precedents which they believe to be unjust. They distinguish the case from the earlier one by finding some difference in the facts or the law. Sometimes they pour cold water on the reasoning in the earlier case or say that it is too widely stated. They find some reason for departing from the previous decision such as saying that things are different now that law and equity are fused.

As a result precedents proliferate, all depending on slightly different facts. English lawyers are wedded to precedent. They search for a precedent and are satisfied when they find one. They seldom raise their eyes to any other aspect of the case. They often fail to dig down to find the principle established by the case. In the eighteenth century Lord Mansfield said: 'The law does not consist of particular cases: but in general principles which run through the cases and govern the decision of them.'[3]

Denning dissented in two cases in the House of Lords in 1959 and 1960 on the question of precedent. In the first case he said:

> It seems to me that when a particular precedent, even in your Lordship's House, comes into conflict with a fundamental principle, also of your Lordship's House, then the fundamental principle must prevail. This must at least be true when on the one hand, the particular precedent leads to absurdity or injustice, and on the other hand, the fundamental principle leads to consistency and fairness. It would, I think, be a great mistake to cling too closely to a particular precedent at the expense of fundamental principle.[4]

Here Denning was emphasising the importance of principle; that it should have priority over particular precedents. As Sir John Holt said in the seventeenth century: 'The law consists not of particular instances and precedents, but in the reason of the law.'[5] The precedent should be an illustration of the principle. The other case in the 1960s dealt with the subject of double taxation. Denning said:

> The doctrine of precedent does not compel your Lordships to follow the wrong path until you fall over the edge of the cliff. As soon as you find that you are going in the wrong direction you must at least be permitted to strike off in the right direction, even if you are not allowed to retrace your steps.[6]

Rebuffed in his judicial efforts for the reform of precedent in the House of Lords Denning sought other means to persuade his colleagues and the legal profession. In 1959 he was invited to be the Romanes lecturer at Oxford and delivered the lecture in the Sheldonian Theatre on 21 May. He used the opportunity to put forward his views on how the doctrine of precedent might be modified and the lecture was entitled 'From precedent to precedent'. He compared a lawyer seeking justice to a scientist seeking truth. A lawyer should take his precedents and from them build principles. These principles should be modified when found to be unsuited. He said that the House of Lords, sitting judicially, as delegate of the Sovereign, was the fountain of justice and commanded to correct errors and determine what is right and ought to be done according to the law and custom of the realm.

Denning was concerned about the effect of the law on the community at large a, subject seldom considered by many judges and lawyers. He said:

Many a lawyer will dispute the analogy with science. 'I am only concerned,' he will say, 'with the law as it is, not with what it ought to be.' For him the rule is the thing. Right or wrong does not matter. That approach is all very well for a working lawyer who applies the law as a working mason lays bricks, without any responsibility for the building which he is making. But it is not good enough for the lawyer who is concerned with his responsibility to the community at large. He should ever seek to do his part to see that the principles of law are consonant with justice. If he should fail to do this, he will forfeit the confidence of the people. The law will fall into disrepute; and if that happens the stability of the country will be shaken. The law must be certain. Yes, as certain as may be. But it must be just too.[7]

Denning emphasised how the law had been improved when lay people had some say in the matter:

You will have noticed how progressive the House of Lords has been when the lay peers have had their say, or at any rate, their vote on the decisions. They have insisted on the true principles and have not allowed the conservatism of lawyers to be carried too far. Even more so when we come to the meaning of words. Lawyers are here the most offending souls alive. They will so often stick to the letter and miss the substance. The reason is plain enough. Most of them spend their working lives drafting some kind of document or another – trying to see whether it covers this contingency or that. They dwell on words until they become mere precisians in the use of them. They would rather be accurate than clear. They would sooner be long than short. They seek to avoid two meanings, and end – on occasions – by having no meaning.[8]

The Romanes Lecture was a very cogent argument for the House of Lords to be allowed to review its own decisions. The rule of practice – that the House could not reverse a ruling of its own on a point of law – was only laid down in 1861, when the House decided not to depart from an earlier ruling. Some of the judges, however, thought the former ruling wrong.[9] Denning gave examples from history, when lay lords had sat and when the House frequently departed from earlier decisions. He said that the House of Lords made the law by creating new precedents where none previously existed and by correcting old precedents. He also quoted cases within his own experience, including the case of workmen's compensation, an occasion on which the House had changed its mind. He said that if a court below went wrong the House of Lords could correct the error but it could not correct its own errors. He pointed out that the Judicial Committee of the Privy Council had always had power to reconsider its own decisions, so too has the Supreme Court of the United States of America, the Supreme Court of South Africa and the Supreme Court of Israel. He urged that the House recapture the vital principle of growth.

It must, of course, correct the errors that have been made in the courts below, but it should do more. It lays down, or should lay down, the fundamental principles of law to govern the people; and whilst adhering firmly to those principles, it should override particular precedents that it finds in variance therewith. Then only shall we be able to claim that 'Freedom broadens slowly down from precedent to precedent.'[10]

The subject of precedent was the subject of much discussion and concern in the early 1960s when articles appeared in learned journals on the subject.[11] In a case in 1962 Denning said:

The doctrine that your Lordships are bound by a previous decision of your own is, as I have always understood it, limited to the decision itself and to what is necessarily involved in it. It does not mean that you are bound by the various reasons given in support of it, especially when they contain propositions wider than the case required.[12]

As long as Lord Simonds was Lord Chancellor there could be no change but on 17 October 1964 Lord Gardiner was appointed by the incoming Government. His great interest was law reform and he had edited a book with Andrew Martin, published in 1963, entitled *Law Reform Now*. His most important contribution to law reform was the establishment of the Law Commission in 1965. He also applied his mind to a relaxation of the law relating to precedent. The rule that the House of Lords could not depart from a previous decision of its own was not a precedent in the strict sense but a rule of practice that the House had laid upon itself. It was not laid down by Parliament. Rules of practice may be altered by the judges who make them. Each Division of the High Court and the Court of Appeal issues its own Practice Directions and cancels them when they are no longer appropriate. Practice is constantly being changed in an attempt to improve it. The initiative for change in the practice in the House

of Lords came from Lord Gardiner and on 26 July 1966 a Practice
Statement was published stating:

Their Lordships nevertheless recognise that too rigid adherence to
precedent may lead to injustice in a particular case and unduly restrain
the proper development of the law. They propose, therefore, to modify the
present practice and, while treating former decisions of the House as normally
binding, to depart from a previous decision when it appears right to do
so. This announcement is not intended to affect the use of precedent elsewhere
than in this House.

By this time Denning was back in the Court of Appeal as Master
of the Rolls.

In 1944 a full Court of Appeal of six judges had held that the
Court of Appeal was bound to follow its own decisions.[13] There were,
however, three exceptions to this rule:

1 The court is entitled to decide which of two conflicting decisions
of its own it will follow.
2 It is bound to refuse to follow a decision of its own which cannot
stand with a decision of the House of Lords.
3 It is not bound to follow a decision of its own if given *per incuriam*
[when a case or statute has not been brought to the court's attention
and the decision was given in ignorance thereof].

A full Court of Appeal has no greater power than a division of
the court but in this case the court was laying down a practice direction
for the future business of the court. Here was a rule of practice laid
down many years before and endorsed by the House of Lords.

Denning struggled long and unsuccessfully against this fetter on
the powers of the Court of Appeal. He tried to read the statement:
'This announcement is not intended to affect the use of precedent
elsewhere than in the House of Lords' as: 'We are only considering
the doctrine of the precedent in the House of Lords. We are not
considering its use elsewhere.' The House of Lords would have none
of this and confirmed that the 1944 rules still stood.[14] The issue came
to a head in *Davis* v *Johnson* in 1978.[15] The Domestic Violence Act
1976 gave the County Court a new jurisdiction for the protection
of battered wives. Two divisions of the Court of Appeal had held
that the court had no power to grant an injunction excluding Johnson
from the house owned jointly by Davis and Johnson. The judges
had obeyed all the rules. They had not looked at *Hansard* and had

construed the statute strictly saying that the statute did not affect property rights.[16] Denning thought that the judges were not following the spirit of the statute and the intention of Parliament. He convened a five-judge court to try the appeal, one of whom was Sir George Baker, the President of the Family Division who had wide experience of family business. The court divided – three judges: Denning, Baker and Shaw, held that the County Court had power to grant an injunction excluding Johnson from the house, even though he owned a half share of the house. Two judges: Goff and Cumming-Bruce, dissented. They held that the 1944 case was a precedent that bound them. The majority held that a practice direction about precedent was made by a full Court of Appeal in 1944 and that a full Court of Appeal in 1978 was entitled to amend that direction by adding an additional reason. It was not a precedent in the true sense of the word.

Johnson appealed to the House of Lords. The House dismissed the appeal saying that s1 of the Act gave power to grant the injunction but reaffirmed the 1944 case that the Court of Appeal must follow its previous decisions. This was said by the House: 'expressly, unequivocally and unanimously'. Lord Diplock referred to Denning's 'one man crusade' to free the Court of Appeal from its obligation to follow its previous decisions. The majority of the Court of Appeal had considered the 1944 case and had come to the conclusion that what they wanted to do would not come within the exceptions laid down in 1944. They added another exception of their own: that the court was not bound to follow a previous decision if satisfied that the previous decision was clearly wrong and could not stand in the face of the will and intention of Parliament, expressed in simple language in a recent Act of Parliament passed to remedy a serious mischief. The decision of the House of Lords was Gilbertian. The decision of the majority of the Court of Appeal was right but they had no power to make it. In 1944 the Court of Appeal was right to make a practice direction about its power to review its previous decisions but in 1978 it had no power to alter such practice direction.

Denning's one man crusade had much to be said for it. The problems raised by the 1944 judgment could have been solved by the House of Lords making another Practice Statement that a division of the Court of Appeal of five judges could overrule a decision of three judges if the decision was clearly wrong. At the Annual Meeting of 'Justice' in 1961 Lord Evershed, with his experience of both the House of Lords and the Court of Appeal, suggested that consideration should be given to abolishing the appellate jurisdiction of the House of Lords and giving jurisdiction to a Court of Appeal of five judges to reconsider any previous decision of the Court of Appeal.[17] The Court of Appeal was the final court of appeal in England from the date of the Judicature Act in 1873 until the Appellate Jurisdiction Act was passed in 1876. In 1963 Lord Gardiner and Lord Elwyn-Jones were in favour of a strong and final Court of Appeal able to reconsider any previous decision.[18]

The need for the Court of Appeal to be able to review its own decisions becomes more urgent as the court now sits in many more divisions because of the increase of work. This means that the chance of error increases. Perhaps English lawyers could adopt the more relaxed attitude to precedent as is the case in Scotland. As Professor T.B.Smith of Edinburgh University said:

Why should a court, which in the past clearly refused to be strictly bound by precedent (and has subsequently tied its own hands) not resume the earlier and more equitable practice? It is astonishing to observe the most eminent legal minds of the country reacting to the prison of precedents (of precedents which they recognise as unjust) like a child who has shut himself in a room and screams to be let out – presumably by the legislature.[19]

It is an anomaly that a High Court judge is not obliged to follow the decision of a brother High Court judge and the House of Lords need not follow a decision of its own. It is only the Court of Appeal that is bound by its own earlier decisions.

Denning sometimes dissented from a previous decision of the House of Lords with the object of getting a change in the law. An example of this occurred in 1967 in connection with Crown privilege.[20] Michael Conway was training to be a police constable. The Police Superintendent, with no sufficient grounds, accused Conway of stealing another trainee's torch. Conway was acquitted but sued the Police Superintendent for damages. Conway's lawyers wanted to see the reports that the Superintendent had, from time to time, made on Conway. The defence claimed Crown privilege. In 1942 judgment had been given in the case of *Duncan* v *Cammell Laird* when the Lord Chancellor had presided in the House of Lords with all six law lords.[21] It was held that a Minister of the Crown had the right to object to the production of any document 'where the practice of keeping a class of document secret is necessary for the proper functioning of the public service'. If the Minister objected the court could not overrule his objection. The majority of the Court of Appeal could see no way in which this ruling could be challenged. Conway could not appeal to the House of Lords without legal aid. A dissenting judgment in the Court of Appeal would help him to get legal aid. Denning said that the doctrine of precedent in the House of Lords had been transformed by the Practice Statement of 1966 and this was a case where the power should be used. The extent of Crown privilege extends only so far as the common law permits and it is for the judges to define its ambit, as was being done in Commonwealth countries. The Home Secretary did not suggest that the contents of the reports would in any way harm the public interest. The 1942 case had been decided in wartime and when the House of Lords came to reconsider the case and looked at the documents they could see no reason why they should not be disclosed. Denning felt that his dissent had given the House the chance to reconsider their earlier decision.

Denning's attitude to precedent can best be summed up in his own words:

Let it not be thought from this discourse that I am against the doctrine of precedent. I am not. It is the foundation of our system of case law. This has evolved by broadening down from precedent to precedent. By standing by previous decisions we have kept the common law on good course. All that I am against is its too strict application, a rigidity which insists that a bad precedent must necessarily be followed. I would treat it as you would a path through the woods. You must follow it certainly, so as to reach your end. But you must not let the path become too overgrown. You must cut out the dead wood and trim off the side branches, else you find yourself lost in the thickets and the brambles. My plea is simply to keep the path to justice clear of obstructions which impede it.[22]

Perhaps the last word may be said by the late Professor Rupert Cross: 'There should be a simple rule that neither the House of Lords nor the Court of Appeal is absolutely bound by its own decisions.'[23]

Nine

ABUSE OF POWER

*Properly exercised the new powers of the Executive lead to the Welfare
State: but abused they lead to the totalitarian state.*[1]

Denning

Two world wars and the growth of the Welfare State had led to
a great increase in administrative action. Tribunals abounded and
the State encroached more and more on the freedom of the individual.
In England there is no special court dealing with the relationship
between the State and the individual, such as the Conseil d'Etat in
France, and it was left to the common law to give the protection
needed. As early as 1949 in his Hamlyn Lecture 'Freedom under
the Law' Denning was saying that our procedure for securing our
personal freedom was efficient but our procedure for preventing the
abuse of power was not.[2]

The Court of King's Bench exercises control over public bodies
by means of the prerogative writs. As I have already mentioned
certiorari is a writ directed to an inferior tribunal requiring the record
of the proceedings to be transmitted to the King's Bench to be dealt
with there. Mandamus is a command by the King's Bench to an
inferior tribunal to do something which it has a public duty to do.
There was no doubt that the court could interfere to prevent a tribunal
from exceeding the jurisdiction which Parliament had conferred on
it by means of the writ of *certiorari*, but had it any power when
the tribunal had gone wrong in law? In 1952 the Court of Appeal
dealt with the case of Thomas Shaw who lost his job as clerk to
the West Northumberland Joint Hospital Board.[3] He was aggrieved
by the amount of the compensation awarded by the tribunal. Denning
said:

The Court of King's Bench has an inherent jurisdiction to control all
inferior tribunals, not in an appellate capacity, but in a supervisory capacity.

This control extends not only to seeing that inferior tribunals keep within their jurisdiction but also to seeing they observe the law. Control is exercised by means of a power to quash any determination by the tribunal which on the face of it offends against the law. The King's Bench does not substitute its own views for those of the tribunal as the Court of Appeal would do. It leaves it to the tribunal to hear the case again.

The Court of Appeal held that in Shaw's case there had been an error in law which had deprived Shaw of the compensation to which he was entitled. The Court of Appeal, consisting of Singleton, Denning and Morris, unanimously quashed the award and there was no appeal. To reach this result the court had to circumvent a Court of Appeal decision of 1944; this was done. Denning regarded this as one of his most important cases.

Ministers were anxious to prevent the courts from interfering with the decisions of tribunals and frequently inserted 'ouster clauses' in Acts of Parliament making the decision of the Minister 'final'. In 1957 Denning said:

> The remedy is not excluded by the fact that the determination of the Board is by statute made final. Parliament only gives the impress of finality to the decisions of the Board on condition that they are reached in accordance with the law: and the Queen's Courts can issue a declaration to see that the condition is fulfilled.[4]

In another case in the same year he said that 'final' means 'without appeal' and does not mean without recourse to certiorari.[5] He said that certiorari was never to be taken away by any statute except by the most clear and explicit words.

The Executive must have thought that they had succeeded when they inserted this sentence in s4(4) of the Foreign Compensation Act 1950: 'The determination by the Commission of any application made to them under this Act shall not be called in question in any court of law.' In 1964 Denning and Harman allowed a case under this section to go to trial; Diplock dissented. The Court of Appeal was upheld by the House of Lords; it said that in the particular case the Commission rejected the claim on a ground which they had no right to take into account.[6]

English judges have tended to take a restrictive attitude to the standing of persons entitled to apply for a prerogative writ, confining it to those whose rights had been affected. Denning took a more liberal view: that the words 'persons aggrieved' included persons with a genuine grievance – their interests had been prejudicially affected. These interests could extend to amenity interests. In 1966 Mr Raymond Blackburn was concerned about the way the big London gaming clubs were being run. He complained to the Commissioner of Police without success as the Police had taken a policy decision not to prosecute. In the event it was held that he had standing to ask that the law should be enforced and the court held that the Police must see that it was enforced.[7] As a result of this case the Home Secretary at the time, Mr James Callaghan, invited Denning to see him to discuss the reform of the law and a system of licensing was introduced.

Denning tried to extend the category of persons who could apply for declarations and injunctions as well as the prerogative writs. For historical reasons these were equitable remedies employed in the Court of Chancery and where the relief was to enforce a public duty the Court required the applicant to apply to the Attorney-General for his consent to bring a 'relator' action. If the Attorney-General consented the action proceeded as an action by the Attorney-General. On Tuesday 16 January 1973 Ross McWhirter came to the Court of Appeal at 3 p.m. and told them that a film was to be shown on television about Andy Warhol. The Attorney-General attended and said that he did not consent but, despite his refusal, an injunction was granted.[8] Denning held that a citizen aggrieved had a *locus standi* to come to the courts.

In 1977 this did not find favour with the House of Lords in the Gouriet case.[9] On Friday 14 January 1977 at 5.30 p.m. Denning was about to leave for home when his clerk told him that there was an urgent application to be made on Saturday morning. It was an appeal from a Queen's Bench judge who had refused an injunction against the Post Office Union. The Court of Appeal sat on Saturday 15 January 1977. On 13 January the General Secretary of the Post Office Union said that the Union would stop all transmission of mail to South Africa from Sunday for one week. On 14 January Mr Gouriet's solicitor went to the Attorney-General's chambers for his consent to bring an action to stop the proposed breach of the law. The Attorney-General refused and Mr Gouriet applied to the judge in chambers in the Queen's Bench Division. The judge refused, saying that without the consent of the Attorney-General he could do nothing.

The Court of Appeal granted the injunction which was obeyed. The trade union appealed to the House of Lords which held that the Court of Appeal had no power to grant the injunction and the proceedings should have been struck out. There is no doubt that historically the Attorney-General had an absolute discretion whether or not to act in such a case. This was a rule of practice which the House of Lords could have altered if they so desired. Denning's views are forcibly expressed in one paragraph of his judgment:

When the Attorney-General comes, as he does here, and tells us that he has a prerogative, a prerogative by which he alone is the one who can say whether the criminal law should be enforced in these courts or not, then I say there is no such prerogative. He has no prerogative to suspend or dispense with the laws of England. If he does not give his consent, then any citizen of the land, any one of the public at large who is adversely affected, can come to this court and ask that the law be enforced.

It is unfortunate that the word prerogative was used. The Attorney-General has no prerogative but only the Crown. By custom there was a rule of practice that the Attorney-General's discretion with regard to relator actions was absolute.

In January 1978 new Rules of Court were brought into force introducing a comprehensive system of judicial review enabling an application to include the prerogative writs and also a declaration and an injunction. On the question of *locus standi* an applicant must have 'a sufficient interest in the matter to which the application relates' but no attempt is made to define this. Denning's efforts to widen the scope of *locus standi* were successful although his attempt to curb the absolute discretion of the Attorney-General in relator actions was not. However relator actions became of less importance as declarations and injunctions could in future be obtained by means of judicial review.

The principles used by the judges to control the powers of public bodies were natural justice and fairness. The two elements of natural justice are that a man must not be a judge in his own cause and that a party must have an opportunity of having his say. The first element is illustrated by a case in 1969.[10] Lannon was a rent officer who adjudicated on a case with the landlords of Regency Lodge. He was a tenant of the landlords and was in dispute with them about the rent of his own flat. Denning, sitting in the Court of Appeal, said that a man might by disqualified from sitting in a judicial capacity if he had a direct pecuniary interest in the subject matter or if he was biassed in favour of one side or against the other. The court held that Lannon's connection with the tenants of Regency Lodge was such as to give an impression of bias. Justice must not only be done but must be seen to be done.

The second element, that a man must be given the opportunity to be heard, occurs much more frequently in practice and raises many more difficult questions. Does it mean a right to an oral hearing and the right to have counsel? In *Kanda* v *Government of Malaya* Kanda was not supplied with a copy of the report of a board of inquiry which contained matters highly prejudicial to him.[11] The court held that there had been a failure to afford Kanda a reasonable opportunity of being heard and that his dismissal from the Government service of Malaysia was null and void. Denning said:

If the right to be heard is to be of real right which is worth anything, it must carry with it a right in the accused man to know the case which is made against him. He must know what evidence has been given and what statements have been made affecting him; and then he must be given a fair opportunity to correct or contradict them.

Does the right to be heard include the right of legal representation? Denning held that it was part of natural justice if a case involved the possible deprivation of a man's livelihood,[12] but it should normally be excluded in the case of a domestic tribunal.[13] Generally he was against legal representation before tribunals. In one case he said:

Parliament intended that the Supplementary Benefit Act 1966 should be administered with as little technicality as possible. The courts should hesitate long before interfering by *certiorari* with decisions of appeal tribunals. The courts should only interfere when the decision of the tribunal is unreasonable in the sense that no reasonable tribunal could reach that decision.[14]

Nor was he willing to extend legal representation to cases involving disciplinary hearings in prisons where a speedy hearing was required.[15] The problem with lawyers is that they bring with them technicality not required in most tribunal cases; however, in important cases the subject should have the benefit of professional advocacy provided by the Bar.

Denning was always anxious to extend the rules of natural justice to the hearing of public inquiries despite a decision in 1948 that the Minister's duties were purely administrative, not judicial or quasi-judicial.[16] Lord Thankerton, the Scottish law lord, said that if the Minister 'genuinely' considers the matter, the court will not interfere. In his Hamlyn Lecture in 1949 Denning expanded on the meaning of powers 'genuinely' exercised.[17] The administrator must carefully investigate all the relevant considerations and reject irrelevant ones. He must fairly balance public interest and private right. He must come to an honest decision as to whether he should exercise the power or not, for the purpose authorised by Parliament. Where there was a conflict of interest between natural justice and national security he came down on the side of national security. In a case in 1977 he said that where there was a conflict between these two principles the balance had to be decided by the Home Secretary and not by the courts.[18] He is the person entrusted by Parliament with the task.

What is the position when a minister abuses the discretion given to him by Parliament? Denning's view was that if a minister went wrong in law he was doing something for which he had no jurisdiction. The court could interfere if the minister had gone outside the powers given by the Act; or if he had acted on no evidence; or if he had come to a conclusion which, on the evidence, was not reasonable; or if he had given a wrong interpretation to the words of a statute; or if he had taken into consideration matters which he ought not to have taken into account, or vice versa; or if he had departed from the rules of natural justice; or if he had asked himself the wrong questions.[19] Denning believed that a minister was given jurisdiction on condition that he exercised his discretion in accordance with law. If he went wrong in law he was doing something that he had no jurisdiction to do.

In 1968 Denning gave a dissenting judgment in the case of *Padfield* v *Ministry of Agriculture*.[20] The Milk Marketing Board fixed the price of milk. There were eleven regions in England, each having a different price for milk depending on the cost of transport and other factors. The South East region complained that their differential was too low. S 19(3) of the Agricultural Marketing Act 1958 provided that complaints should be considered by a committee of investigation. The Minister, however, refused to refer the complaint to the committee. Denning said:

Good administration requires that complaints should be investigated and that grievances should be remedied. When Parliament has set up machinery for that very purpose it is not for the minister to brush it on one side. He should not refuse to have a complaint investigated without good cause ... the minister has been influenced by reasons which ought not to have weighed with him. He has not therefore properly exercised his discretion.

Subsequently Denning was upheld in the House of Lords on a different ground, that the refusal would frustrate the policy of the Act.

In the 1970s there were three important cases relating to ministerial discretion. The first one caused a great deal of public interest. This was *Secretary of State for Education & Science* v *Tameside MBC*.[21] The Secretary of State approved a scheme of comprehensive schools in Tameside in May 1976 but after an election the political complexion of the council changed and they wanted some postponement in the proposal. The council agreed that three new comprehensive schools should be built and that sixteen secondary modern schools should become comprehensive. They proposed to postpone plans for five grammar schools to give time for the position to be reviewed and wished to maintain the status quo. The Secretary of State felt that there was not time to carry out any selection procedure by September and sought an order for mandamus to have the scheme carried out. The divisional court of the Queen's Bench Division granted the order sought. The minister was acting under s 68 of the Education Act 1944 which permitted the minister to give appropriate directions 'if satisfied that any local authority was acting unreasonably.' Denning said that he could not find any evidence on which the minister could decide that the council had acted or were proposing to act unreasonably. The Court of Appeal was upheld by the House of Lords.

The second case was in 1976.[22] The Home Secretary proposed to increase television licences from £12 to £18 on 1 April 1975. On 26 March 1975 Mr Congreve applied for a £12 licence and got it. Overlapping licences were granted to 24,000 licence holders. The Home Office wrote to each holder saying that unless a further £6 were paid the licence would be revoked. Mr Congreve did not pay and his licence was revoked. The Home Office had power under s 1(4) of the Wireless Telegraphy Act 1949 by notice to revoke a licence. Denning said that the court could intervene if the power was exercised arbitrarily or improperly. The action of the Minister was unlawful. The Court of Appeal granted a declaration that the notice of revocation of the television licence was unlawful. During the course of argument counsel for the Crown, Roger Parker, said: 'If the court interferes in this case it would not be long before the powers of the court would be called in question.' Commenting on this in his judgment Denning said: 'We trust that this was not said seriously but only as a piece of advocate's licence.' On 5 December Bernard Levin wrote exultantly in *The Times*: 'Blow the loud trumpets of victory for US over THEM in the TV Licence War' and on 6 December *The Times* had a leading article: 'Not advocate's licence'. On 9 December Mr Parker had the court specially reconvened to make an apology. He said that there was no intention by the Home Secretary to threaten the court that the powers of the court would be curtailed and apologised if it should have sounded like that. The incident was brought to a happy ending by the Home Secretary, Roy Jenkins, who announced in the House of Commons on 9 December that he was not asking for leave to appeal to the House of Lords. He said that it was unthinkable for any Home Secretary to question the vital independence of the judiciary or propound the doctrine that the executive was in any way above or outside the law.

The third was the celebrated case of Freddie Laker.[23] One of the objects of the Civil Aviation Act 1971 was to permit at least one major British airline to compete with the State airline. The Civil Aviation Authority granted Laker a ten-year licence to fly to the USA from 1 January 1973 and on the strength of this Laker ordered planes and incurred heavy expenses. In July 1975, under different political masters, the Secretary of State reversed the previous policy and decided not to encourage competition between the State airline and private airlines. Laker was told that 'Skytrain' could not begin flying. Two main issues arose. Firstly whether the Minister could completely reverse the previous policy and decide not to encourage competition. The Court of Appeal held that the Minister could not do so as he could not alter the statutory purpose of the Act, the encouragement of competition. The second issue was whether the Secretary of State could withdraw Laker's designation as a carrier under the prerogative power. Both the judge of first instance and the other two judges in the Court of Appeal held that the provisions of the Civil Aviation Act 1971 fettered the use of the prerogative. Denning was willing to go further and to challenge the prerogative power directly: 'If it is found that the power has been exercised improperly or mistakenly so as to impinge unjustly on the legitimate rights or interests of the subject then the court must so declare.'

There was one case in which discretion was checked for the lack of 'careful investigation'. It can be regarded as the use of the 'substantial evidence' test.[24] A local authority declared a 'clearance area' and included four shops and six flats, which were in good condition. Under s 43(2) of the Housing Act 1957 a local authority may purchase any land adjoining a clearance area which is 'reasonably necessary' for dealing with the cleared land. The Inspector recommended that the shops and the flats should be excluded from the clearance area but the Minister rejected his advice and confirmed the compulsory purchase order. The Court of Appeal held that there was no evidence that the acquisition was 'reasonably necessary' for the satisfactory development or use of the cleared land and the Minister's decision was held to be *ultra vires*. It was held that the reasonable necessity of including the land was a question of fact, not policy. This was a pioneering decision similar to the American rule insisting that ministerial decisions must be based on 'substantial evidence'. It has been followed frequently since 1971.

In 1982 there was a case of great political sensitivity. Labour gained control of the Greater London Council and moved to reduce London Transport fares by 25% which would entail extra money being found by the London boroughs. Bromley Borough Council objected and took proceedings.[25] Both the Court of Appeal and the House of Lords unanimously granted *certiorari* to quash the precept. Denning asked the question whether the GLC had given 'genuine consideration' to the rights of all parties. He accepted that the GLC felt impelled to fulfil their election manifesto and considered that they had a mandate to do so. This was held to be misconceived and that an election manifesto should not be 'taken as gospel'. The GLC had not given genuine consideration to the rights of other parties affected by the decisions.

The duty to act fairly and to observe the law was not only applied to ministers and to public authorities but also to domestic tribunals. Two cases in the 1950s illustrate Denning's attitude. Mr Abbott was a cornporter in London who went to work when six other members of his gang stayed away. The trade union committee fined him 10 shillings and ordered him to pay the day's money to the other six. He felt aggrieved and hit the convenor of the committee on the nose.

The convenor called the committee together and struck Abbott's name off the register of cornporters. This meant that he could not make his living in the London Docks where he worked. The judge did not award him damages as he could not find any legal peg on which to award damages. The Court of Appeal upheld the decision of the judge; Denning dissented.[26] Denning said: 'I should be sorry to think that if a wrong has been done, the plaintiff is to go without a remedy simply because no one can find a peg to hang it on.' In this he has the support of the great judges of an earlier time. In 1757 Lord Mansfield said: 'There is no injury or wrong for which the law does not provide a remedy', following a dictum of Sir Edward Coke in the seventeenth century.[27]

The other case also related to the activities of a trade union committee.[28] Frank Lee ran a roundabout called 'Noah's Ark' and had a pitch at Bradford Summer Fair which was claimed by William Shaw. The trade union committee found in favour of Shaw and, finding Lee guilty of 'unfair competition', fined him £100. Lee failed to pay the fine and was expelled from the union. The Court of Appeal held that the committee's decision was invalid. As Lee had been expelled from the union he was deprived of his right to earn his living as a showman on fairgrounds controlled by the union. Denning said: 'A man's right to work is just as important to him as, if not more important than, his rights of property. The courts intervene every day to protect rights of property. They must also intervene to protect the right to work.' It was held that on the true construction of the trade union rules Lee's conduct could not be unfair competition and the fine and expulsion were ultra vires and void.

Denning's efforts from his earliest days aimed to protect the individual from the abuse of power from whatever source. Parliament gave great discretionary powers to ministers and he felt that the courts must be the bulwark protecting the subject from the arbitrary exercise of this power. How were such powers to be kept within recognised channels? What were such channels to be? The major principle established was that the minister's decision must be in accordance with law. There must be proper evidence to support his decision and he must act fairly. The minister must observe the principles of natural justice and must give reasons. An official must not go outside the powers given by statute. Denning was successful in broadening the class of person able to apply for the prerogative writs but was unsuccessful in challenging the Attorney-General's right to decide whether or not it was in the public interest to act in a relator action.

The duty to act fairly and to observe the law was applicable not only to ministers and officials but also to domestic tribunals. Denning upheld a man's right to work. The actions of domestic tribunals can affect a man's livelihood and they were not permitted to act arbitrarily and unfairly. Legal representation was not desirable for tribunals but where a man's right to work was at stake he should have the opportunity of employing a professional advocate. In his Hamlyn Lecture, 'Freedom under the law', which dealt with justice between man and the State, Denning said: 'We must see to it that the stream of British freedom, which has been kept clear by the decisions of the judges, does not perish in the bogs and sands of departmental decisions.'[29]

Ten

MASTER OF THE ROLLS
1962–82

*I am glad that you have got your wish and managed to get back to
the Court of Appeal where I am sure you will be happier, if only because
it will be nearer reality. . . . What tigers for work the Dennings are.*[1]

Sir Rodger Winn

In 1962 Lord Evershed, the Master of the Rolls, resigned and was
appointed a Lord of Appeal in Ordinary. Denning explained what
happened:

Who was to succeed him? We all wondered. When at lunch one day in
the Lords, the Lord Chancellor, Lord Kilmuir, (when the others had left
the table) said to me: 'I hear that you would like to be Master of the Rolls
yourself. Is that so?' Now I had mentioned this to no one – unless it were
to Lord Parker – in 1957 – five years before. I said at once that I would.
It was the opportunity I wanted. Lord Goddard often told me that he enjoyed
his time in the Court of Appeal best of all. So had I. It was with a glad
heart that I returned to it. Some would say that I moved down.[2]

The appointment took effect from 19 April 1962 and at that time
the salary was £9000 a year. The Master of the Rolls was President
of the Court of Appeal and, as few appeals go beyond it to the House
of Lords, it is an appointment of great importance in the law.

The Bar was delighted by the appointment as it meant that they
would have more opportunities to appear before him. The only counsel who regretted the move were practitioners in the Privy Council.
Sir Dingle Foot wrote: 'We shall miss you a great deal in the Privy
Council more especially when we are dealing with the subtle intricacies
of West African law.'[3] A number of judges felt that it would give
greater scope to his powers and that this was a job which offered
the greatest opportunity to influence the development of the law.
Leslie Scarman (later Lord Scarman) said: 'As Master of the Rolls
you have an unrivalled vantage point for guiding and moulding the
law.' Mr Justice Melford Stevenson wrote: 'It is obvious that the

vital contribution you have made to the structure of the law may be more effectively given by underpinning the foundations than by working on the top of the scaffold.' The Q.C. Leonard Caplan said: 'The office should fit you like a glove.'

The other side of the coin was put by Sir Frank Soskice Q.C.: 'It must be gratifying and exciting to have held practically all the highest judicial offices. This one, I think, is not only the most exacting but the most responsible of all.' Professor H.W.R.Wade wrote:

I feel that you will be moving back to the real centre of gravity of the law, where your creative powers can be of the greatest service. ... I have a presentiment that your escape from the House of Lords, if you will forgive me so putting it, will be the great event of the legal history of our time. The odds against enlightened decisions have now shortened once more!

The element of escape from the House of Lords was echoed by Desmond Ackner (later Lord Ackner): 'When you spoke at the Circuit Dinner given in your honour in 1957 you said that the House of Lords was like heaven – one should not go there until one was dead. We are delighted to welcome you back to the land of the living.'

Robert Riches, the Librarian of the Bar Library, a very old man at the time of writing, who had held his post from time immemorial, said: 'I hope that you will preside in Court 3 and not in Court 1 as it is in that court that Lord Esher sat for the whole period that he was the Master of the Rolls. I well remember the last two years of his life 1895–97, thus I have seen all the Masters of the Rolls who have ever sat in the Royal Courts of Justice.' Denning sat in Court 3 and was fond of recalling a letter received from an Indian student in 1973: 'I will ever remain grateful to you if you would kindly help me to begin my professional career with your company, the Rolls Royce Motor Company Ltd.'

In medieval times there were twelve Masters of the Chancery and the senior Master had the custody of the rolls or records of the Court of Chancery. There is an appointment recorded as early as 1295. The senior Master was called the Master of the Rolls and in course of time became a second judge in the Court of Chancery, subordinate to the Lord Chancellor. He took precedence after the Chief Justice of the King's Bench and before the Chief Justice of the Common Pleas. So it remains today; after the Lord Chief Justice and before the other judges. In the reorganisation of the courts which took place in the 1870s a Court of Appeal was established as part of the Supreme Court of Judicature and the title of Master of the Rolls was retained by the President of that court.

In Denning's time the Master of the Rolls still retained vestigial functions in relation to the custody of the rolls. He was head of the Public Record Office. He had extensive jurisdiction relating to solicitors and the roll of solicitors. He was responsible for manorial records under the Law of Property Acts and for all the documents under the Tithe Act 1936. He was the rule-making authority under various Acts of Parliament. He was by statute Chairman of the Advisory Committee on Public Records and the Royal Commission on Historical Manuscripts which dealt with the preservation of private records. Denning took a great interest in all these duties and personally signed the admission certificates for every newly qualified solicitor.

By virtue of his office he was appointed Chairman of a departmental committee on legal records which was appointed in 1963 and reported in 1966.[4] The committee consisted of one judge – Sir Denys Buckley, one academic – Mr Cecil Fifoot, and officials. They had twenty-seven meetings over a period of three years. Until the nineteenth century all courts were required to keep all their records. In 1838, by the Public Record Office Act 1838, the Master of the Rolls was given power to gather all records into one depository and the Public Record Office in Chancery Lane was built. In 1952 the responsibility for the Public Record Office was transferred from the Master of the Rolls to the Lord Chancellor's Department. The committee found that the main problem was the accumulation of Chancery records and original wills. The original wills accumulated in the Principal Probate Registry since 1858 occupied over six miles of shelving. The committee recommended that registered copies should be permanently retained but that originals, more than fifty years old, should be destroyed. On the chancery side they recommended that certain key documents should be kept permanently. Certain selected documents of interest and a random selection of sample papers should be preserved. The remaining documents should be destroyed after specified periods of time.

The Council of the Advisory Committee on Public Records met once a quarter and the subjects dealt with included the allocation of records to the new Public Record Office at Kew and the thirty-year rule for the examination of departmental records. The Council had to check the efficiency of the departmental systems for keeping records. The weakness lay in the fact that it had no direct communication with departments but had to work on reports from an officer from the Public Records Office. In 1982, giving evidence to an all party Commons Select Committee which was enquiring about policy relating to public records, Denning suggested that the evidence in the Profumo affair should not be disclosed for fifty years. He also supported a proposal made in 1981 by the Wilson Report on Public Records that each Ministry should have a 'Sector Panel' as pioneered by the Ministry of Defence, consisting of outsiders who would advise on what material should be proscribed. He also agreed with the Wilson idea of a committee of Privy Councillors to examine sensitive materials that Departments wished to retain beyond the thirty year period. Neither suggestion appealed to the Government and both were ruled out.

Another unexpected result of being Master of the Rolls was that *ex officio* he was President of Queen Elizabeth College, Greenwich. When William Lambard founded the Queen Elizabeth Almshouses in Greenwich in 1574, in memory of his first wife, he appointed the Master of the Rolls as *ex officio* President and two wardens of the Drapers' Company as governors or trustees. Lambard, who was the author of *Perambulations in Kent,* lived at Westcombe Park, Greenwich, and was a Master in Chancery. What was more natural than that he should appoint his senior colleague, the Master of the Rolls, as President of his College? The College still flourishes and Denning took his duties seriously. Once a year there was a Visitation to the College when the roll was called, the rules were read out in the chapel and the President gave a short address to the residents. In 1970 a new building, known as Lambard House, was built on College land – in Blind Man's Garden – and Denning spoke at the opening. The Queen was present when he unveiled a stained glass window on the occasion of the 400th Anniversary on 19 November 1974.

Becoming Master of the Rolls meant a change in the private life of the Dennings. They rented a flat at 11 Old Square, Lincoln's Inn. They had 62 stairs to climb and no lift. It had three good-sized rooms with a tiny kitchen. They spent all the week there, only going to the country at the weekends. They much enjoyed the gardens of the Inn:

One of the great privileges of a flat in the Inn is the pleasure of the garden. In the very heart of London are the well-kept lawns, studded with trees and bordered with flowers. A lovely row of pink cherries topping the bank of the old wall. Magnolias and white cherries in the garden of New Square. Camellias in hundreds behind the War Memorial. Crocuses in profusion opposite the New Hall. Flowers changing with spring, summer and autumn. Joan and I walk here in the evenings. Often we meet our friends. For the Inn is full of our friends.[5]

Late in 1960 Denning's sister, Marjorie, told them that 'The Lawn', Whitchurch, might be sold. In 1963, after much deliberation, they sold 'Fair Close', Cuckfield, and bought 'The Lawn'. Denning kept the land and plantation at Cuckfield when the house was sold. 'The Lawn' had been built during the Regency period and had been sold by auction in 1868 for £7000. During the war the house had been requisitioned, first by the Bank of England and later by the Army Pay Corps. As a result it was in a very dilapidated condition and the garden was a wilderness. The Dennings pulled down half the house and added a new wing. They converted the drawing room into a library and turned the stables into living accommodation. The house was converted into two self-contained halves, one for themselves and the other an annexe for the family when they came to stay.

The Dennings derived great pleasure from the restoration of the garden:

Let me describe our garden and what we did. From the French casements of my library, you walk out to a wide open lawn which slopes down to the water. It is why the place is called 'The Lawn'. You then come to an island in the river. It is crossed by two charming old bridges – one of wood in an arch – the other of wrought ironwork. The island has many fine trees. Beyond the island is the main stream – and the far bank is full of willows, poplars and hazels. When we took the place over, the island, the paddock and the paths were all thick with dense undergrowth. You could not get along at all. The banks of the river were falling in ... We set to work – Joan and I and the family. We cut away the undergrowth – hacking our way through it. We cleared the paths. Joan and I wheeled down rubble to fill in the banks of the river. The strong youngsters of the family got old railway sleepers and lined the banks – driving in stakes to do so. At first the far bank was in other hands: but we acquired 20 acres and planted poplars there. The youngsters made a bridge across. We used big stones which had been discarded on the repair of the old gateway of Lincoln's Inn ... Then there is the kitchen garden, walled, and running down to the river: fine soil and very fertile. The border of box hedges well clipped. A large Victorian greenhouse – very expensive to maintain. Few people can find gardeners nowadays. We have a good man. More than enough fruit and vegetables for our own use.[6]

In summer the Church Fête and another for the Cricket Club were held in the garden; 800 or more people would attend. Friends were invited to come and fish in the River Test. In June 1972 Joan Denning gave an interview to a newspaper which gives some idea of their life at this time:

My husband always says justice should be done before law. I felt he did the right thing. He is entirely unpolitical as a person and not just because he is a judge. He is interested in a broad outlook no matter what party is in power. He is always on the side of the little man especially if he thinks the Establishment has been too heavy. He does not want to do things to offend public opinion, but he says that good public opinion is what the right thinking man and woman in the street are thinking.

We spend every weekend at Whitchurch and the legal vacations when we are not travelling. My husband gets his exercise cutting the lawn for an hour. He can think at the same time. And he loves his trees. He grows poplars in the water meadows. I'm his chauffeur. He hasn't had a licence since the war, so everywhere he goes I go. My husband does not drink or smoke and I have to drive him home. He is a man of equable temper with a keen sense of humour. A man of great humility. ... His mind is totally immersed in his work. I have to remind him to remember small things. Many times he goes to the station with no money in his pocket and I have to go up later and pay the train fare. I try to cushion him against the irritating domestic affairs and I do all the household accounts. He hates going into shops. It is as much as I can do to persuade him to buy a new shirt. I wouldn't call him a sentimental man; no, I wouldn't. But he is generous .... I have no staff in town but a housekeeper in the country during the week. I do all the work. He [Denning] likes good simple English food, roast beef and plain fish. And he is very fond of rice pudding. He is really quite a religious man. We both are. We go to early morning service every Sunday and we try to live our lives by Christian principles, although I can't say we always succeed![7]

As Denning was the President of the Court of Appeal he controlled how the work was done and often selected the most important cases for his own court. Out of six hundred cases a year at that time only perhaps twelve were important. He felt that these were few but could change the conditions of English social and communal life. His clerk acted as clerk of the lists assisted by a clerk from Chancery Chambers. He had been criticised for not running the court on American lines with a strict rota system for cases as well as judges. In the Court of Appeal the President of each Division remained in charge of his Division but the other two Lord Justices changed individually, going from one Division to another every three weeks. But Denning was unrepentant. He said:

> The work of the Court of Appeal is so varied that it is important to see that the cases are heard by judges who are conversant with the subject matter. If it is a Chancery case, one or two should be experienced in chancery work. So with commercial cases, or cases on planning or family law. It is desirable as far as possible to arrange the work to suit the court and conversely man the court to suit the work.[8]

The work of the Court of Appeal has continued to grow. Before 1947 there were only six appeal judges. In 1947 the number was increased to nine and by 1981 there were eighteen. The administration has also grown. After Denning's retirement a Registrar of Civil Appeals, a barrister, was appointed with a staff of civil servants. In his time the judges sat five days a week, all day. Only about one case in ten was reserved and reserved judgments had to be written at the weekend. Some of the judges found the pace too hot. Now the judges are free on Fridays to write their judgments. Denning was always a very hard worker and expected others to keep up the same pace. Henn Collins had often warned him about the danger of overwork and on one occasion sent him a short rhyme to press the point home.

> My brother pray be warned by me
> And always rise in time for tea
> And when you feel you must sit late
> Remember my untoward fate
> Don't go on sitting until seven
> But sit next morning at eleven.[9]

Henn Collins retired early because of heart trouble; this was his 'untoward fate'.

The machinery of judicial administration in the Court of Appeal in Denning's time was rudimentary but he saw little need for change. He was interested in changes of practice which improved the law but was not interested in the minutiae of administration. There was a very good spirit amongst the judges when he was Master of the Rolls. He was considerate to the other judges and never asked them to do anything that he would not do himself. If the judges sitting in the long vacation wanted help he would come up himself to do the extra work. He was friendly and informal and willing to change his mind if persuaded that the other judges were right. This was particularly so if they could persuade him that the merits of the case lay with them. There were occasional Saturday morning hearings when he thought the public interest required it.

Denning was a good friend of the Press, believing that the reporter was the watchdog of justice. He said that, so long as newspapers do not impute improper motives, they have full freedom to criticise magistrates and judges.[10] Speaking in Adelaide in 1967 he criticised the provisions of the Criminal Justice Bill, which prohibited full reporting of committal proceedings in the Magistrates Courts. He said: 'Every court should be open to every subject of the Queen. I think it is one of the essentials of justice being done in the community. Every judge, in a sense, is on trial to see that he does his job properly.'[11] Again he once said: 'Reporters are there, representing the public, to see that magistrates and judges behave themselves. Children's courts should also be open. Names should be kept out but the public should know what happens to the child and proceedings should never be conducted behind closed doors.'[12] This does not happen in the High Court, even today. Proceedings about the custody, care and control, access and maintenance of children are held in private. Ninety per cent of High Court work is done privately, in chambers, by Masters and Registrars. Speaking on the radio in the 1960s Denning said:

'Somehow I believe, in the words of old Jeremy Bentham, that in the darkness of secrecy all sorts of things can go wrong. And if things are really done in public you can see that the judge does behave himself, the newspapers can comment on it if he misbehaves – it keeps everyone in order.'[13]

Denning believed that all legal proceedings should be held in public:

It is of first importance that all proceedings should be held in public and this includes the delivery of judgments together with the reasons for them. This is so that everyone who wishes to do so can come into court and hear what takes place: and also that the reported cases can be taken down by reporters for their own use.[14]

The other point of view was well put by Sir John Donaldson (later Lord Donaldson and Denning's successor as Master of the Rolls). He wrote that in a recent case he had spent one hour and forty minutes reading his judgment in the presence of counsel and solicitors for all parties. He suggested that the Court of Appeal should follow the practice of the House of Lords and send written copies of their judgments to the parties as this would reduce the cost and time taken for appeals. He finished: 'Reading of judgments in cases which are of little public interest serves one purpose only, namely to prove that the judge can read and this is widely assumed without further proof.'[15]

Although Denning was in favour of the freedom of the press he was not afraid to act against newspapers if he thought they were abusing their powers. In 1963 Lord Radcliffe was conducting an inquiry into the Vassal affair which related to questions of security at the Admiralty. The Tribunal asked a journalist to give the source of his information and he refused. The Attorney-General took proceedings and Mr Justice Gorman sentenced the journalist to six months imprisonment for contempt of court.[16] On appeal to the Court of Appeal Denning said: 'There is no privilege known to law by which a journalist can refuse to answer a question which is relevant to the inquiry and is one which, in the opinion of the judge, it is proper for him to be asked.' This case was followed by the Granada Television case in 1980.[17] The judge, the Court of Appeal and the House of Lords all held that the media had no immunity based on public interest which protected them from the obligation to disclose their source of information when disclosure was necessary in the interests of justice. Only Lord Salmon dissented, on the grounds that the 1963 case related to national security which had a higher priority than freedom of the press. In the Granada case he thought that the freedom of the press should have the highest priority.

In his ill-fated book, *What Next in the Law*, Denning wrote that he had changed his mind about the Granada case:

On reconsideration, therefore, I think that in cases of investigative journalism, save in most exceptional circumstances, the newspaper or television company ought not to be ordered to disclose the source of information: first, because it impedes the flow of information concerning matters of public interest; and second, because such an order is apt to be mere *brutum fulmen* – which Addison in *The Spectator* described as an empty noise.[18]

Denning was a serving judge at the time of writing and it was unfortunate that he should say that one of his reported judgments in an important case relating to the public interest was wrong. Section 10 of the Contempt of Court Act 1981 confirmed the law as laid down in the two cases above: that disclosure is not required unless the court thinks it necessary in the interest of justice, or national security, or for the prevention of disorder or crime.

There was one other case where the press thought that they had been hard done by. In *Home Office* v *Harman*[19] Harriet Harman, then a practising solicitor, wrote to the Home Office during the course of litigation: 'I am well aware of the rule that requires documents obtained on discovery should not be used for any other purpose except the case in hand.' She obtained an order for discovery and production of documents from the Home Office which were produced in court and read out. Despite her implied undertaking she allowed a press reporter to take copies of the documents read out. The journalist wrote an article based on these documents which was very critical of the Home Office. The question for the decision of the court was: does the implied undertaking apply to documents which have ceased to be confidential in that they have become public knowledge by being produced and read out in the course of a public trial? The Court of Appeal and the House of Lords held that the fact that the documents were read out at the hearing in open court did not bring the implied undertaking to an end. Harriet Harman was guilty of contempt in passing on such documents to a journalist. For the judges the highest priority was the conduct of a member of the legal profession and any rights of the press were secondary. *The Times* came out with a headline 'Contempt ruling a bad day for the press'. It all depends on the angle from which the conduct is considered. Ms Harman took her case to the Court of Human Rights at Strasbourg which held that the overriding principle (from its point of view) was the freedom of the press to deal with matters of public interest which had been ventilated in a court of law.

Denning was tolerant of criticism of himself and of the Court of Appeal and was personally one of the judges who heard the case of *R* v *Commissioner of the Police for the Metropolis* in 1968.[20] Quintin

Hogg (later Lord Hailsham) wrote an article in *Punch* criticising the courts as follows:

> The legislation of 1960 and thereafter has been rendered virtually unworkable by the unrealistic, contradictory and, in the leading case, erroneous, decisions of the courts, including the Court of Appeal. ... It is to be hoped that the courts will remember the golden rule for judges in the matter of *obiter dicta*. Silence is always an option.

Mr Blackburn applied in person on a Monday morning to commit Mr Hogg for contempt of court. After hearing argument the court gave immediate judgment. Denning said:

> This is the first case, so far as I know, where this court has been called on to consider an allegation of contempt against itself. It is a jurisdiction which undoubtedly belongs to us but which we will most sparingly exercise: more particularly as we ourselves have an interest in the matter.
>
> Let me say at once that we will never use this jurisdiction as a means to uphold our own dignity. That must rest on surer foundations. Nor will we use it to suppress those who speak against us. We do not fear criticism, nor do we resent it. For there is something far more important at stake. It is no less than freedom of speech itself ....
>
> Exposed as we are to the winds of criticism, nothing which is said by this person or that, will deter us from doing what the occasion requires, provided that it is pertinent to the matter in hand. Silence is not an option when things are ill done.
>
> So it comes to this: Mr Quintin Hogg has criticised the court, but in so doing he is exercising his undoubted right. The article contains an error, no doubt, but errors do not make it contempt of court. We must uphold his right to the uttermost. I hold this not to be contempt of court, and would dismiss the application.

Denning was willing to temper judgment with mercy when dealing with contempt of court arising out of political and industrial disputes, and to act quickly. Some Welsh students from Aberystwyth University, enthusiastic for the Welsh language, were upset that programmes to Wales on the BBC were being broadcast in English and not in Welsh. They came up to London on 4 February 1970 and invaded one of the courts. Very unwisely they chose the court in which Mr Justice Lawton (later Lord Justice Lawton) was sitting. They flocked into the well of the court and the gallery. They shouted slogans, scattered pamphlets and sang songs. The judge had to adjourn the hearing. When order was restored the judge sentenced all those who would not apologise to three months imprisonment. The appeal was started on Monday 9 February, and was completed on 11 February.[21] Denning sat with Lord Justice Salmon and Lord Justice Arthian Davies – not only a Welshman but one who could speak Welsh. The court held that the law had been vindicated by the sentence which the judge had passed on 4 February. The students had already served a week in prison and they were no ordinary criminals. They were released forthwith but bound over to be of good behaviour, to keep the peace for twelve months. Public opinion in Wales was relieved and satisfied.

Denning spoke frankly about making policy decisions and other lawyers were disturbed about his candour in this respect. They thought it was wrong to speak so openly on the subject. All judges know that they have to operate policy but are reluctant to admit it. They say that, if it were admitted, people would lose confidence in the law. Hugo Young has said:

It seems to me to Denning's credit that he should speak frankly about making policy. For the pretence that other judges never do, besides being hypocritical, also conceals the fact that some judges do much less than they might to develop the law in its social content. The fact is that all judges make policy decisions, if only to preserve unnecessarily a status quo which may be obscure, unjust and out of date. There is a strong case for saying that judges would be improved, and the law along with them, if they had a greater sincerity in articulating the social consequences of what they are doing.[22]

What strikes the observer is how much time Denning spent on public duties. Apart from his work as a judge and lecturing at home and abroad he chaired committees on divorce procedure; legal education of students in Africa; and legal records. He was Chairman of the Royal Commission on Historical Manuscripts; the Advisory Committee on Public Records and, single-handedly, wrote the Denning Report on the Profumo Affair. He received no award from the Government but received recognition from universities and public institutions all over the world. Denning has received Hon LLD: Ottawa 1955; Glasgow 1959; Southampton 1959; London 1960; Cambridge 1963; Leeds 1964; McGill 1967; Dallas 1969; Dalhousie 1970; Wales 1973; Exeter 1976; Columbia 1976; Western Ontario 1979; British Columbia 1979; Sussex 1980; Tilberg (Netherlands) 1983; Buckingham 1983; Nottingham 1984; Hon DCL Oxford 1965.

He has also been appointed Deputy Lieutenant, Hampshire 1978; Hon Fellow of the British Academy 1979; Hon Fellow of Nuffield College, Oxford 1982. He had been an Hon Fellow of his own College, Magdalen, Oxford since 1948. He became a Bencher of his own Inn, Lincoln's Inn, when he was appointed a judge in 1944 but had the unusual honour of being elected an Hon Bencher of all the other Inns of Court: Middle Temple 1972; Gray's Inn 1979 and Inner Temple 1982.

It would be tedious to compile a list of all the societies for which Denning was President or Patron but a list of some gives an idea of the width of his interests: Vice-President, Queen's University Law Society, Belfast; Patron, Legal Research Foundation, University of Auckland; Patron, United Law Clerks' Society; Patron of Commonwealth Legal Education Association; Vice-President, Society of Genealogists; Hon President of Council for the Protection of Rural England; Patron, The Woodland Trust; Patron of the Theatre Royal, Windsor; Hon President, Glasgow University Dialectics Society; President of Whitchurch Cricket Club; Patron of The National Law Library Trust; Hon President of the City of London Polytechnic; Patron of the Victorian Society, Hampshire Group.

Although Denning has, in general, been a supporter of government and of law and order he has never been an establishment man. Such a man is careful not to put a foot wrong and not to offend his superiors in any way. From the Government point of view he could not be regarded as a safe man. Lord Chancellors were, on many occasions, offended by his words and judgments. Judicial restraint was not his strong suit. Lord Simonds frequently rebuked him in public judgments. Lord Jowitt wrote to him to say that judges should not write books. Lord Hailsham suggested that he should not rely on the authority of *Hymns: Ancient and Modern*. None of this, of course, affected his popularity with students and the young but rather enhanced it. It is Denning's unique privilege to be commemorated on numerous T-Shirts. This is what he says about them himself:

Yet I am the proud possessor of T-Shirts from universities all over the world. On them is reproduced a photograph of me in my full-bottomed wig – or a cartoon – with Lord Denning MR underneath. Then an appropriate caption such as:

Toronto: Leave to appeal refused
Manitoba: Equity

Alberta: It was bluebell time in Kent
Malaysia: Braddell Memorial Lecture
The University of British Columbia put in a team for their race with T-Shirts inscribed:
Denning's Demons
9th Annual Trike Race
UBC Law[23]

People like to be amused and interested; in all his talks and lectures Denning has tried to amuse as well as instruct. He likes people and is appreciative of their efforts. He remembers names and what people have done. He is both courteous and affable – the Profumo Affair produced one of the celebrated remarks by Mandy Rice-Davies: 'Quite the nicest judge I've ever met'. He has generally been both liked personally and admired professionally for his achievements.

Eleven

THE PROFUMO AFFAIR
1963

*I have heard these terrible things being said about all sorts of people
which if allowed to go on, will destroy not only this side of the House
of Commons but the other side of the House.*[1]
Harold Macmillan

Stephen Ward was an osteopath by profession with consulting rooms
at 38 Devonshire St, London W1 and a flat nearby at 17 Wimpole
Mews. He had a gift for portraiture and made pencil sketches of
many well-known people. He was a man of loose morals who associated with women of the demi-monde. He was financially irresponsible,
keeping no bank account and dealing in cash transactions. He used
a firm of solicitors to cash cheques and to pay some of his bills.
He had a number of famous patients who included the American
Ambassador, Winston Churchill and King Peter of Yugoslavia. Early
in the 1950s he added another famous name to his list of patients,
Lord Astor, who came to him after suffering a back injury when
hunting. This connection was good for his practice as Astor recommended him to many of his friends.

   In 1956 Astor let Ward have a cottage in the grounds of Cliveden,
his country house in Buckinghamshire, on the understanding that,
when there, he would be available to give professional treatment to
Astor and to any of his guests who needed it. Astor had no liking
for Ward's political views which were pro-Russian. Ward often
expressed the wish to go to Moscow and draw portraits of personal-
ities there, in particular Mr Krushchev. The editor of a newspaper,
a patient of his, knew of his interest in Russia, and on 20 January
1961 invited Ward to lunch in order to meet Captain Ivanov, naval
attaché at the Russian Embassy; he was also an Intelligence Officer.
Ivanov spoke English fluently, drank heavily, was fond of women
and soon became a great friend of Ward.

   Christine Keeler, an attractive young woman, and the other principal character, was at this time living intermittently with Ward.

Astor allowed Ward and his friends to use the swimming pool at Cliveden and on a hot Saturday afternoon, 18 July 1961, Ward and Christine Keeler were at the swimming pool when a party of Astor's guests walked down. Among this group was the Secretary of State for War, John Profumo. The following day there was a bathing party at the pool enjoyed by both the guests of Ward and Astor. Mr Profumo was clearly attracted by Christine Keeler and determined to see her again. A relationship developed but ceased four months later.

Later in 1961 Christine Keeler started associating with coloured men and, on 27 October 1962, the jealousy between two coloured men, 'Lucky Gordon' and John Edgecombe, led to violence. The police arrested Edgecombe and charged him with assault but he disappeared. In December 1962 Edgecombe again quarrelled with Gordon but on this occasion the police caught up with him and charged him with shooting and slashing Gordon. On 26 January 1963 the police went to warn Christine Keeler that she was wanted to give evidence at the trial of Edgecombe. She voluntarily gave the police a statement about Ward and Profumo. The police reported to the Special Branch as they thought that there might be some security implication. On 1 February 1963 an appointment was made for the police to see Christine Keeler at her flat when officers of the Special Branch and the Drug Squad would be present. This appointment was, however, cancelled. The Special Branch thought that if it became known that they were questioning Christine Keeler it would cause a lot of speculation in the Press and decided that it would be better if she was seen only by the Criminal Investigation Department. From the point of view of the police they could see no good purpose in the interview as no crime had been committed and they were not concerned with the morals of ministers.

On the security aspect of the affair Captain Ivanov told Ward in July 1961 that the Russians knew as a fact that the American Government had taken a decision to arm West Germany with atomic weapons; he asked Ward to find out through his influential friends when this decision was to be implemented. A critical question at the later inquiry was whether Ward had asked Christine Keeler to obtain from Mr Profumo information on when the Americans intended to supply these weapons. Denning believed Ward when he said: 'Quite honestly nobody in their right senses would have asked somebody like Christine Keeler to obtain any information of that sort from Mr Profumo – he would have jumped out of his skin.' On 31 July 1961 the Head of the Security Service suggested to Sir Norman Brook, the Secretary of the Cabinet (later Lord Normanbrook), that it might be useful for him to see Mr Profumo and warn him about Ward and Ivanov. This he did on 9 August 1961. On the very same day that Sir Norman spoke to him Mr Profumo wrote the ill-fated note to Christine Keeler which subsequently fell into the hands of the press. This letter started 'Darling' and broke an engagement to see her on 10 August. This was the beginning of the end of the association between Mr Profumo and Christine Keeler; he stopped seeing her in December 1961.

In January 1963 Christine Keeler was busy trying to get her memoirs published and everyone else was trying to stop her. She had signed a conditional contract to sell her story to the *Sunday Pictorial* for £1000, £200 of which was paid in advance. She told her entire life story to two *Sunday Pictorial* reporters. The reporters saw how 'the spy interest' would heighten the story. They re-wrote the story and Christine Keeler signed every page as being true and correct. Ward and Astor did everything in their power to stop her. Solicitors were instructed in an attempt to get her to withdraw from her contract and to go abroad immediately the Edgecombe trial was over. In return she was to be paid compensation for loss of the contract and expenses. The sticking point was money. Christine Keeler wanted £5000. This offer was passed on to Profumo's solicitors but they considered it to be extortion and advised against payment. Eventually Ward telephoned the *Sunday Pictorial* saying that the major facts in the story they had were wrong and that he, Profumo and Astor would take action if the article were published. The newspaper backed down and did not publish the article.

Government ministers were very concerned about the rumours that were circulating about Mr Profumo and other ministers. On the night of 28 January 1963 Mr Profumo went to see the Attorney-General, Sir John Hobson, at his home. Sir John pressed him to be absolutely frank as if there was any truth in any of the rumours he would have to resign. He advised him to consult a solicitor and suggested that Derek Clogg of Theodore Goddard & Co was particularly experienced in this type of case. A day or two later Sir John Hobson, accompanied by the Solicitor-General, Sir Peter Rawlinson (later Lord Rawlinson), visited Mr Profumo in his room at the Ministry.

Mr Profumo emphatically denied that there had been any impropriety with Christine Keeler. Thereafter there were discussions between the Attorney-General, the Chief Whip, Martin Redmayne, the Prime Minister's Principal Private Secretary, Tim Bligh, and the Prime Minister himself, Harold Macmillan. The Prime Minister never saw Mr Profumo as it was thought that this could be better done by others. On 3 February Mr Profumo consulted Derek Clogg and instructed him to take proceedings for libel against any newspaper or other person publishing the libel.[2]

On 4 February Ward himself telephoned the Marylebone Lane Police Station reporting that two photographs had been stolen from him. They were photographs taken in the swimming pool at Cliveden. On 5 February Ward was interviewed at the police station when he made a statement. He mentioned the association of Christine Keeler and Mr Profumo and also that he was a friend of Ivanov. The Marylebone Police made a written report which they sent to the Special Branch. The Special Branch sent a copy to the Security Service. The Security Service decided that there was no security interest involved to warrant any action by them. Ivanov had left the country and there was no doubt about the loyalty of Mr Profumo.

On 8 March Christine Keeler disappeared before the trial of Edgecombe. She went to Spain accompanied by Paul Mann, a racing driver and journalist. They were eventually traced to a remote fishing village on the coast of Spain. On 25 March Christine Keeler appeared at a police station in Madrid; she asked to stay the night as she was being besieged by reporters. Paul Mann negotiated a contract on her behalf. She was to get £2000, £500 of which was to be paid to Mann. On 28 March she returned to England with the reporters but Mann prudently remained in Spain until 12 June.

The trial of John Edgecombe opened on 14 March but the chief prosecution witness, Christine Keeler, had disappeared. Because of lack of evidence Edgecombe was acquitted of wounding 'Lucky Gordon' and on the shooting charge he was also acquitted. He was, however, convicted of being in possession of a firearm with intent to endanger life and sentenced to seven years imprisonment. Rumours began to circulate that Lord Astor or Mr Profumo had been responsible for Christine Keeler's disappearance. Later Denning was to say that he was completely satisfied that neither of them had paid any money to spirit her away.

The spotlight was now turned on Mr Profumo. Fleet Street was looking for a story. On 20 March there was a break-in at Lord Astor's London home and on 21 March Ward's cottage at Cliveden was ransacked. At 11 p.m. on 21 March George Wigg MP raised the matter in the House of Commons implying that Mr Profumo had been responsible for the disappearance of Christine Keeler. The Chief Whip found Mr Profumo and told him of the accusations. The Chief Whip believed this to be an opportunity for Mr Profumo to scotch the rumours by making a personal statement to the House. He telephoned the Prime Minister who agreed. Mr Profumo was woken at 2.45 a.m. and went back to the House. The Leader of the House, Iain Macleod, was present with Sir John Hobson, Sir Peter Rawlinson and Mr Profumo's solicitor, Derek Clogg. Lord Rawlinson wrote:

Jack Profumo and Derek Clogg joined the five of us who were still in the House. The three lawyers then went into another room, and we drafted the statement. Derek Clogg did indeed require that it should be comprehensive so that it met all the known rumours and gossip which had been circulating for so many weeks and he ensured that its terms would not prejudice the litigation that had been launched. I wrote out the draft statement.[3]

It had been arranged that the statement should be made at 11 a.m. on the next morning. By 4 a.m. the draft was ready and at 4.30 a.m. they all went home to bed.

Shortly after 11 a.m. on Friday 22 March 1963 Mr Profumo made his personal statement to the House. He refuted the charge of being responsible for the disappearance of Christine Keeler and said: 'There was no impropriety whatsoever in my acquaintanceship with Miss Keeler.' On 25 March George Wigg appeared on television saying that security was the main consideration in the Profumo affair. The Home Secretary wanted to be kept up to date on the affairs of Ward and on 27 March he sent for the Head of the Security Service and the Commissioner for the Police. The Head of the Security Service said that as Invanov had left the country the security interest had ceased. This meeting led to two official decisions. The Security Service decided not to prosecute Ward under the Official Secrets Act. The Commissioner for Police decided to investigate Ward to see whether he was engaged in any criminal activities.

Police investigations were set on foot on 1 April. The police were receiving anonymous communications about Ward alleging that he was living on the immoral earnings of women and was being protected by his friends in high places. The police took statements from Christine Keeler on 4 and 5 April. On 7 May Ward telephoned the Prime Minister's private secretary and asked to see him. An appointment was made for that evening with an officer of the Security Service present. Ward wanted to have the police enquiries called off and said that he was in a position to expose Profumo's association with Christine Keeler. This proving unsuccessful he took to writing letters and on 19 May he wrote to the Home Secretary without any effect. He complained that the police were questioning his patients and friends and were damaging his professional and social life. He wrote to his own MP and to the leader of the Opposition, Harold Wilson. These letters did have an effect. Questions were tabled in Parliament for the Home Secretary to answer but were subsequently withdrawn. There was a great deal of speculation in Fleet Street. The Prime Minister and the Chief Whip became involved. On 29 May the Prime Minister asked the Lord Chancellor, Lord Dilhorne, to look at all the relevant papers relating to the security aspect and report to him. During the week 27–30 May both the Chief Whip and the Prime Minister's private secretary saw Mr Profumo separately and on 31 May Parliament adjourned for the recess.

Mr and Mrs Profumo left for a short holiday in Venice on 31 May and at London Airport they were besieged by reporters. On arrival in Venice the Profumos dined together at their hotel and after dinner Mr Profumo told his wife the truth about his affair with Christine Keeler. Mrs Profumo advised an immediate return to face up to whatever was in store. They returned the next day on the night train to avoid reporters. They arrived in England on Whit Sunday and motored down to Suffolk to stay with friends. On Tuesday 4 June Mr Profumo saw the Chief Whip and the Prime Minister's private secretary saying: 'I have to tell you that I did sleep with Miss Keeler and that my statement in that respect was untrue.' He then sent his letter of resignation to the Prime Minister which was accepted.[4]

On 9 June the *News of the World* started to publish the Christine Keeler Story by instalments for which they agreed to pay her £23,000. In the meantime the police enquiries had been completed and on 7 June a conference was held with the Director of Public Prosecutions and counsel. On that evening information was received at Scotland Yard that Ward was about to leave the country. He was arrested on 8 June and remained in custody throughout the proceedings before the magistrate which were concluded on 3 July. He was then committed for trial and allowed bail in spite of objections by the police. The trial started on 22 July and continued for eight days. On 30 July the judge started his summing up but had not finished when the court adjourned. Contrary to the usual practice Ward was not kept in custody but spent the night at a friend's flat in Chelsea. In the morning the friend found him unconscious having taken an overdose of drugs. He was rushed to St Stephen's Hospital, Chelsea. The judge concluded his summing up in Ward's absence and the jury found him guilty of living on the earnings of prostitution. The judge postponed sentence until Ward was fit to appear but he never regained consciousness and died on 3 August 1963.

On the 21 June the Prime Minister asked Denning to undertake an inquiry with these terms of reference:

To examine, in the light of the circumstances leading to the resignation of the former Secretary of State for War, Mr J.D.Profumo, the operation of the Security Service and the adequacy of their cooperation with the Police in matters of security, to investigate any information or material which may come to his attention in this connection and to consider any evidence there may be for believing that national security has been, or may be, endangered and to report thereon.

On Monday 24 June he started work and on Tuesday 25 June he started hearing witnesses. Hearings continued for forty-nine days and evidence was taken from one hundred and sixty people. In order to enable every witness to speak frankly he had to assure them that what they said was in strict confidence and would only be used for the inquiry report. Denning had a room in the Treasury in Whitehall with two secretaries, T.A.Critchley of the Home Office, and A.J.M. Chitty of the Treasury Solicitor's Department, and two shorthand writers. He sat at a long polished wood table flanked by the two secretaries. The witnesses sat opposite and could have their legal advisers with them if they so desired. The witnesses were ushered in through the back passages of the Treasury Building.

Denning came to the conclusion that the primary responsibility must rest with Mr Profumo for associating with Christine Keeler as he did and telling lies to his colleagues and deceiving them. His gravest fault was the false statement to the House of Commons. The

Security Service came to the conclusion that there was no security interest but only the moral behaviour of a minister and they were under no duty to report this to anyone. The police were also slow to act as there was no apparent criminal activity. Denning said that ministers did not ask themselves the proper question. They concentrated on the question whether Mr Profumo had in fact committed adultery whereas the proper question was: was his conduct, proved or admitted, such as to lead ordinary people to believe that he had committed adultery? He drew an analogy from the civil law. If a man commits adultery his wife may have just cause for leaving him, but it does not depend on his in fact committing adultery. If his wife reasonably believes he has committed adultery she has just cause for leaving him. The reason is because his conduct is such as to destroy the confidence and trust which should subsist between them. He said: 'It was the responsibility of the Prime Minister and his colleagues, and them only to deal with the situation: and they did not succeed in doing so.'[5]

Lord Shawcross believed the analogy to be quite false, as did Sir John Hobson, the Attorney-General. He claimed that Denning had turned the rule inside out so that on this basis people should be condemned if there were reasonable grounds for believing they had done wrong even if their judges believed them innocent.[6] Lord Hailsham protested on television and the Prime Minister and Mr Macleod said that it would have meant condemning a colleague on suspicion. Lord Rawlinson wrote: 'The only courses open were dismissal, because of conviction that this Minister was guilty: or support, either because of confidence in his innocence, or at worst, because the charge was not proven.'[7] Denning's analogy was perhaps unfortunate but he was saying that the question was not whether or not Mr Profumo had committed adultery with Christine Keeler. What mattered was his admitted association with her and Stephen Ward had given rise to rumours which ordinary people might reasonably believe and which brought discredit to his colleagues and to the Government. His conduct was so indiscreet as to affect the confidence which people should have in cabinet ministers. This was the conduct that ministers should have dealt with but did not.

Denning worked very hard on the report during the long vacation of 1963 and the 70,000 word report was signed by Denning on the 16 September and published on the 26 September. It proved a bestseller and 105,000 copies were sold. As it was Crown copyright Denning received no personal benefit from the sales. People queued up outside the Stationery Office to buy copies. The *Daily Telegraph* published the report in full as a supplement. John Sparrow, then Warden of All Souls, described it as 'surely the raciest and most readable Blue Book ever published.'[8] It has, of course, been much criticised as a whitewash operation but Dennning himself made a robust defence of the report:

> While the public interest demands that the facts should be ascertained as completely as possible, there is a higher interest to be considered, namely the interest of justice to the individual which overrides all others. At any rate, speaking as a judge, I put justice first.[9]

He said that this form of inquiry had two great disadvantages: first, being in secret, it did not have the appearance of justice; secondly, he had to be inquisitor, advocate and judge.[10]

One of the objects of the inquiry was to quell the rumours that were circulating in London at the time and this was why a proper judicial inquiry was not appropriate. If an independent person of high standing could hear in private what was said and make his report, it was hoped that the rumours would subside. You cannot deal with rumours in a public inquiry or in a court of law without hurting innocent people. The circumstances were exceptional and it is difficult to see what other course the Government could have taken. In 1966 a Royal Commission on Tribunals and Inquiries under the chairmanship of Lord Justice Salmon (later Lord Salmon) said:

> Lord Denning's report was generally accepted by the public. But this was only because of Lord Denning's rare qualities and high reputation. Even so, the public acceptance of the report may be regarded as a brilliant exception to what would normally occur when an inquiry is carried out under such conditions.[11]

Professor Heuston thought that the choice of Denning to conduct the inquiry was a curious one as, at the Bar, he had had almost no experience of criminal work.[12] This is not borne out by an examination of his fee books.[13] Although the bulk of his work was civil there is a good sprinkling of criminal work. As a King's Bench judge and Chairman of the East Sussex Quarter Sessions he had many cases of crime to deal with. In any event a knowledge of criminal law was not necessary for this inquiry. In most inquiries it is the experience of the judge in sifting the evidence to arrive at the truth which is the important factor. Denning had been a judge for nearly 20 years in 1963 and was one of the most experienced judges on the bench at the time. Perhaps the first choice of the Government would have been Lord Radcliffe but he had just finished the tribunal and inquiry into the Vassall case and had been in constant demand to head inquiries since 1946.

Denning wanted the evidence from his inquiry to be destroyed and thought that this had been done. However, in 1977, the matter was raised in the House of Commons and the Prime Minister, James Callaghan, said in reply that the evidence had not been destroyed and was still retained in the Cabinet Office.[14]

Harold Macmillan's biographer believes Macmillan never got over the Profumo affair. He wrote:

As it was, coming in the wake of so many other misfortunes and reverses, he never quite got over it. To colleagues he suddenly seemed older, and more alone, and never regained his former deftness. It may well have exacerbated the illness that finally drove him from office only weeks later.[15]

In an interview on BBC1 on 26 September 1973 Macmillan said:

Public life is quite different from private life. Nobody has any right to enquire into the private life of ordinary citizens and subjects, it's their affair. They live their life. They're not imposing themselves on you. But if you go into public life, become Prime Minister, become Foreign Secretary, become a member of the Cabinet, nobody asked you to; nobody asked you to stand for Parliament. Nobody asked you to carry the burdens that I describe here. You have to be careful about complaining about them. There are plenty of people who will take them from you. But you set yourself up to do something different from other people. And to take a very great responsibility, moral responsibility of coming into a position of leadership. And I think that does imply certain parallel duties. You can – you owe it, if you step in the front line, and if you can use a very reactionary, an old-fashioned sentence, which hasn't done much harm to our country through many centuries, you should behave like an officer and a gentleman.[15]

This, after all, is what Denning had said.

Twelve

TRADE UNIONS

*They [trade union statutes] are to be construed with due limitations,
to keep the immunity within reasonable bounds. Otherwise the freedom
of ordinary individuals to go about their business in peace would be
intruded upon beyond all reason.*[1]

Denning

Denning has sometimes been thought of as anti-trade union but this
is not the case. He was against the abuse of power given to trade
unions by Parliament. His position was that the judiciary was there
to hold the balance between those given great power, such as ministers
and trade unions, and the innocent bystander who is affected by their
actions. His attitude to trade unions was the same as his attitude
to any body which is given great power: to ensure that, by the exercise
of that power, they do not hurt others. His method was to restrict
the statutory immunity so that it would not apply if the unions made
demands which were wholly extortionate, or utterly unreasonable,
or quite impossible to fulfil. He said that powerful bodies must act
responsibly towards society at large and not purely out of sectional
interest of their own. The stress in these cases is not upon finding
out the intention of Parliament but restricting the powers given to
powerful bodies to protect the rights of innocent parties. He also
sought to protect the individual's right to work and not to belong
to a trade union. In his own defence he said:

As I myself have been accused I would say that I have never been a
member of a political party. I have never voted in a parliamentary election.
I have refused invitations to any meeting, fête or dance sponsored by a
political party. I regard this of the first importance so that all should know
that I am independent of any political party whatsoever.[2]

Trade unions and their officials have been given by Parliament immunity from legal action in respect of certain actions in contemplation
of and in furtherance of trade disputes. It is not unlawful for trade
unions to induce a breach of contract of employment or any other

contract. Any such action, however, must be in contemplation of or in furtherance of a trade dispute. In 1977 in *BBC v Hearn* a dispute arose about televising the Cup Final to South Africa.[3] The union objected because of its anti-apartheid policy. The Court of Appeal granted an injunction to ensure that the Cup Final was televised. Denning said:

> The officers of the union are going to call on their members to break their contract of employment with the BBC and to induce the BBC to break its contracts with all those countries overseas. That is what they are asking their members to do. It is beyond doubt lawful for the trade unions, or their officers, to do this, provided always that it is in contemplation of or in furtherance of a trade dispute.

He said that this was not a trade dispute. It was coercive action unconnected with a trade dispute. It was nothing to do with the terms and conditions of employment. This was a clear-cut case and was one of the few cases relating to trade unions where he was upheld by the House of Lords. In the 1970s there were many trade union disputes and he was nearly always at odds with the House of Lords.

In 1972 a Conservative Government was returned to power pledged to curb the powers of trade unions. The Industrial Relations Act 1971 came into force on 28 February 1972. It set up a register of trade unions giving immunity to those who registered. It also set up the National Industrial Relations Court to enforce the new law. The court was manned by a High Court judge, Sir John Donaldson, and two or more lay members; it was given the powers of the High Court. It had a separate building of its own, the members sat informally round a table and counsel wore neither wigs nor gowns. Most unions refused to register under the Act and refused to nominate any lay members for the court. They refused to acknowledge its authority and would not appear before the court. If it made orders they would not obey them.

In 1972 the first case arose under the 1971 Act.[4] Heaton's was a road haulage company with a warehouse in St Helen's, Lancashire where containers were stuffed and stripped. This was done not by dock workers but by their own men. The dockers at Liverpool were incensed that they were losing work to men who worked outside the docks. They decided to black all lorries carrying goods from such a warehouse to the docks. On 20 March 1972 a Heaton's employee took his lorry to the docks in Liverpool. A man at the entrance asked to see his union card. The driver produced it but it was not stamped. The man refused to let the driver in saying that he was on their black list. The black list was unofficial, having been prepared by shop stewards at the Liverpool docks without authority from the union. Heaton's took action in the Industrial Relations Court against the union: the Transport and General Workers' Union. The union had not been registered as a trade union under the 1971 Act and were not represented at the hearing. The court made an order restraining the union from blacking Heaton's lorries, but made no order against the shop stewards who continued the blacking. In March and April 1972 the court held that the union was guilty of contempt of court on the ground that the union had continued the blacking. The court fined the union £5000 at first and subsequently £50,000 but still the blacking continued.

At this stage the union obtained lawyers to represent it and appealed. The Court of Appeal allowed the appeal and set aside the fines. Denning said:

> According to the law as I believe it to be, a union, registered or unregistered, is not responsible for the conduct of its shop stewards when they call for industrial action, if in so doing these shop stewards are acting outside the scope of their authority. They were undoubtedly liable themselves but the union is not.

The judgment was given on 13 June and on 14 June *The Times* had the headline 'Appeal Court ruling on shop stewards seen as blow to Government aims'. In a leading article entitled 'The Denning Decision' *The Times* said: 'If there are any who really believe that the judiciary is systematically prejudiced against their interests, they now have before them a notable instance of contradiction of that belief.' The result of this decision was that Denning became very unpopular in Government circles. But the judgment had a very short life as on 26 July the House of Lords gave a single unanimous judgment. They held the union liable, developing a theory of authority conferred on the shop stewards from below, meaning from the membership as a whole, but they were not authorised to do anything outside union policy. The House restored the fines of £55,000 imposed by the Industrial Court and on the same day the Industrial Court

136

accepted that fines and not imprisonment was the appropriate sanction in trade union cases.

Some employers tried to get at the shop stewards as well as at the unions, for instance in the Churchman case which was being heard at the same time as the Heaton's case.[5] At Chobham Farm in London there was a depot where men were employed to stuff and strip containers. The dockers complained that this was their work but the dispute was complicated by the fact that the men at Chobham Farm and the men at the London Docks all belonged to the same union: the Transport and General Workers' Union. The dockers had their own shop stewards and three of them picketed the depot. The men at the depot went to the Industrial Court for redress. The three dockers who picketed did not attend the court and were not represented. On 14 June 1972 the Industrial Court made a committal order against the three dockers. At 2 p.m. on 16 June all the 35,000 dockers in England stopped work as a protest against the threatened imprisonment of the men. At 1.55 p.m. on Friday 16 July Peter Pain, instructed by T&GWU, came to see Denning on his return from lunch. He said that he had some points to argue against committal but could not get instructions as the three dockers had gone to ground. Denning telephoned the Official Solicitor who said that he already knew about the case and had retained counsel. At 3.15 p.m. counsel appeared before the Court of Appeal instructed by the workers at the depot and also by the Official Solicitor on behalf of the three dockers. The court quashed the order for committal on the grounds that the evidence before the Industrial Court was insufficient to prove a breach of the court's order. This was the reason given but it may be that the judges were swayed by the political and industrial problems which would have arisen if the committal order had been enforced. They were not anxious to make martyrs of the dockers.

A Labour Government was returned to power in 1976 with an overall majority. It passed the Trade Union and Labour Relations (Amendment) Act 1976 in which the words 'trade dispute' were defined in comprehensive terms so as to cover nearly every dispute in which a union was likely to be engaged. In 1978 a bulk carrier was about to sail from Glasgow to Antwerp.[6] She had a Greek crew paid at the rates agreed with the Greek seaman's union. She was flying the Liberian flag and on that account the International Federation of Seaman's Union took objection. They demanded that the owner should pay the Federation rates and blacked the ship until their demands were met. The owners were prepared to pay but the crew refused to sign the articles. The Court of Appeal granted an injunction to stop the blacking. Denning said:

If we were to give the words 'an act done by a person in contemplation or furtherance of a trade dispute' their full meaning they would cover almost every difference or demand by a trade union. But judicial decisions have put some limit on these words and the court can look at the motive for which the action is taken.

The House of Lords reversed the Court of Appeal. The Court of Appeal had erred in holding that it was necessary to place some limitations upon the words of s 29(1) of the Act: none was needed and none was intended by Parliament.

Another important case was heard in 1978, namely *Express Newspapers Ltd* v *McShane.*[1] All journalists were members of the National Union of Journalists. Some worked for local newspapers in the provinces, others for the Press Association in London. Local journalists in the provinces wanted more money and their union called the local journalists out on strike. This had little effect as the provincial newspapers got their news from other sources including the Press Association in London. The union called on its members at the Press Association not to send copy to the provincial newspapers. Only some of its members agreed. The union called on the journalists on the *Daily Express* not to accept copy from the Press Association. The *Daily Express* applied for an injunction against the union leaders which the Court of Appeal granted. Denning said:

When Parliament granted immunities to the leaders of trade unions it did not give them any rights. It did not give them the right to break the law or to do wrong by inducing people to break contracts. It only gave them immunity if they did. In construing the immunity the correct approach was shown 70 years ago in *Conway* v *Wade* (1909) AC 506. The House then showed that the words of the statute are not to be construed widely so as to give unlimited immunity to lawbreakers. They are to be construed with due limitations so as to keep the immunity within reasonable bounds. Otherwise the freedom of ordinary individuals to go about their business in peace would be intruded upon beyond all reason.

The House of Lords took a quite contrary view and adopted a strictly intellectual position. Having found out what they thought to be the intention of Parliament they followed it. Lord Diplock said: 'The test of whether an act was done 'in furtherance of' is a purely subjective one. If the party who does the act thinks at the time he does it that it may help one of the parties to a trade dispute to achieve those objectives and does it for that reason, he is protected by the section.'

Union activities affect everyone and Denning tried to do all in his power to protect the public and innocent third parties. In 1978 in *Express Newspapers* v *Keys* there was another strike of journalists, members of the National Union of Journalists, at the *Daily Mirror*. The union, SOGAT, ordered their members at the *Daily Express* not to handle any additional output during the *Daily Mirror* strike.[7] Denning asked whether the acts done by the union were in furtherance of the *Daily Mirror* dispute. He thought that an act done in furtherance of a trade dispute must be directly in furtherance of it. He said:

> You cannot chase consequence after consequence in a long chain and say that everything which follows a trade dispute is in furtherance of it. ... So it seems to me that the action taken by the *Daily Express* in handling and distributing extra copies was not in furtherance of a trade dispute. It was a consequence of it. So the next step, of Mr Keys telling SOGAT members not to distribute extra copies, was not in furtherance of a trade dispute. It was a consequence of a consequence. It is far too remote to be protected by statute.

The House of Lords reversed the Court of Appeal on all grounds and held that any restrictive interpretation of the Trade Union Acts could not be supported. They held that the policy of the Acts was to strengthen the role of recognised trade unions in collective bargaining and to exclude trade disputes from judicial review by the courts. No consideration was given by the House to the question of the rights of innocent people who had their lives and businesses disrupted by trade union activity.

In April 1979 Denning went to London, Ontario, to receive an Honorary Doctorate of Civil Law at the University of Western Ontario. He said at the ceremony: 'The greatest threat to the rule of law today is posed by the big trade unions. One of the biggest problems is how to restrain the misuse or abuse of power.' This caused a political furore as there was a General Election pending.[8] Journalists who had been waiting for Denning at Heathrow Airport followed him down to Whitchurch by car. Mr Callaghan, the Prime Minister, protested and Michael Foot, leader of the House of Commons, said that Denning had made an ass of himself. In May 1979 the Conservative Government, who had again come to power, pledged to curb the powers of the trade unions. In December 1979 the House of Lords reversed the Court of Appeal decision in *Express Newspapers* v *McShane*. On 18 December 1979 *The Times* had a leading article very critical of the House of Lords entitled 'The leaky umbrella'. It said that its admiration went to Lord Denning and not to the House of Lords:

In recent years there has been some concern that the House of Lords, in its judgments, has been unnecessarily supportive of authority at the expense of the individual .... It is crucial that such a law [about trade unions] be interpreted restrictively .... It is unfortunate that Lord Diplock, perhaps inadvertently, favoured the subjective test.

The Times did not think that the House of Lords took the liberty of the subject sufficiently seriously.

At lunchtime on 23 January 1980 Lord Justice Lawton said to Peter Post, Denning's clerk: 'Peter, I am disappointed in you. I have been sitting with Lord Denning since the start of term [11 January], nearly a fortnight, and you have failed to produce any drama, *cause célèbre* or even a constitutional crisis.' On Friday 25 January at 7 p.m. papers were delivered to Lawton for hearing the next day, Saturday 26 January. Peter Post said to Lawton: 'Do you think I am improving?' Lawton replied: 'Yes, but don't overdo it.' The papers related to the important case of *Duport Steels Ltd* v *Sirs*.[9] It was regarded as being of such urgency that a Saturday sitting was required. Before the Conservative Government could bring any bill into Parliament about trade union reform there was a strike in the steel industry. The industry was then divided into two sectors: the public sector owned by the British Steel Corporation and the private sector. The men in both sectors were members of the same union. The men in the public sector were dissatisfied with their wages whilst in the private sector there were no complaints. The union called a strike in the public sector but it was not fully effective as the men in the private sector continued working. The union therefore called the men in the private sector out on strike although there was no dispute with the private sector employers. The employers in the private sector issued a writ on Thursday, 24 January 1980 and the motion for an injunction was heard by Mr Justice Kenneth Jones on Friday 25 January. He refused an injunction. On 26 January the Court of Appeal, consisting of Denning, Lawton and Ackner, held a special Saturday sitting and granted an injunction. An injunction can be granted as temporary relief pending the trial of an action and when deciding whether or not to grant the injunction the judges would consider, among other things, the public interest. The Court of Appeal then refused leave to appeal to the House of Lords.

The union applied to the House of Lords for leave to appeal on 31 January and on 1 February the appeal was heard and allowed. On 7 February the House of Lords gave their written reasons. The union immediately called the workers out on strike and serious damage was inflicted on the steel industry. In *Express Newspapers* v *McShane* the House of Lords had decided that secondary picketing was lawful. They had power under the Practice Statement to change their minds. They didn't change their minds because they were sure that they were right. Lord Diplock said:

> There may be some who would deplore this conduct; harsh words descriptive of it may come readily to the tongue; but it seems to me that, whatever else may be fairly said about it, it cannot be said with any plausibility that it was not done in furtherance of the existing dispute with British Steel Corporation.

From the point of view of the House of Lords there was an important constitutional point at issue: what was the proper place of the Court of Appeal in the hierarchy of the courts? Judges of the lower courts must be obedient to the decisions of the House of Lords. The House said: 'The keystone of *stare decisis* is loyalty throughout the system to the decisions of the Court of Appeal and this House.'

In granting the injunction the Court of Appeal had given priority to the public interest over the rules of precedent. Denning was interviewed on radio and television on 7 February 1980. This brought him a hundred or more letters from the general public approving the judgment and hoping that he would not retire in the near future.[10] One correspondent gave the advice: 'Keep going, take plenty of rest and some exercise to keep fit.' Another wrote: 'I would like to point out that I served in the last war to stop one man making his own laws.'

Less than two weeks after the House of Lords decision the text of a Government working party on secondary industrial action referred with approval to the Court of Appeal's decisions in the period 1977–79 and proposed to restore the effect of those decisions in legislation. But the task of putting into legislation any law on secondary picketing was daunting. Denning himself found s 17 of the Employment Act 1980 bewildering. All the judges concerned with interpreting the section have complained about the tortuosity of s 17 of the Act. It is by no means certain that legislation is the best way to deal with trade union matters. If the House of Lords had supported the Denning approach in 1977–79 there might have been no need for legislation. The common law has many advantages over statute law in dealing with industrial action as it is more flexible and can be more easily applied to particular situations.

Under the Employment Act 1980 secondary picketing was declared unlawful but the same questions arose as to what action was secondary picketing. In *Hadnor Productions Ltd* v *Hamilton* the plaintiffs, who produced music and other programmes which they sold to television companies, had made an oral agreement with the union to permit this.[11] Later the union changed its mind and decided to black Hadnor. The union told Thames Television that it ought to make its own music and other programmes instead of buying films from facility companies. The question was whether the blacking was permitted under the new Act. The judge of first instance refused to grant an injunction. The Court of Appeal reversed him on the ground that it was an attempt to dictate to Thames Television how they should run their business. There was an implied threat that if Thames Television attempted to show the programme they would black it. The House of Lords unanimously reversed the Court of Appeal on the ground that it was quite clear that the action was in contemplation of a trade dispute, as buying films from outside might affect the work of the men in Thames Television.

Sometimes the chips were stacked so heavily against the individual that there was nothing Denning could do. Trade unions are often in conflict with one another and the TUC attempted to bring in some order to prevent one union poaching from another. In 1939 a code of conduct was worked out; it was called the Bridlington Principles. Whenever there was a dispute between two unions on this subject, which they could not resolve themselves, the dispute was referred to the TUC to arbitrate and their decision was final.

The union member himself was not a party to the arbitration – he was merely a pawn in the struggle between two unions.

In *Cheall* v *APEX* Mr Cheall was employed by Vauxhall Motors as a security officer and was a member of T&GWU.[12] He became dissatisfied with the union, resigned and applied to join APEX. APEX welcomed him but this was in infringement of the Bridlington Principles. T&GWU complained to the TUC who found in favour of T&GWU without paying any regard to what Mr Cheall said or thought. APEX did as they were told by the TUC and terminated Mr Cheall's membership. He did not re-join the T&GWU and took proceedings in the courts against APEX. In the Court of Appeal the majority, including Denning, declared that APEX were at fault for expelling him without giving him an opportunity of having his say, as this was a breach of natural justice. Denning said: 'I take my stand on something more fundamental. It is on the freedom of the individual to join a trade union of his choice. He is not to be ordered to join this or that trade union without having a say in the matter. He is not to be treated as a pawn on a chess board.' He referred to Article 11(1) of the Convention for the Protection of Human Rights and Fundamental Freedom: 'Everyone has the right to freedom of peaceable assembly and to freedom of association with others, including the right to form and join trade unions for the protection of his interests.' The Industrial Relations Act 1971, which had been repealed, gave the right to be a member of such trade union as he may choose. The House of Lords rejected this argument. They held that natural justice did not apply as the Bridlington Principles were a matter for the trade unions alone to make representations. They somewhat weakened their case by saying that different considerations might apply if the effect of Mr Cheall's expulsion from APEX were to have put his job in jeopardy because of a closed shop or otherwise.

The Bridlington Principles came into play in another case in 1982.[13] Mr Taylor was a milk roundsman employed by a dairy. By virtue of the Bridlington Principles all members of the T&GWU who were employees of the dairy company were required to join the USDAW. Mr Taylor refused to give up his membership of the T&GWU and was dismissed by the dairy. He complained of unfair dismissal by the dairy to the Industrial Tribunal but his complaint was dismissed. The Court of Appeal held that the employers' action was not unfair dismissal under the Acts. Denning said that Mr Taylor was subject to a degree of compulsion which was contrary to the freedom guaranteed by the European Convention on Human Rights but under the Trade Union Acts of 1974 and 1976 his treatment could not be regarded as unfair dismissal.

In a similar case a workman took his case to the European Commission of Human Rights at Strasbourg. The court held that there had been a breach of Article 11 of the Convention and that the United Kingdom should pay to the applicant compensation for the loss of his job. The United Kingdom Government provided compensation for Mr Taylor and others who had lost their jobs under a scheme introduced by the Employment Act 1982. On 21 June 1983 *The Times* newspaper reported that 400 people had applied under the Act and 207 were found to be eligible.

Denning saw the existence of a 'closed shop' as further reason for construing trade union immunities narrowly. A union member could be put in a cleft stick if he wished to choose for himself what he should do. If he failed to comply with the instructions of the union he could be expelled and lose his job. His right to work would have gone. Denning's instinct was to do what he could to help the workman. As early as 1954 an important case arose about the closed shop.[14] Bonsor was a member of the Musicians' Union and got in arrears with his union subscriptions. The secretary expelled him without referring the case to the committee. The Court of Appeal held that his expulsion was invalid but the majority held that they were bound by a decision of 1915 that Bonsor could not recover damages against the union. Denning dissented saying: 'Nowadays exclusion from membership [of the union] means exclusion from his livelihood without having redress for the damage thereby done to him.' Denning's dissenting judgment was subsequently followed by the House of Lords. His view that a trade union should be liable for damages in a civil action has since been implemented by statute[15] and is accepted by everyone as fair and reasonable.

Denning was again in a minority in *Faramus* v *Film Artistes' Association*.[16] Faramus was aged forty and of good character; he had been a member of the Film Artistes' Association for eight years. Someone in the union had a grudge against him and found out that twenty years before, when Faramus was in Jersey during the German occupation, he had been sentenced to six months imprisonment for getting unemployment pay for his wife. The officer of the union said that as a result of this he was not, and never had been, a member of the union, as the union had a rule that no one who had been convicted of a criminal offence should be eligible for or retain membership. Faramus claimed that the rule was unreasonable and invalid and sought a declaration that he was still a member. The judge of first instance gave him the declaration sought. The majority of the Court of Appeal construed the union rule literally and refused the declaration. Denning, dissenting, sought a way out by way of public policy holding that it was an unreasonable restraint of trade. He said:

This trade union is a 'closed shop'. No one can enter this trade unless he is a member. Insisting as it does on a monopoly it is, in my opinion, unreasonable that it should shut out absolutely from membership, or expel automatically without a hearing, anyone who has a conviction recorded against him anywhere, no matter how long ago, how trivial, and how irrelevant it may be. He may under this rule, as they construe it, be debarred from entering this trade by reason of a conviction which may be just as irrelevant to membership as the colour of his hair.

This case is a good illustration of Denning's strong desire to do justice, also his willingness to give a sensible interpretation to a rule or a contract. To deceive the Germans in wartime could be regarded as a sign of patriotism and not as a crime. When the case reached the House of Lords they agreed with Denning that the rule was an unreasonable restraint of trade but held that they could not intervene because s 3 of the Trade Union Act 1871 gave the union exemption from actions in respect of restraint of trade.

The importance of the right to work is a continuing theme in Denning's judgments. In *Nagle* v *Fielden* the Court of Appeal refused to strike out a statement of claim seeking an injunction against the Jockey Club for refusing to transfer a trainer's licence to a woman.[17] Denning said:

The common law of England has for centuries recognised that a man has a right to work at his trade or profession without being unjustly excluded from it. He is not to be shut out from it at the whim of those having the governance of it. If they make a rule which enables them to reject his application arbitrarily, or capriciously, or not reasonably, that rule is bad. It is against public policy.

Denning was also alert to see that the powers of professional or workers' associations were not used arbitrarily to the detriment of individual members. In *Dickson* v *Pharmaceutical Society* the Society wanted chemists to dispense medicines and sell traditional articles such as photographic material but nothing else.[18] Boots objected and took the case up to the House of Lords. Every court held that the rule was invalid. Denning said:

Suppose this Society was to make a rule that no pharmacist should sell any goods other than pharmaceutical goods. Such a rule would be unreasonable and bad. ... The chemist has to go into trade to live. And once he goes into trade it is for him to decide what goods he shall sell. His colleagues cannot say to him 'You must trade in these goods and not in those'. That would be too great an interference with his freedom.

The reasons given in the judgment were that the rule was unreasonable and against public policy as a restraint of trade. The public interest required that people should have freedom to trade subject to any reasonable limitations.

The giving of reasons is an important element in justice. If a trade union committee is to act fairly it must give the reasons for its decisions. In *Breen* v *AEU* Breen was elected a shop steward but the district committee refused to approve his appointment.[19] The union had a rule that a shop steward could not function until approval was given. Breen had been accused of misappropriation of funds but the accusation was completely unfounded and the committee was activated by prejudice against Breen. Denning said that a statutory body entrusted with a discretion must act fairly and he thought that this applied also to a domestic tribunal. Even though its functions were not judicial or quasi-judicial but only administrative, if the rules give a domestic tribunal a discretion it must be exercised fairly. He held that if a man had some right or interest, or some legitimate expectation, he should be given a fair hearing and reasons given for the decision. He said:

The giving of reasons is one of the fundamentals of good administration. ... If they had something against him they ought to tell him and give him a chance of answering it before turning him down. It seems to me intolerable that they should be able to veto his appointment in their unfettered discretion.

Denning was always concerned about the harm done by groups of people, industrial companies or trade unions to third persons and the public at large. By the common law any group of people can combine together to further their own interests so long as they are seeking their own advantage and not doing it out of spite to injure others. The groups must not use unlawful means or pursue unlawful ends. Knowingly to induce the breach of a contract is using 'unlawful means'. Denning first attempted to stretch the word 'knowingly' in 1966.[20] Higgs and Hill employed some bricklayers as sub-contractors. The union threatened to call all the union men off the site. They picketed the site and staged a token half day strike. The object was to terminate the 'labour only' contract. Denning said:

> This 'labour only' sub-contract was disliked intensely by this trade union and its officers. But nevertheless it was a perfectly lawful contract. The parties to it had a right to have their contractual relations preserved inviolate without unlawful interference by others . . . . If the officers of the trade union, knowing of the contract, deliberately sought to procure a breach of it, they would do wrong . . . . Even if they did not know of the actual terms of the contract, but had the means of knowledge – which they deliberately disregarded – that would be enough. Like the man who turns a blind eye . . . The Trade Disputes Acts, 1906 and 1965, do not avail the defendants, for although this may have been a 'trade dispute' nevertheless this 'labour only' contract is not, as it appears to me at present, a 'contract of employment' within s 3 of the Trades Disputes Act 1906, or s 1 of the Trades Disputes Act 1965. The words 'contract of employment' in this context seem to me prima facie to denote a contract between employer and workman; and not a contract between an employer and a sub-contractor, even though he be a sub-contractor for labour only.

An interlocutory injunction was granted to Higgs and Hill against the union.

Three years later Denning extended the meaning of the word 'breach' in the expression 'inducing a breach of contract'. The Imperial Hotel at Torquay got all its oil from Esso but there was a clause in the contract which excused Esso if they were hindered from delivering the oil by labour disputes. The hotel employed no union members but the Transport and General Workers' Union thought they should. The union 'blacked' any oil being delivered to the hotel and put pickets outside the hotel, knowing that the drivers of the oil lorries would not cross the picket lines. Denning said: 'The interference (which is unlawful) is not confined to the procurement of a breach of contract. It extends to a case where a third person prevents or hinders one party from performing his contract, even though it be not a breach.'[21]

Denning believed that: '"unlawful means" includes intimidation, inducing breach of contract, preventing or hindering the performance of a contract, collective boycott, and "blacking". All these are unlawful at common law.'[22] Denning's views in the Torquay hotel case were approved by the House of Lords in 1983.[23]

What meaning should be given to the expression 'unlawful means'? Assault, trespass, violence, threats of violence, molestation and nuisance are all 'unlawful means'. Mass picketing is usually unlawful but what about peaceful picketing? An interesting case arose in 1976. A group of social workers thought that a firm of estate agents were harrassing tenants. They peaceably picketed the offices of the estate agents and made a demonstration. The judge said: 'The sole issue before me has been whether or not the use of the highway for picketing which is not in contemplation or furtherance of a trade dispute is a lawful operation. I have concluded that it is not.' The majority of the Court of Appeal agreed with him. Denning dissented saying:

> This ruling is of such significance that I do not think that it should be allowed to stand. I see no valid reason for distinguishing between picketing in furtherance of a trade dispute and picketing in furtherance of other causes. Why should workers be allowed to picket and other people not? I do not think there is any distinction drawn by the law save that, in the case of a trade dispute, picketing is governed by statutory provisions: and, in the case of other causes, it is left to the common law. But, broadly speaking, they are in line one with the other. Picketing is lawful so long as it is done merely to obtain or communicate information, or peacefully to persuade: and is not such as to submit any other person to any kind of constraint or restriction of his personal freedom .... Here we have to consider the right to demonstrate and the right to protest on matters of public concern. These are rights which it is in the public interest that individuals should possess; and, indeed that they should exercise without impediment so long as no wrongful act is done.[24]

Here the majority could find no precedent and concluded that the action was unlawful.

Denning attempted to stretch the expression 'inducing a breach of contract' to imply that an employer had an obligation to provide work. In *Langston* v *AUEW* Langston was a man of sixty who had worked for Chryslers for many years.[25] He declined to join the union as he objected to the closed shop. Chryslers suspended him on full pay. When he went to collect his money he was pelted with stones, mud and tin cans. The question was whether Chryslers were guilty of a breach of contract in suspending him on full pay. Denning said:

Joseph Langston is playing a lone band. He is at odds with the other workers in the factory. He claims two rights of fundamental importance: first the right not to be a member of a trade union or an organisation of workers: second the right to work at his job. His fellow workers deny him these rights .... To my mind therefore, it is arguable that in these days a man has, by reason of an implication in the contract, a right to work. That is, he has a right to have the opportunity of doing his work when it is there to be done. If this is correct, then if any person knowingly induces the employer to turn the man away, and thus deprive him of the opportunity of doing his work, then that person induces the employer to break his contract.

All the courts can do in trade union cases is to make sure that the unions obey their rule books, comply with the statutes affecting trade unions and act fairly in accordance with natural justice. Imprisonment for breach of court orders was not favoured by the courts when the offence related to trade union affairs. The unions were fined for breach of court orders but how were such orders to be enforced? The Industrial Relations Act 1971 brought back into use the writ of sequestration. This was an old Chancery writ which was brought back into service. All the assets, real and personal, of the unions could be impounded and held by the sequestrators until the fines were paid.

Thirteen

NEW PROCEDURES

Laws are like Princes, those best and most beloved who are most easy of access.[1]

Jeremy Taylor

Access to the law is often as important as the law itself. Jeremy Taylor said:

Princes must provide that the laws must be so administered, that they be truly and really an ease to the people, not an instrument of vexation: and therefore must be careful that the shortest and most equal ways of trial be appointed, fees moderated, and intricacies and windings as much cut off as may be, lest injured persons be forced to perish under the oppression, or under the law, in the injury, or in the suit.[2]

English law provides swift and easy access to a judge by way of motion. A motion is an oral application made to a judge, usually before trial, to obtain urgent relief or directions from the judge. The judge may grant an injunction restraining the other party from taking certain action until after the trial. After the Annual Service and the Lord Chancellor's Breakfast on 1 October every year the Lord Chancellor, the judges and the legal profession used to process through the Great Hall in the Royal Courts of Justice. The Lord Chancellor took his seat in court as the Head of the Chancery Division of the High Court. He asked each Queen's Counsel sitting in court the question 'Mr X, Do you move?' The silk then stood up and bowed to the Lord Chancellor. This was symbolic of the right of counsel to apply direct to the court by way of motion. On one occasion when Lord Hailsham was Lord Chancellor a member of the public arose and addressed him. After listening Lord Hailsham said: 'My brother Pennycuick will hear your application later in the afternoon.' Later he was heard.

New problems are always arising in practice and on 22 May 1975 the Court of Appeal had such a case before them. Japanese shipowners entered into a charter-party with two Greeks. The Greeks did not pay and disappeared. They did, however, have some funds in London and the Japanese feared that the Greeks would transfer the funds abroad. The Japanese issued a writ and applied by motion for an injunction to stop the funds being removed out of the jurisdiction. The judge refused the injuction but the Court of Appeal, with no dissent, granted the injunction.[3] Such an injunction had never been granted before as it had never been the practice for English courts to seize the assets of a defendant before judgment. In 1890 Lord Justice Cotton had said: 'You cannot get an injunction to restrain a man who is alleged to be a debtor from parting with his property.'[4] Denning said:

It seems to me that the time has come when we should revise our practice. There is no reason why the High Court should not make an order such as is asked for here. It is warranted by s 45 of the Supreme Court of Judicature (Consolidation) Act 1925 which says that the High Court may grant a mandamus or injunction or appoint a receiver by way of interlocutory order in all cases in which it appears to the court to be just or convenient to do so. It seems to me that this is just such a case. There is a strong prima facie case that the hire is owing and unpaid. If an injuction is not granted, these moneys may be removed out of the jurisdiction and the shipowners will have the greatest difficulty in recovering anything.

The old practice was in fact altered by this decision as there was no appeal to the House of Lords.

The news soon got round the Temple. On 23 June 1975 the important case of *Mareva* v *International Bulkcarriers* came before the Court of Appeal.[5] Shipowners let their ship, the *Mareva*, to time charterers on terms which required the hire to be paid half monthly in advance. The charters defaulted on the third instalment, but they had money in a London bank. In this case counsel drew the attention of the Court of Appeal to two cases which showed that no injunction could be granted before judgment, but the court ignored the precedents. Denning said: 'If it appears that the debt is due and owing – and there is a danger that the debtor may dispose of his assets so as to defeat it before judgment – the court has jurisdiction in a proper case to grant an interlocutory injunction so as to prevent him disposing of those assets.' There was no appeal. The important point about this case was that the court made the injunction ex parte, without the defendant being present. If the defendant had known of the application the funds would have been removed from the jurisdiction.

It was not until March 1977 that a case arose when both sides were represented and the defendant had the opportunity of arguing his case.[6] In this case Denning used his well tried method of discussing all the old law before the difficult precedent to find the principle that people who give credit to a trader should not be debarred of their remedy by the trader leaving the jurisdiction. The court approved the *'Mareva'* principle but in the particular case refused the injunction. This prevented the case being taken to the House of Lords.

Very shortly afterwards, in May 1977, another case arose, *'The Siskina'*, which caused Denning much disappointment.[7] *The Siskina* was a motor vessel owned by a Panamanian company and managed by Greeks in Piraeus. She was chartered by an Italian firm and the charter-party provided that all disputes should be dealt with by the Italian courts. The cargo had been paid in advance by the buyers. The buyers had also paid the freight for the voyage. The ship was diverted to Cyprus to unload, left Cyprus in ballast and disappeared. The shipping company made a claim for the insurance from London underwriters. The case came before the English court in an unusual way. As the defendants were out of the jurisdiction the plaintiff had to apply to the court for leave to serve the writ out of the jurisdiction. Order 11 of the Rules of the Supreme Court sets out the circumstances in which leave can be given. The case came before Moccatta J. on 2 July 1976 and he gave leave to serve the writ out of the jurisdiction under Order 11 r 1(1) i which provides: 'Service of writ is permissible in an action begun by writ where an injunction is sought to do or refrain from doing something within the jurisdiction.'

The defendants applied to have the writ set aside and the case came before Kerr J. who in a considered judgment set aside the writ. As the writ was set aside the plaintiff could not obtain the injunction sought. The plaintiff appealed to the Court of Appeal consisting of Denning, Lawton and Bridge. The court, by a majority – Bridge dissenting – set aside Kerr's order and gave leave to issue the writ. Denning said:

To my mind this case comes within the principle of the *Mareva* case. I would therefore grant an injunction to restrain the removal of the insurance

moneys (or such part of as would suffice to cover the claim of the cargo
owners) .... It was suggested that this course is not open to us because
it would be legislation; and that we should leave the law to be amended
by the Rules Committee. But see what that would mean. The ship owning
company would be able to decamp with the insurance moneys and the cargo
owners would have to whistle for any redress. To wait for the Rules Committee would be to shut the stable door after the steed had been stolen.
And who knows that there will ever again be another horse in the stable?
Or another ship sunk and insurance moneys here? I ask, Why should the
judges wait for the Rules Committee? The judges have an inherent jurisdiction to lay down the practice and procedure of the courts: and we can
invoke it now to restrain the removal of these insurance moneys. To timorous
souls I would say in the words of William Cowper:

> Ye fearful saints, fresh courage take,
> The clouds ye so much dread
> Are big with mercy, and shall break
> In blessings on your head.

These arguments were not sufficient to melt the hearts of the House
of Lords who reversed the Court of Appeal. They held that in this
particular case the English court had no jurisdiction to make a final
order and consequently it could not make an interlocutory order.
Lord Hailsham expressly rebuked Denning saying:

The second point upon which I wish to comment in the argument of
Lord Denning MR fortified by the authority of a quotation from *Hymns:
Ancient & Modern*, that judges need not wait for the authority of the Rules
Committee in order to sanction a change of practice, indeed an extension
of jurisdiction in matters of this kind. The jurisdiction of the Rules Committee is statutory, and for judges of the first instance or on appeal to preempt
its function is, at least in my opinion, for the courts to usurp the function
of the legislature.

There is no doubt that judges do not have any power to amend the
Rules of Court but there was no need to attempt this in the particular
case. Mr Justice Moccatta and Lord Justice Lawton based their judgments on the plain meaning of the words of Order 11 r 1(1)i and
Denning could quite easily have done the same. The subject matter
of the action was within the jurisdiction. The quarrel between Denning
and the House was not one of practice but whether or not the court
had jurisdiction to make a final order. The House held that it had
no jurisdiction. The decision of the House of Lords was logical but

it was not what the legislature intended. By s 25 of the Civil Jurisdiction and Judgments Act 1982 Parliament gave the court power to grant an injunction in the absence of substantive proceedings.

An important change in practice was made by the Court of Appeal in 1975 that judgments could be stated in foreign currencies as well as in pounds sterling. This was the case of *Schorsch Meir* v *Hennin*.[8] This was firmly supported by the commerical community as at that time sterling was continuously falling and a judgment in sterling was often worth less than its face value when it came to be executed. Denning had a particular difficulty to overcome in this case. In 1961 the House of Lords, of which he was then a member, had affirmed that judgments in English courts must be given in sterling.[9] Must a rule of practice affirmed by the House of Lords be changed only by the House of Lords? Events move quickly and the value of sterling in the currency markets was not the problem in 1961 that it became in 1975. In Dennings own words: 'But I am afraid we did what a great sailor once did. We turned a blind eye to the *Havana* case'.[10] Happily this case proved a turning point and in 1976 in the *'Miliangos'* case the House of Lords itself overruled the *'Havana'* case and approved the practice of giving judgment in a foreign currency. Subsequently Rules of Court were made to regularise the matter. If Denning and the Court of Appeal had not forced the issue it is difficult to see how this valuable reform of practice could have been effected. The *'Miliangos'* case would never have got to the House of Lords and they would not have had the opportunity of changing the practice. The House of Lords did not think it necessary to wait for the Rules Committee before they made this change in practice.

The original *'Mareva'* injunction was applied in the case of foreign defendants who could easily remove their assets outside the jurisdiction of the English courts but it was equally easy for an English defendant to do the same. It was only a matter of time before an injunction would be granted against an English defendant within the jurisdiction. In *Third Chandris Corporation* v *Unimarine* the judge granted such an injunction and was upheld in the Court of Appeal.[12] The *'Mareva'* injunction had the full support of the legal profession and Denning was always careful in matters of practice as in other things not to make any changes that were not supported by the profession. He always had his ear to the ground and followed the current thinking among lawyers. It was not long before Parliament stepped in and by s 37(3) of the Supreme Court Act 1981 the *'Mareva'* principle was given statutory recognition.

Legislation was not the end of the story as legislation has to be interpreted. Section 37(3) of the Act gave power to the court to grant an injunction restraining a party from removing assets from the jurisdiction of the court, or otherwise dealing with the assets. Denning felt that the words 'otherwise dealing with the assets' should be given a wide meaning and not be limited to removing assets from the jurisdiction. In 1982 he said:

So I would hold that a *'Mareva'* injunction can be granted against a man even though he is based in this country, if the circumstances were such that there is a danger of his absconding or a danger of the assets being removed out of the jurisdiction, or disposed of within the jurisdiction, or otherwise dealt with, so that there is a danger that the plaintiff, if he gets judgment, will not be able to get it satisfied.[13]

There is a rule of construction that the court will only grant an injunction to protect some legal or equitable right although Denning thought that this was often an unnecessary clog on the powers given to the courts by statute. There are often borderline cases that arise in practice. An old lady in Tunbridge Wells had money in Grindlays Bank. A man was charged with wrongfully drawing cheques on her account and paying them into his own account. The Chief Constable of Kent feared that the man might draw the money out of the Bank and disappear. He issued a writ and applied ex parte for an injunction.[14] There was a precedent as a judge in the Queen's Bench Division had granted an injunction in a similar case.[15] On appeal to the Court of Appeal Denning relied on s 37(1) of the Supreme Court Act 1981 which says: 'The High Court may by order (whether interlocutory or final) grant an injunction ... in all cases in which it appears to the court to be just and convenient to do so.' He said that anyone with a sufficient interest might apply. Lord Justice Slade could not bring himself to say that the Chief Constable had any legal or equitable right whilst Lord Justice Donaldson sided with Denning by finding that by analogy the Chief Constable had a legal right to recover the property.

About the same time as the controversy over the *'Mareva'* injunctions was taking place a new procedure was being introduced in the Chancery Division. The makers of gramophone records had a problem. They had a music copyright and received royalties on the sale of records. Modern copying methods make it easy to make copies of recordings which can then be sold illegally. In the first case to come before the courts a Mr Pandit had a small shop in Leicester where he sold copies at cut prices. He said that he had only a few copies and bought them from a man in Dublin without any fixed address. He swore his own innocence and produced a letter to prove it. The owners of the copyright found out that Mr Pandit had forged the letter and had a large stock of the infringing material on his premises.[16] On the advice of Mr Hugh Laddie, of the Chancery Bar, they applied ex parte, by motion, for an order enabling them to enter the premises and look for infringing copies. The case came before Mr Justice Templeman (later Lord Templeman), in the Chancery Division. The judge made the order sought and subsequently five judges of the Chancery Division made similar orders.

One of the judges had doubts about the propriety of such an order and refused to make the order in a case about drawings and confidential information.[17] The plaintiff appealed to the Court of Appeal and Denning said:

> It seems to me that such an order can be made by a judge ex parte, but it should only be made when it is essential that the plaintiff should have inspection so that justice can be done between the parties and when, if the defendant were forewarned, there is a grave danger that vital evidence will be destroyed, that the papers will be lost or burnt or hidden, or taken out of the jurisdiction, and so the ends of justice defeated: and when inspection would do no real harm to the defendant or his case.

These orders are known as *'Anton Pillar'* orders. The order is obtained from a judge on affidavit evidence before the writ is served in the absence of the defendant. It is served at the same time as the writ. It catches the 'pirate' unawares before he has time to destroy or dispose of his infringing stock or incriminating papers. It requires him to disclose all relevant material he has and 'freezes' the stock to enable the plaintiff to inspect it.

In the above cases the owners of the copyright sued for infringement of copyright but what about artists who do not own the copyright? In *Ex parte Island Records Ltd*, thirty performers and the recording companies with whom the performers had exclusive contracts, complained of serious damage caused by the activities of recorders of performances who were unauthorised.[18] The judge held that he had no jurisdiction to grant relief as the performers had no right of property in the articles infringed. Denning immediately saw that there was an important principle at stake and asked HM Attorney-General to assist the court as *amicus curiae*. Treasury Counsel, Mr Peter Gibson (later Mr Justice Gibson), appeared at the hearing. The Court of Appeal, by a majority – Denning and Waller – held that where a person could show that a private right was being interfered with by a criminal act there was jurisdiction in equity to grant an injunction to restrain the defendant from damaging that private interest.

In *Rank Film Distributors Ltd* v *Video Information Centre* in 1981 the defendant appeared at the hearing and put up the defence that by disclosing documents they might open themselves to criminal proceedings.[19] Mr Justice Whitford refused to accept the plea of self-incrimination and granted the *'Anton Pillar'* order. The defendants appealed and Denning said that there was sufficient evidence to warrant the inference that there was a conspiracy to defraud at common law. The criminal law is of little use in such cases and seldom used so the plaintiffs had sought relief in the civil courts. The defendants claimed the privilege from self-incrimination and Denning dissenting said:

> To allow wrongdoers to take advantage of their wrongdoing in this case was an affront to justice itself. It is a great disservice to the public interest. It should not be allowed. If this illicit trade is to be stopped strong measures are needed. Whitford J has much experience in cases of this kind. He has made a strong order. I agree with it. I would dismiss the appeal.

The two other judges did not agree and the plaintiff appealed to the House of Lords. The House of Lords upheld the decision of the majority in the Court of Appeal. The House of Lords gave its decision on 8 April 1981 and the Government acted quickly putting in an extra clause in the Supreme Court Act 1981. The clause took away the privilege against self-incrimination in civil proceedings for the infringement of rights relating to any intellectual property or passing off and the Act was passed on 28 July 1981.

At the end of Denning's long career he was again at issue with the House of Lords on the question of delays in arbitrations. In 1981 in the *Bremer Vulkan* case between German shipbuilders and Indian buyers there had been a 12 year delay in arbitration proceedings.[20]

The shipbuilders sought an injunction to restrain the buyers from continuing the arbitration because of inexcusable delay and the judge in the commerical court granted the application. All the judges in the Court of Appeal, including Denning, were agreed on dismissing the appeal. On appeal to the House of Lords the judges were divided, two supported the Court of Appeal and three were against. The majority were of the opinion that the High Court had no inherent jurisdiction to supervise the conduct of arbitrations analagous to its power to control inferior courts. There was an obligation on both sides of an arbitration agreement to keep the claim moving.

In the *'Splendid Sun'* case Mr Justice Lloyd had granted the charterers an injunction restraining the owners from proceeding with the arbitration and the Court of Appeal unanimously upheld him saying that the proper inference to be drawn from the conduct of the parties, in particular the long period of total inactivity, was that the agreement to submit the dispute to arbitration had been abandoned and the charterers were entitled to an injunction.[21] Denning said: 'The Court can find that an arbitration has come to an end by abandonment or by frustration, by mutual default or by repudiatory breach.' Fortunately this case was not taken to the House of Lords so the decision of the Court of Appeal stood.

It was only a year later that another case, the *'Hannah Blumenthal'*, was taken to the House of Lords.[22] The judge in the Commerical Court stayed the arbitration on the ground of frustration of contract. The Court of Appeal by a majority, Denning and Kerr, Griffiths dissenting, upheld the judge. Griffiths only dissented on the ground that he must follow a previous decision of the House of Lords. The House of Lords held that the decision in the Bremer case must be followed. Here again the House of Lords was battling against the legal profession and the commercial community while Denning followed the current thinking in the profession and the trade. In the *'Anton Pillar'* case he said: 'Mr Justice Whitford has much experience of cases of this kind.' In the 'Bremer' case he said: 'Mr Justice Donaldson and Mr Justice Lloyd have pointed the way. Both are most experienced in the ways of arbitrations.' By 1988 the House of Lords had still not resolved this question.[23] A commentator has remarked: 'In a spirit of resigned hopelessness the House said that legislation was the only satisfactory way to remedy the law as it has been stated in the 'Bremer' case.'[24] All the judges in all the courts have felt that power to dispose of long delayed arbitrations was necessary but the House could not find sufficient justification to overrule the 'Bremer' case. Lord Diplock, in 'Bremer', had given an intellectually satisfying reason for asserting that the courts could not interfere with arbitrations and the House could not see any way round.

Denning was very much aware of the danger of the strict intellectual approach to judgment. Many judges accept that law is based on logic and feel that if logic is not followed to the end this implies a lack of intellectual honesty on the part of the judge. A very good example of this attitude to judgment is found in *Re Pritchard decd.*[25] The Rules of Court provided that a summons by a dependant for provision out of the estate of a deceased person must be issued in London. By mistake the solicitor for the widow issued such a summons out of a District Registry in the country and not in London. He paid the fee and the official at the District Registry issued the summons. The District Registrar, the High Court judge and two of the judges in the Court of Appeal, Upjohn and Danckwerts, held that the issue of the summons was a nullity. The effect of this was that if the widow issued a new summons in London she would be out of time as the law provides that such applications have to be made within six months of death. She would lose her claim to share in her husband's estate.

Denning dissented saying:

My fellow judges think that the defect is fatal: that the widow must be driven from the judgment seat without a hearing. I greatly regret that this should be so. Quite recently the proud boast of Lord Justice Bowen had been recalled: 'It may be asserted without fear of contradiction that it is not possible in the year 1887 for an honest litigant in Her Majesty's Supreme Court to be defeated by any mere technicality, any slip, any mistaken step in his litigation.' The present case shows that in the year 1963 this assertion can no longer be made. We have not followed the handwriting of our predecessors. We have marred our copy-book with blots, and the more's the pity of it.

One small improvement in practice introduced by Denning had a good effect on the administration of justice. Judges and masters frequently make orders that unless a party takes a certain step in the action by a fixed date the action or the defence will be struck out. It is a useful stick to get the action moving if one of the parties is dilatory. Formerly when such an order was made the action was at an end when the time expired and could not be extended.[26] In

1976 Denning said that he did not agree with the reasoning behind this case. He said that even though the action may be said to cease to exist the court always had the power to bring it to life again by extending the time.[27] It was a grave injustice to a litigant that if his solicitor failed to carry out what he was ordered to do, by even a small margin of time, his action would be struck out. It is a poor consolation for a litigant to be told that he has an action against his solicitor. The court has an inherent jurisdiction and also power under the Rules of Court to extend the time within which a person is required to do any act in any proceedings.

New procedures are constantly needed to deal with new problems and new ideas come from the judges and the legal profession. Parliament is not interested in the practice of the courts and if judges are hesitant little can be done. *'Anton Pillar'* orders came in because counsel thought of the method, the judges acted and the Court of Appeal supported them. Denning encouraged new ideas and developed them. The Rules Committee usually comes in at a later stage to formalise any changes made by Parliament or the judges. *'Mareva'* injunctions and *'Anton Pillar'* orders became statutory by the Supreme Court Act 1981. The power given to the Rules Committee to make rules given by the Judicature Act 1873 does not affect the inherent right of the court to govern its own practice. The head of each Division of the High Court continues to issue practice directions relating to the practice of his own Division and to amend them from time to time. This inherent power was exercised by the House of Lords when it laid down guidelines on how judges should exercise their discretion in granting interlocutory injunctions,[28] or the Practice Statement about precedent. Opportunity usually only knocks once and Denning was always keen to seize the chance when it arose to improve the practice of the courts.

Fourteen

A LEAKY UMBRELLA

*If our liberties had to be protected by them [the House of Lords] they
would prove a leaky umbrella.*
The Times, 18 December 1979

Denning was frequently in conflict with the House of Lords throughout his judicial career and an attempt will be made to examine the
causes of this conflict. Denning once said:

> My root belief is that the proper role of the judge is to do justice between
> the parties before him. If there is any rule of law which impairs the doing
> of justice, then it is the province of the judge to do all that he legitimately
> can to avoid the rule, even to change it, so as to do justice in the instant
> case before him. He need not wait for legislation to intervene because that
> can never be of help in the instant case.[1]

The first case in which Denning was rebuked by the House of Lords
was in 1951.[2] During the war, in 1941, film distributors agreed to
supply their newsreels to cinemas for ten guineas a week to support
the war effort. The question was whether the agreement was still
effective in 1950 as it had been expressed to remain in full force and
effect during the Cinematographic Film (Control) Order 1943. That
order was still in force in 1951. The Court of Appeal consisting of
Denning, Bucknill and Roxburgh held that the parties were no longer
bound by a contract if there had been an unexpected turn of events
which might fall within the literal meaning of the words of the contract
but outside the true intention of the parties. Denning relied on a
dictum of Lord Wright that in frustration cases the court really exercised a qualifying power to qualify the absolute literal terms of the
contract to do what was just and reasonable in the circumstances.
Denning said:

> When the ensuing turn of events was so completely outside the contem-
> plation of the parties when they made their agreement that the court was

satisfied that the parties as reasonable people could not have intended that the contract should apply to the new situation, then the court would read the words of the contract in a qualified sense .... Even though the contract was absolute in terms it was not absolute in effect: supervening events had struck away its foundation.

The House of Lords held that the words of the contract must be strictly followed and Lord Simon said that 'Phrases occur which give us some concern.' Simon wrote a letter to Denning explaining why he felt that he had to give the rebuke. Lord Simonds denied that the court could really exercise a qualifying power in order to do what was just and reasonable in the new situation. Here the conflict was on the method of construing contracts.

Very soon afterwards, later in 1951, Denning again clashed with the House of Lords, but this time on the construction of statutes.[3] Denning said:

We do not sit here to pull the language of Parliament and of Ministers to pieces and make nonsense of it .... We sit here to find out the intention of Parliament and of Ministers and to carry it out, and we do this better by filling in the gaps and making sense of the enactment than by opening it up to destructive analysis.

Lord Simonds expressed strong disagreement saying:

The general proposition that it is the duty of the court to find out the intention of Parliament, and not only Parliament but Ministers also, cannot by any means be supported. The duty of the court is to interpret the words that the legislators used .... these words may be ambiguous, but even if they are, the power and the duty of the court to travel outside them on a voyage of discovery are strictly limited.

It appeared to him that Denning's approach was 'a naked usurpation of the legislative functions under the guise of interpretation .... If a gap is disclosed the remedy lies in an amending Act.' Simonds was genuinely shocked that anyone could take a contrary view, especially a judge of the Court of Appeal. He adopted the method of strict construction to all statutes while Denning adopted a more liberal attitude. But it was more than this. Denning's attitude was positive, to do justice and make sense of the material available.

In 1954 he gave a strong dissenting judgment in the Court of Appeal in the case of *Chapman* v *Chapman*.[4] The majority of the judges in the Court of Appeal and all the judges in the House of Lords decided that the court had no power to vary a trust even when it was desirable in the interests of the infant beneficiaries to do so. The case started in the Chancery Division by a Chancery judge holding that in the particular circumstances he had no jurisdiction to vary a trust on behalf of an infant. The object of the exercise was to reduce the tax liabilities of the trust. No case on all fours had ever come before the court. The House of Lords based its judgment on a case of 1901.[5] In that case the judge had said that in a case of emergency the court may do something not authorised by the trust. The House of Lords held that in *Chapman* v *Chapman* there was no emergency to justify the exercise of this power. Lord Oaksey, who said that he had no experience of Chancery law, agreed with the others only with the greatest hesitation.

This was the sort of case that Denning most enjoyed. The case of 1901 was not a precedent in the true sense which had to be circumvented. He indicated that the principle governing the Chancery jurisdiction over children was the benefit to the child. He said that whenever the Court of Chancery of its own motion placed limitations on its own jurisdiction, as it did on a few occasions in the second half on the nineteenth century, the legislature had intervened to remove these limitations. He referred to an unreported decision of Lord Simonds in chambers when, as a Chancery judge, he had exercised such a jurisdiction as was sought. He said that the practice of the profession in these cases was the best evidence of what the law was. It would be most disturbing if the court was to say that Chancery judges for many years had been acting without jurisdiction. This was an argument that comes up time and again in Denning's judgments. The law should follow the practice of the profession. In this case it was what the Chancery judges had been doing for years. In other cases it was practice of the commercial or patent judges. This particular case had been brought under s 57 of the Trustee Act 1925 but apart from the Act the court has always had an inherent jurisdiction to act on behalf of children as they had no power to act on their own. Chancery barristers were so concerned about the decision of the House of Lords that the Lord Chancellor referred the matter to the Law Reform Committee who made the comment: 'It was the fact that there were no adequate precedents for the jurisdiction claimed, rather than any conviction that the court ought not to have such jurisdiction, that moved their Lordships to deny its existence.'[6] The committee recommended that the court should have jurisdiction.

Chapman v *Chapman* was a case in which the House of Lords could, without any straining of the law, come down on Denning's side. The Court of Chancery had, from time immemorial, approved settlements and compromises on behalf of children. The court acted on behalf of the child who was not legally capable of entering into a binding contract. The exact circumstances of this case had not occurred before but in law this is always happening. Old principles are applied to new situations. All the adult beneficiaries in *Chapman* v *Chapman* had agreed to vary the trust in order to save tax but only the court could agree on behalf of the infants. If the court approves settlements on behalf of children, as it does, surely it has power to approve a variation of the settlement on the child's behalf. The result of this case was that Parliament intervened and passed the Variation of Trusts Act 1958. This was drafted very economically. There are only three sections and s 1 provides that the court may on behalf of persons under a disability approve of any arrangement varying or revoking trusts or enlarging the powers of trustees for the benefit of such persons. The House of Lords, by failing to exercise the powers it undoubtedly had, caused Parliament to pass an Act spelling out those powers in detail. Denning always maintained that legislation would not have been necessary if Chancery judges had dealt with such cases in court rather than in private, in chambers. Cases would have been reported and the profession at large would have known what was happening. As it was, only the Chancery judges and the practitioners at the Chancery Bar knew what was happening and knew how cases were dealt with under s 57 of the Trustee Act 1925. After the Variation of Trusts Act 1958 came into force the Chancery judges decided that cases under the new Act should be held in open court. A good number of cases were reported for the guidance of the profession.

The next case when there was a difference with the House of Lords led to legislation twenty years later. In 1957 Denning was a member of the House of Lords, as a law lord, and took part in the case of *Rahimtoola* v *Nizam of Hyderabad* when he dissented.[7] He thought that the House of Lords was the one place where it should be possible to restate the principles and clarify the law, and that this should be done before 'the law gets any more enmeshed in its own net'. In 1932 Lord Atkin had restated the law of negligence in the famous case of *Donoghue* v *Stevenson* although this had been done by a majority of three to two.[8] One of the two judges, Lord Buckmaster, thought that the majority had passed the permissible limits of judicial law-making.

In the 1957 dissent Denning said that he had considered some questions and authorities which had not been mentioned by counsel and that sovereign immunity should not depend on whether or not a foreign Government was implicated, but on the nature of the dispute. If the dispute concerns the commercial transaction of a foreign Government, immunity should not be granted. Lord Simonds was highly incensed that Denning had given his views on cases not cited by counsel and rebuked Denning publicly in his judgment. This rule of practice has a good reason. If a judge bases his judgment on law not argued before him there is an apparent lack of fairness to counsel and his client. Counsel does not have the chance of arguing that the judge was wrong. All judges do private research of their own but are careful not to give any indication of this in their judgment. Denning's point of view was that counsel vary very much in their ability and he did not think that their client should suffer by any oversight or mistake of counsel. If a new point arose which would alter the outcome of the case, then counsel should be informed and the case be put in the list for further hearing. But if it was just an elaboration of existing points there was no such need.[9] Denning always tried to get to the reality of any situation. If counsel does not do his job properly the only other person who can do it is the judge, if justice is to be done to the client, whatever the rules may say. It is sometimes said that an important duty of the court is to protect the client from the actions or lack of action by his lawyers. The majority of the House of Lords disapproved of any restatement of the law by the House, also of Denning's failure to adhere to the rule of practice that the court should base its judgment only on cases that counsel has had an opportunity to consider.

Denning made great efforts to get adopted the principle that when a contract is for the benefit of a third party, then it could be enforced by the third party. This had been recommended by the Law Revision Committee in 1937. In 1962 Denning was again a dissenter in the case of *Scruttons Ltd* v *Midland Silicones Ltd.*[10] The plaintiffs were stevedores who were lowering a drum from an upper floor of a dock transit shed, dropped and damaged it when delivering it to a consignee in accordance with the bill of lading. Part of the contents were lost, to the value of £593. The consignee sued the stevedores for £593. The stevedores, relying on the bill of lading, claimed that their liability was limited to £500. Denning held that the stevedores were entitled to rely on the bill of lading although they were not parties to the bill. He suffered another rebuke from Simonds who said that it was an elementary principle that only a party to a contract could sue on it and if this was to be changed it could only be done by Parliament. Denning was very disappointed but thought the dissent was worth while as by 1975 the House of Lords, led by Lord Wilberforce, had bypassed the decision by their judgment in *Eurymedon*.[11]

In Denning's last case in the House of Lords as in his first he dissented. In this case he was in good company as he was joined by Lord Reid, a judge of the highest reputation. It was the case of *Griffiths (Inspector of Taxes)* v *J.P.Harrison (Watford) Ltd* and related to dividend stripping.[12] The object was to get a dividend in hand on which tax had already been paid and secondly to get losses in hand which would serve as a basis for a claim for the repayment of tax. The losses had to be sustained in the exercise of a trade. Denning said that the commissioners were entitled to see these people as they really are, prospectors digging for wealth in the subterranean passages of the Revenue. Simonds asked the rhetorical question: 'If this is not a trade, what is it?' The majority: Simonds, Morris and Guest, allowed the dividend strippers to keep their ill-gotten gains but twenty years later the climate of opinion in the House of Lords had changed so much that Denning and Reid would have been in the majority.

The 1960s was a period of turbulence in matrimonial law with Denning's efforts to bring in the deserted wife's equity. The House of Lords decided in *National Provincial Bank Ltd* v *Ainsworth* (*see* p. 51) that there was no such right.[13] It was fair comment to say that this was a matter for Parliament but what was to happen in the meantime? Denning attempted to use the judicial power to cushion the plight of deserted wives until such time as legislation could be brought in. It is arguable that this is a proper function of the judiciary. One of the objects of equity is to ameliorate the harshness of the common law. From 1952–65 Denning succeeded in softening the harshness of the law but the decision of the House of Lords compelled Parliament to intervene.

In *Pettitt* v *Pettitt* in 1970 the House of Lords finally took the opportunity of quelling the Denning heresy that the Married Women's Property Act 1882 should be taken seriously.[14] All the law lords were against Denning. Section 17 of the 1882 Act provided that in case of any question between husband and wife as to the title to or possession of property the judge might make such order with respect to the property as he thinks fit. None of the judges could agree that s 17 empowered the court to take property from one spouse and allocate it to another. They held that it was quite impossible to construe the words of the section as conferring upon the judge a jurisdiction to make an order declaring the title to any property. The rights of the parties must be decided by the courts in the ordinary way. They held that all s 17 did was to empower the court to deal with matrimonial disputes in a summary fashion. It was procedural only. The law lords could not believe that Parliament would give authority to deal with any property rights summarily especially as the powers could be exercised by county court judges. Denning's position was simple. Section 18 of the Act provided that s 17 should not apply where there was a marriage settlement defining the legal rights of the parties. But where the parties had not considered their rights the court was authorised to transfer property from one spouse to another. The efficacy of the 1882 Act was destroyed by this judgment and Parliament had to act hurriedly to put something its place. In 1970 the Matrimonial Proceedings and Property Act was passed and by s 4 the court was empowered on or after divorce to make an order transferring assets from husband to wife and vice versa.

The differences in the 1970s related to the doctrine of precedent and the interpretation of trade union legislation. In 1944 a full Court of Appeal had set out conditions for the use of precedent in the Court of Appeal. In 1978 in *Davis* v *Johnson* (*see* p. 95) a full Court of Appeal purported to add another condition.[15] All the law lords reaffirmed the obligation of the Court of Appeal to follow its own previous decisions. The power to correct a decision of the Court of Appeal lay only with the House of Lords and not with the Court of Appeal itself. Confusion was caused by using the word 'precedent' to cover a rule of practice. The House of Lords insisted that the Court of Appeal must stick to a rule of practice about precedent that the Court of Appeal had laid down in 1944. The House of Lords was in effect extending the frontiers of its jurisdiction in *Davis* v

Johnson. It said that the Court of Appeal was not entitled to alter a practice direction about precedent made by it in 1944 but this could only be done by the House of Lords. The *Hannah Blumenthal* case (*see* p. 158) was a case where the majority of the Court of Appeal, Denning and Kerr, refused to follow a previous decision of the House of Lords and the House naturally decided that its decisions must be followed.[16]

Denning found himself at odds with the House of Lords over the interpretation of trade union legislation. The Trade Union and Labour Relations (Amendment) Act 1976 defined the term 'trade dispute' in very wide terms. The House of Lords tried to discover the intention of Parliament and carry it out. Denning looked at the question from a different point of view. What about innocent people who are affected by the wide powers given to trade unions? Is it not the duty of the judge to see that they are not unnecessarily hurt by the actions of groups of fellow citizens who have been given great power by the State? Denning's method was to interpret trade union legislation strictly. It was this method that did not find favour with the House of Lords. The dispute came to a head in *Duport Steels Ltd* v *Sirs* (*see* p. 140) when the Court of Appeal ignored earlier House of Lords decisions.[17] The House took swift action to overturn the judgment of the Court of Appeal and it was on this occasion that the House of Lords was accused by *The Times* of being a leaky umbrella.

In 1981 when an *Anton Pillar* injunction came before the court the defendant put up the defence that by disclosing documents he might lay himself open to criminal proceedings (*see* p. 157). This was a defence of no real merit and Denning treated it as such. Denning dissented from the majority of the Court of Appeal but the majority decision was upheld by the House of Lords. The Government had to take hurried action to put the matter right and a clause was inserted in the Supreme Court Act 1981 which was then going through Parliament.

Can any conclusions be drawn from an examination of these cases? The first area of dispute in the early days was over the construction of contracts and statutes. The House of Lords construed contracts strictly whilst Denning tried to discover the truth of the transaction. His object was to get at the reality of the dispute. On the interpretation of statutes Denning followed the principle laid down by Aristotle who allowed judges: 'to do as the legislator would do if he were present, and as he would have provided if the case had occurred to him.'[19] He held that it was the duty of the court to find out the intention of Parliament and to fill in the gaps to make sense of the statute. In the 1950s the House of Lords held that statutes must be interpreted strictly but later moved to what is called the 'purposive approach'. They never went so far as to agree that the courts should fill in the gaps and make sense of the statute.

Denning wanted to use the power of the court to adapt the law to new situations, which is the way the common law develops. Theoretically the House of Lords accepted that this was the way the law develops but often seemed afraid to exercise its undoubted powers. Denning did this on many occasions but the House of Lords refused to follow this road. Parliament had to intervene on numerous occasions, passing the Variation of Trusts Act 1958; the Matrimonial Causes Act 1973; the State Immunity Act 1978; the Employment Act 1980; the Supreme Court of Judicature Act 1981; the Civil Jurisdiction and Judgments Act 1982; all of which contained clauses carrying into effect the decisions of Denning that had been overturned by the House of Lords. When receiving an honorary degree as Doctor of Law at the University of Wales on 21 July 1973 the orator said: 'When Lord Denning fails to carry the House of Lords with him he can afford to bide his time for the likelihood is that Parliament will intervene to re-direct the course of the law.'[20]

Denning received no encouragement from the House of Lords in his desire to restate the existing law in a more logical way. He wished to bring out the relevant principles where a multitude of reported cases causes ambiguity. An academic has written: 'After all, rearranging the various elements of the system in an ordered structure is almost as creative as making them in the first case.'[21] When he was a member of the House of Lords, Denning attempted this without any success. Giving an interview in 1981 he said: 'One of the main functions of the House of Lords should be to develop the law and they overturn me because I try to develop it in the right way.'[22]

The main area of dispute, however, was in relation to the doctrine of precedent in the Court of Appeal. Denning struggled long and unsuccessfully to free the Court of Appeal from the shackles of this doctrine. A full Court of Appeal in 1944 had voluntarily limited its own powers. In 1978 the House of Lords refused to allow another full Court of Appeal to modify the limitations imposed on itself in

1944. The House of Lords Practice Statement of 1966 had relaxed the rule of precedent so far as the House was concerned but was jealous of allowing such relaxation to the Court of Appeal. A higher branch of the judiciary is seldom willing to concede any of its powers to a lower branch. Here lies the crux of the dispute: the authority of the House of Lords.

Denning was sometimes too cavalier and failed to respect the susceptibilities of the House of Lords. The most notorious case was that of *Broome* v *Cassell* in 1971.[23] In the course of argument doubts were expressed about an earlier House of Lords decision: *Rooks* v *Barnard*. In his judgment Denning said that the judgment relating to exemplary damages of the House of Lords in *Rooks* v *Barnard* was wrong. Later he bitterly regretted saying this and was rebuked by the House of Lords. Lord Hailsham said: 'The fact is, and I hope it will never be necessary to say so again, that in the hierarchical system of courts which exist in this country, it is necessary for each lower tier, including the Court of Appeal, to accept loyally the decisions of the higher tier.'

Part of the problem arises out of the two tier system of appeals imposed by the Appellate Jurisdiction Act 1896. As the House of Lords is the head of the legal heirarchy it cannot have a lower tier refusing to accept its rulings. Two tiers for appeals make the legal system a lottery. It all depends whether a case reaches the House of Lords. Often a decision of the Court of Appeal is not taken further as the parties have not the means or the inclination to pursue their claim by further litigation. In a letter to *The Times* on 14 March 1978 Professor Glanville Williams wrote: 'It would be an excellent reform if the appellate committee of the House of Lords were wound up by transferring its members to the Court of Appeal.' The two main advantages of the present system are the presence of Scottish law lords who bring another point of view to final appeals and the House performs a 'long stop' function putting right the mistakes of the Court of Appeal. Some of the disadvantages could be mitigated by giving the Court of Appeal power to revise its own decisions.

The layman wants the law to move with the times and to protect him from oppression by Government and bureaucracy or by other groups given great power by the State. The general opinion is illustrated by the following conversation between Harold Macmillan and Roger Gray QC:

Macmillan:	What on earth has happened to the judges? Denning is the only one who speaks for the people.
Gray:	Most people would agree with you but not all the law lords.
Macmillan:	Who is the senior law lord now?
Gray:	Lord Diplock.
Macmillan:	Funny name.[24]

In a leading article in *The Times* on 18 December 1979 the writer said:

Once great power is granted there is a danger of it being abused. Rather than risk such abuse it is the duty of the courts to construe the statute so as to see that it encroaches as little as possible upon the liberties of the people of England .... If the revising power is to be confined to the House of Lords they must show that they are willing to move with the times too, in appropriate cases, something they have not always been capable of.

The House of Lords adopted a negative attitude and failed to do things which it had power to do. For the law to be kept up to date it is necessary for both Parliament and the judges to play their part. Not everything can be left to legislation and Parliament is entitled to expect the House of Lords to do all in its power to amend the law without recourse to Parliament. Case law is judge made law which can and should be amended by the courts. The House of Lords would never consider restating the law in areas where this could have been done.

Fifteen

AMBASSADOR AT LARGE

*Lord Denning continually reminds us that it is not enough for our laws
to be justly administered; it is no less necessary that our laws should
be just.*[1]

Sir Hugh Wooding

Denning played a great part in bringing together people of all races
and cultures and was an ambassador for the common law. From
1954–77 he travelled tirelessly during the law vacations to the United
States of America and other countries, lecturing and taking part in
conferences sponsored by universities, the British Council, charitable
bodies and the Government. Always interested in comparative law,
he was Chairman of the Society of Comparative Legislation and International Law. This Society was originally founded in 1886 by Parliamentary draftsmen to help them in their work. In 1952 he spoke
at their Annual General Meeting saying that the common law should
be kept harmonious throughout the Commonwealth. He stressed that
a centre or institute for all concerned with comparative law was
needed.[2] In 1958 this society joined with the Grotius Society, founded
by the legal members of the Foreign Office, to form the British Institute
of International and Comparative Law. The new Institute was supported by Sir Gerald Fitzmaurice QC of the Foreign Office; Maurice
Bathurst (later Sir Maurice Bathurst QC); Sir Hartley Shawcross
(later Lord Shawcross); Richard Wilberforce (later Lord Wilberforce); Professor R.H.Graveson and others. A headquarters was
acquired in Charles Clore House, Russell Square, London. Denning
was President of the Institute from 1959–86 and his step-daughter,
Lady Fox, became the director in 1982. Lawyers from overseas call
in at the Institute when in London and the Institute has correspon-
dence with lawyers all over the world.

The first of Denning's journeys overseas took place in 1954. He
was invited by the Nuffield Foundation to visit the six universities
of South Africa. He was accompanied by his wife, his son, and his
step-son John. They travelled by sea on the *Athlone Castle* starting

by visiting Witwatersrand University and ending with Capetown University. After the visit the Foundation wrote: 'You succeeded in bringing together academic lawyers, the Bench and serving members of the Bar in a way not done in South Africa before.'[3] August 1955 was spent on a visit to the United States of America as a guest of the American Bar Association, Philadelphia, and he was elected an Hon Member of the American Bar Assocation. In Canada he was the guest of the Canadian Bar Association and awarded the Hon LLD at the University of Ottawa. In 1954 he was sponsored by the Nuffield Foundation to meet South African lawyers and in 1959 by the British Council to meet Indian lawyers. At other times in the 1950s he was the guest of the American Bar Association and foreign universities.

In 1958 Denning visited Israel and went on from there by sea to Poland. This was out of the ordinary as he was a participant in a colloquium on the conception of Socialist legality. He thought that the Polish system was much like the French and other European systems. He was surprised by the large number of women sitting as judges and how poorly they were paid. The Poles were equally surprised at how well paid the English judges were. He visited a prison in Warsaw and approved their system of paying prisoners for the work they did as he thought it was a good means of re-education. The visit to Poland resulted in his conversion from sea to air travel. In the 1950s air travel was regarded as somewhat risky and people made their wills before venturing aloft. Denning had his son, Robert, to think about. He found Poland very drab and uncomfortable, the food was poor and their room was bugged. He welcomed an opportunity to come home by air. From then onwards the Dennings always travelled by air on their journeys.

In the 1960s one country after another was acquiring independence and new constitutions were being framed. This led to interest in the development of the law in Africa. At the beginning of 1960 Denning was Chairman of a Conference held in London on 'The future of law in Africa'.[4] As well as discussing legal problems the conference considered the subject of legal education. The problem was that African lawyers were usually trained in London and knew nothing about African customary law which would form a substantial part of the law they must practise in Africa. This meant that there was urgent need for legal education to be provided locally. In West Africa a separate Department of Law had been set up at the University College of Ghana. There were no law schools in East Africa. The London Conference finally recommended the setting up of a committee under the chairmanship of Denning to consider what facilities should be provided for additional instruction and training that might be required to ensure that African lawyers qualified in England possessed the knowledge and experience required to fit them for practice in Africa.

In the second half of 1960 Denning was fully occupied with his work as Chairman of the Committee on legal education for students in Africa.[5] At that time there were over three thousand students from overseas studying in England, most of them at one or other of the Inns of Court. The University of Ghana had fifty-six students in the first and second years. In West Africa a school of law had just been set up in Accra, but the facilities for study in both East and West Africa were very rudimentary. The Inns of Court had done valiant work in taking African students and call to the Bar in England was accepted as being a qualification for practice in most African countries. In their anxiety to help, the Inns of Court had not been strict enough in their requirements for entry to the Bar examination. Many students were admitted to take the examination who had not sufficient general education or intelligence to be successful in the examination. The committee was told of sad cases where the whole village had saved up to send a student to England to become a barrister but the student was incapable of passing the Bar examination. Very few students took the examination to qualify as solicitors although the qualifications would have entitled them to practise in Africa. In those days the examination was harder than the Bar examinations.

On 25 July 1960 Denning agreed to act as Chairman of the Committee and in August visited Lagos and all the regions of Nigeria. In September he visited Uganda, Kenya, Tanganyika and Zanzibar. The first meeting of the Committee took place on 14 October 1960 and ten meetings were held. The report was dated 16 December 1960 and was published in January 1961 at the price of 1/6d. Two judges sat on the committee, Sir Seymour Karminski and Sir Kenneth Diplock (later Lord Diplock) and among others was Professor J.N.D. Anderson. The committee recommended that the Inns of Court revise the conditions of entry to ensure that no student would be admitted who had not sufficient education to pass the Bar examination. The examination should be remodelled to include alternative subjects suited to students from overseas. They recommended a substantial period of practical training in chambers or in a solicitor's office, in England or Africa, before being allowed to practise. Barristers and solicitors in England were to be encouraged to take overseas students for six weeks for practical training. This was not a major inquiry but is a good example of Denning's speed in the despatch of business. His visit to Africa gave him the background information needed and ten meetings in two months provided the evidence required. About this time – the winter of 1960 – a resident in the Temple heard an unusual noise and went outside to investigate. He pushed open the door of Middle Temple Hall and found it full of African students giving Denning a standing ovation. He closed the door and crept away while the hubbub continued.

In 1961 there was a visit to Israel to give the Lionel Cohen Lecture at the Hebrew University of Jerusalem (*see* Chapter 7) and 1963 was taken up with the Denning Report on the Profumo Affair (*see* Chapter 11). Despite all this work he was away in Pakistan in the Christmas Vacation of 1963. There was another visit to the American Bar Association in New York in 1964 and a tour of South America sponsored by the British Council. The highlight of 1965 was the Magna Carta Celebrations which took place in Washington in September. 1965 was the 750th Anniversary of the signing of the Magna Carta in the meadows of Runnymede on the banks of the Thames. In 1215 the Master of the Rolls was there to record the Charter. Denning as Master of the Rolls was ex officio Chairman of the Magna Carta Trust and in 1965 a memorial was placed on the field of Runnymede by the American Bar Association which is maintained by them. In September Denning went to Washington and opened an Exhibition entitled 'Great Instruments of Law' at the National Archives which included a copy of the Magna Carta. Many copies of the Magna Carta were made and sealed with the Great Seal of the Realm. There are two copies in the British Library, one in Lincoln Cathedral, one in Salisbury Cathedral and one with the Duchy of Lancaster. It was this last copy which was on display in the United States of America.

In 1966 Denning visited Malta and Auckland; in 1967 he went to Montreal and Adelaide to give the Turner Memorial Lecture in Sydney. It was on the visit to Auckland that the Dennings were unwittingly involved in a murder hunt.

Mrs Marjorie Ellingham was born in England but married a New Zealand student and went to live in New Zealand. In 1966 she was fifty-four and a well known hostess. She gave a buffet lunch for sixteen visiting judges at her lakeside home at Taup – the Dennings were invited. After the lunch several guests became ill and Mrs Ellingham died as did David Davies, the eleven-year-old son of Ronald Davies, an Auckland QC. The police interviewed 1,400 people including the Dennings. The coroner found that Mrs Ellingham was the victim of chronic depression and took her own life. To spare her family she administered small doses of arsenic to her guests so that it would look like food poisoning. She took ten times as big a dose as she gave to anyone else. The police took samples of hair from all at the party including the Dennings. The boy, David Davies, ate chicken brought home from the party for him by his mother. After four previous parties given by Mrs Ellingham guests had been taken ill with apparent food poisoning. Mrs Ellingham prepared the food for all her parties herself.[6]

Visits were made to Delhi in January 1968; to Allahabad and Toronto in April 1969. The major activity was the Fiji Sugar Arbitration in August and September 1969. This related to a dispute between the growers of sugar in Fiji and the Australian sugar millers. In 1960 there had been trouble in the sugar industry in Fiji and in 1961 a commission under Sir Malcolm Trustram Eve had recommended a form of contract between the growers and the millers. The contract was due to come to an end on 31 March 1970 but the parties were unable to agree on the terms of a new contract. They agreed to go to arbitration but could not agree on an arbitrator. Under the terms of the contract, in the absence of agreement, an arbitrator would be appointed by the Chief Justice of Fiji. The Chief Justice appointed Denning and he agreed to act.

Denning sat for twenty-one days in Fiji, from 19 August to 19 September, from 9 a.m. to 4.15 p.m. with one week's break in San Francisco. He was assisted by representatives of the millers and the growers who sat with him as advisers but had no vote. He was also assisted by an English accountant, Robert McNeill, formerly the President of the Institute of Chartered Accountants, who examined the books of the millers and made his report to Denning. Sadly he died before the arbitration report was published. Initially there were complaints about Denning's conduct of the arbitration but by the end he had won his critics round. In October 1969 the *Pacific Islands Monthly* reported:

Lord Denning poured oil on troubled waters. He charmed everyone with his smile and made exactly the right remarks when a difficulty arose. Initially the millers' and growers' counsel had been concerned about the way Lord Denning was handling the proceedings. They felt that he was too lenient and allowed irrelevant issues to arise. But by the time the tribunal ended it was generally agreed that Lord Denning's technique had been the right one. No one can complain of being gagged.[7]

The sugar industry was the backbone of the economy of Fiji. There were 15,000 growers but only one miller. The average holding was only ten acres. Most of the growers were Indian by origin but there were an appreciable number of Fijians. Rightly or wrongly they felt that they were being exploited for the benefit of the Australian shareholders. They thought that the 1961 agreement was unjust and there was a lack of trust between the parties to the dispute. The price formula established by the Eve Commission was very complex. In s 19 of his report Denning wrote:

The Eve Commission said 'Our system is, we hope, easy to understand'. Their hopes are vain. None of the growers has understood it in the least. Few of the lawyers have been able to fathom it. It takes an expert accountant to know what it is all about. It was subject to a searching analysis before me. Some defects were disclosed in it.[8]

The formula gave a big slice of the cake to the millers before it was divided. The millers received all the proceeds of sale and took all the expenses as a first charge on the proceeds before the cake was divided. The millers carried no risk of loss while the growers had to pay all their costs before receiving their slice of the cake.

Denning's final conclusion was that the Eve formula should not be the basis of the new contract. There was to be a new formula, 65% to the growers and 35% to the millers, each paying their own costs and expenses out of their share. The formula was to include not only sugar but molasses and other sugar products. The growers were to receive a guaranteed price, part to be paid within five weeks of delivery, and part after the end of crushing at the mill. The growers were to have a qualified accountant to examine the books and accounts of the millers. Denning said: 'If I have erred at all, I think it will be because I have been too favourable to the growers. The millers have not gone short. The growers have. In settling the terms of the new contract I have tried to restore the balance.'[9]

The arbitration award was not popular with the millers but the growers were well pleased. A.D.Patel said on their behalf:

I am delighted to note that for the first time in the history of the sugar industry in Fiji the growers' legitimate rights have been recognised and by a person [Lord Denning] who has become a legend in his lifetime .... He undertook this great responsibility without any fee or remuneration and I would like to express on behalf of my colleagues and the growers our everlasting gratitude.[10]

Twelve years later Lord Hailsham was again to use the phrase 'a legend in his lifetime' in his description of Lord Denning. On 17 February 1970 the newpaper *Pacific Review* said: 'If the millers refused to accept the new contract and decided to go out of business it was probably for the good of Fiji.'[11] This did, in fact, happen. The report led to the withdrawal of the Australian millers and the nationalisation of the industry. It is important to note that the old contract provided for arbitration in the event of differences and Denning made a binding arbitration award in 'Fiji Sugar Cane Contract Dispute 1969'.[12]

There was to be no let up for Denning. In March 1970 he was approached by Lord Chalfont, on behalf of the Government, to conciliate between the Jamaican Banana Board and the Fyffes Group. The object was to obtain an agreement for the supply, shipping and marketing to the United Kingdom of bananas from Jamaica and to report to the Government. Denning replied that anything he did would have to be done in the law vacations. He first met representatives of both parties at Marlborough House during the Easter Vacation, 25 March–7 April 1970 and visited Jamaica during the Whitsun Vacation, 15–24 May. During this period he managed to fit in a lecture to the Bar Association and Law Society of Jamaica on 22 May. He also visited ripening rooms in England during this vacation. He heard evidence from people in the trade during the Long Vacation of 1970 and a final meeting was held with the parties in September.

Banana growing was Jamaica's fourth biggest industry supporting 80,000 people and supplying 80% of the country's foreign currency. The United Kingdom imported an average of 350,000 tons of bananas a year from Jamaica and the Windward Islands. The Windward

Islands industry was healthy and prosperous apart from a setback arising from a recent hurricane. The Jamaican industry was sick and losing money both for Jamaica and Fyffes. Fyffes complained of the poor quality of the bananas from Jamaica. The industry had been inefficient for many years. The previous Chairman of the Jamaican Banana Board had wanted to introduce a number of reforms but these were vetoed by the Jamaican Government on social grounds.

Fyffes and the Jamaican Banana Board had been on bad terms for years and in December 1969 Fyffes gave notice to determine the contract with the Board. Denning found the greatest difficulty in getting the parties to agree to anything and in the end had to impose his own solution. Looking at a French precedent he suggested an Advisory Council for the banana industry with an independent chairman appointed by the Government of the United Kingdom. If the advice of the Council was not accepted on any new contract the decision was to be made by the Jamaican Minister. The Jamaican Banana Board wanted certain qualifications to be made which Fyffes could not accept. Fyffes thought that the proposal contemplated a surrender by each party of any right to judge for itself the basic essentials of a banana purchase contract. This they could not accept.

Denning's final conclusion was gloomy:[13]

Seeing that none of my proposed solutions are acceptable I can do no more. I must leave it to the Governments of the United Kingdom and Jamaica to bring peace and stability to the industry, if they can. It is nigh a hopeless task because of the suspicion and distrust which exists on both sides. Yet each side needs the other. If they go on as they are each will pull the other down. I only hope that good sense will prevail in time to save them.[14]

The report was not published but was sent to the Foreign Office on 2 November 1970 with a covering letter from Denning: 'I regret that my efforts to conciliate have failed.' The Government had changed since Denning had been appointed to do this work and on 6 November 1970 the Foreign Secretary, Sir Alec Douglas-Home, replied thanking him for his report and all the work he had done. It must be emphasised that this was only an attempt at conciliation and he had no power to enforce his conclusions on the parties as in an arbitration.

All the hard work was not wasted as Denning had feared. A new agreement was reached in March 1971 between Fyffes and the

Jamaican Banana Board. The Board knew exactly what was required to put its house in order and as a result of the report set about doing it. On 4 March 1971 Fyffes wrote to Denning:

May I say how much we at Fyffes appreciate your kind and patient efforts in this matter and assure you that we believe that your inquiry and consequent report has contributed significantly to the successful outcome. We believe your report has been a major factor in persuading the Jamaicans to recognise all that needs to be done if the banana industry is to be restored to prosperity.[15]

In August 1972 he visited Bellagio for a conference and in August 1973 attended the Third Commonwealth Magistrates' Conference in Nairobi. The title 'Magistrate' in the Commonwealth had the connotation of professional judge rather than lay magistrate. The first conference had been held in London in 1970 and had had the backing of Lord Gardiner, the Lord Chancellor. By 1972 only five countries had joined the Commonwealth Magistrates' Assocation and it was clear that what was required was the support of the Government and the senior judiciary. The Third Conference was held in Nairobi from 26–31 August 1973. Denning gave the opening address and reviewed the progress of law in Africa. He ended with the words: 'So you see how great is the responsibility which rests upon the lawyers. They represent the right minded members of the community in seeking to do what is fair, not only between man and man, but also between man and the State.'[16]

This conference was of particular interest as the representatives from all the Commonwealth countries took part in a sentencing exercise. It transpired that there was a very wide disparity between the maximum penalties which could be imposed in different countries for the same offence but there was a surprising measure of agreement in the proper level of punishment. Denning took part in all the proceedings in Nairobi. Sir Thomas Skyrme wrote:

In Nairobi we had Lord Denning. Lord Denning is more revered overseas than in his own land and in most Commonwealth countries he was regarded as the greatest legal luminary of the century. The news that Lord Denning was to attend the conference was sufficient to draw leading lawyers and judges from far and wide. From 1973 onwards he was tireless in his support of the Commonwealth Magistrates' Association and took a leading part in all its activities.[17]

The fourth Commonwealth Magistrates' Conference was held at Kuala Lumpa, Malaysia, from the 10–16 August 1975. Denning combined attendance at the conference with giving the Braddell Memorial Lecture at the University of Malaysia on 9 August. He also addressed the closing session of the conference. The Lord Chancellor, Lord Elwyn-Jones, was also present and this gave the occasion an added importance. The Malaysian Government was lavish in its hospitality which made it particularly enjoyable. The Fifth Conference was held at Christ Church, Oxford, in 1979 and was attended by the Chief Justice of India, the Lord President of Malaysia, the Chief Justice of Trinidad and Tobago and many others. Denning again spoke at the final session. He was elected an Honorary Life Member of the Association at the Third Conference and subsequently made Honorary Life Vice-President.

Denning visited Trinidad and Tobago to lecture in January 1974 by which time he had been travelling the world for twenty years. Once a Customs Officer asked Denning his name. Denning gave it and the officer replied: 'Yes, I knew your father.' The summer of 1974 was spent in a trip round the world lecturing. They started with ten days in South Africa at the beginning of August; then on to Australia, via Mauritius, for a week; and on again to New Zealand, Japan and Canada, arriving home on 20 September. As well as the Conference of the Commonwealth Magistrates' Association in 1975 he visited Nigeria and Ghana in April 1975; Ghent, Belgium in May 1975; Bar Council, New Delhi in January 1976; American Bar Association, Atlanta, Georgia in 1976; Luxembourg in September 1976; Hong Kong in April 1977; Tilburg, Holland in November 1977. What was the effect of all these lectures and visits? Perhaps it can be expressed by an African judge after a visit to the Caribbean in 1974: 'One judge said this morning that it was only after listening to you that he was conscious of how inadequate he was and the necessity to arise above being an ordinary man.'[18] Denning provided stimulus and a spur to judges, practitioners and students alike to make and keep the law and its administration relevant and just.

Suddenly all this travelling overseas came to an end. In 1977 Joan Denning suffered an attack of angina. She had accompanied her husband on all his journeys and he was completely lost without her. He naturally wanted to spend as much time as he could with her at home. They had been able to snatch brief holidays when abroad but for Joan Denning there must have been long periods of tedium at lectures and conferences. It was only after 1977 that Denning turned author and the writing of books is the subject of the next chapter.

Denning crossing Carey Street, leaving the Law Courts as Master of the Rolls.

Where the Master of the Rolls sits: Court 3, Royal Courts of Justice.

Lord and Lady Denning at the ceremony making him Master of the Rolls, 27 March 1962.

Sifting through the Profumo inquiry evidence with his two secretaries, 1963.

A cartoon in the *Sun*, 20 April 1977, following Michael
Foot's description of Lord Denning as an 'ass'.

Lord Denning at the Magna Carta Exhibition, Washington, 1965.

India 1969 – Lord Denning is garlanded.

Talking to students, Nairobi, 1973.

Arriving with Lady Denning in Sierra Leone.

With Lord and Lady Elwyn Jones at the opening of the
new Public Record Office at Kew.

One of the famous T-shirts, Toronto, 1979.

At Robert's wedding to Elizabeth Chilton.

Legal Sunday at Winchester Cathedral.

Lord Denning and his wife stand either end of their bridge over the River
Test, with their family in between.

Lord and Lady Denning on his 90th birthday, 23 January 1989.

Sixteen

AUTHOR

He writes in short staccato sentences . . .. This style does not waste words. It is very infectious.[1]

John Mortimer

A busy barrister has little time for writing. Denning's first efforts were editing legal text-books. In 1929, six years after his call to the Bar, he was one of the two assistant editors of *Smith's Leading Cases*. His job was to rewrite and bring up to date the notes on certain specified commercial cases. Editing a text-book is no easy matter. In one as old as '*Smith*' it was particularly difficult. The editor has to decide where the law has been changed since the last edition and a good deal of re-writing is necessary. But editing a legal text-book does give the editor the opportunity of restating the law. In 1935 he was the joint editor of Bullen & Leake's *Precedents for Pleading in the King's Bench Division*. The junior editor did most of the work but it was good experience for a common law barrister. He also wrote six articles on legal subjects for the *Law Quarterly Review* between 1925 and 1949.

When at the Bar Denning made no speeches, save in court, nor did he give any lectures. Even after he become a judge it was four years before he gave a lecture. Then he was invited to speak to law students at Queen's University, Belfast. It was only after he became a member of the Court of Appeal that he was in demand as a lecturer. The first important public lecture was given under the auspices of the 'Hamlyn Trust' established under the will of Miss Hamlyn of Torquay. She died in 1941 and came from an old Devon family, her father having practised as a solicitor in Torquay for many years. She gave the residue of her estate to establish a lecture to enable the common people of England to realise the privileges they enjoy in law in comparison with other European peoples and to recognise the obligations attaching thereto. This lecture was given at Senate

House, London University, in October and November 1949 and was entitled 'Freedom under the Law'. Denning sets the stage by saying:

> Whenever one of the King's judges takes his seat, there is one application which by long tradition has priority over all others. Counsel has but to say 'My Lord. I have an application which concerns the liberty of the subject.' and forthwith the judge will put all matters aside and hear it first.[2]

Denning raises a number of questions that form a constant theme in all his writing: personal freedom; freedom of mind and conscience; justice between man the State; the power of the Executive. This lecture, published by the Trust, ran into many impressions and proved far the most popular of any of the Hamlyn lectures. Lord Jowitt was Lord Chancellor at the time and wrote reprimanding him, saying that judges should not write books. Denning said that he was induced to do it because one of the government departments did not like what he had said.[3]

After this lecture Denning found himself much in demand at universities and his lectures and addresses to students were brought together and published in 1953 in a book entitled *The Changing Law*. The reason given by Denning for the title was that many people think that the law is certain and can only be changed by Parliament. He said:

> The truth is that the law is often uncertain and it is continually being changed, or perhaps I should say developed by the judges. ... If the common law is to retain its place as the greatest system of law the world has ever seen, it cannot stand still while everything else moves on. It must develop too. It must adapt itself to new conditions.[4]

The titles of these lectures were: 'The Spirit of the British Constitution'; 'The Rule of Law in the Welfare State'; 'The Changing Civil Law'; 'The Rights of Women'; 'The Influence of Religion'. These subjects were of general concern at the time; the encroachment of the State on the rights of the individual, the rights of women and changes in the civil law. Young audiences heard his views on how the law should develop.

In 1954 Denning went as Nuffield visitor to the Universities of the Union of South Africa under the auspices of the British Council to give his first overseas lectures. In 1955 he visited Canada and the United States of America. In 1955 these addresses were collected together and published under the title *The Road to Justice*. The individual lectures were: 'The Road to Justice', 'The Just Judge', 'The Honest Lawyer', 'The Free Press', 'Eternal Vigilance'. The opening words of 'The Honest Lawyer' are worthy of quotation: 'If there is one thing more important than any other in a lawyer it is that he should be honest. He must be honest with his clients. He must be honest with his opponents. He must be honest with the court. Above all he must be honest with himself.' Denning thought that the administration of justice depended on the quality of the men who are ready to undertake it. He took very seriously the duty of a judge to assist in legal eduction. These visits to universities at home and abroad were part of his work for legal education – to teach the young the basic principles. In the preface he says: 'It is to those who are about to enter the profession that I would address these lectures.'

In 1959 there was a change of emphasis. He was invited to deliver the 'Romanes' Lecture in the Sheldonian Theatre, Oxford, on 21 May 1959, and he chose as his title 'From Precedent to Precedent'. He used this lecture as an opportunity to attack the too strict adherence to precedent, especially in the House of Lords. He used examples from history to show that in the past the House had not been bound by its own precedents and urged that if the law was to develop and not to stagnate it must recapture the principle of growth. Denning was at that time a law lord and knew what it was like in the House of Lords. It was the first step in his campaign to get English lawyers to treat precedent with less reverence and to think in terms of principle. This crusade went on throughout his judicial life and was only partially successful.

When Denning was Master of the Rolls he was too busy to do any writing although he delivered a great number of speeches. It was nearly twenty years before another book *The Discipline of Law* was published in 1979 by Butterworths. In the preface Denning says that his object is to impart instruction in the principles of law, as they are, and as they should be. It is a review of the cases in which he has taken part, indicating where changes in the law put forward by him had been made, and where they had been rejected. He was eighty years old when the book was published and it was the summing up of his successes and failures in the law in the thirty five years that he had been on the Bench. It was a book for lawyers about the law. Its theme was that the law laid down for the social conditions in the nineteenth century needed moulding and changing to the needs of the twentieth century. Dennings's eightieth birthday on 23 January 1979 was marked by family celebrations and a reception at Butterworths to mark the publication of *The Discipline of Law*. The next day, between 4.30 p.m. and 8 p.m., he signed four hundred copies of the book in Butterworths bookshop in Bell Yard. Many people waited for three hours in a queue which stretched two hundred yards up Bell Yard and along Chancery Lane.

After 1979 books by Denning came out each year. In 1980 *The Due Process of Law* was published, designed as a companion volume to *The Discipline of Law*. This book was about the practical working of the law and discussed procedural matters and the law of husband and wife. In the preface he wrote:

In the choice of topics, I have tried to do – what the cobbler should do – stick to his last – to those topics which I have most experience. I have chosen them also for their general interest. Not bookish law which depends on the interpretation of Statutes and Rules of Court. But the law in which persons count.

In the late 1970s Denning had given some judgments which were not very popular with trade unionists and when it was proposed that he should sign copies of the book at Blackwell's bookshop in Oxford, posters appeared saying 'Mass picket Denning'. On the advice of the police and the proctors the event was cancelled.

In his epilogue to *The Discipline of Law* Denning wrote:

It is something to have lived through this century – the most dangerous century in the history of the English people. Our family has done its part. All five brothers fought in the wars. Two were lost. They were the best of us. Three survive. One to become a General. One an Admiral. And me, the Master of the Rolls. Some day, if I have time, I will tell you the family story. But that must wait. I must get on with the next case. Nothing must be left undone.

Two years later, in 1981, *The Family Story* was published. This is an autobiography but it also tells the story of his four brothers and their distinguished careers. There are fascinating photographs of Whitchurch in the early years of the twentieth century, of the First World War and of members of the family. The story is anecdotal with much quotation from poetry and there is some marvellous writing. The description of his home (given in chapter one above) is most memorable.

Denning's memory for people and for the law is prodigious. *The Family Story* appeared in the bestseller list for non-fiction.

On 20 May 1982 *What Next in the Law* was published. This was an attempt to look into the future and to discuss where the law needed reform. He said that there had been royal commissions, departmental committees and Blue Books, all recommending reform, but each turned down by the Government for one reason or another. The object of the book was to provide some spur. In the preface he wrote:

> Most of it is controversial – I have deliberately made it so. It is to set you thinking, talking and writing about what I have said. None of it is a final view. It is done without hearing argument. It is done without consulting others. As always, I am ready to change my mind. So agree or disagree. But do please help to get things going.

He considered reforms of the jury system, legal aid, personal injuries, libel, privacy and confidentiality, and the misuse of power. Pages 76 and 77 contained the paragraph which led to Denning's resignation (*see* Chapter 17). The paragraph was withdrawn and the book published without it.

In 1983, after his resignation, Denning published *The Closing Chapter*. In the first part of the book he tells the story of his resignation and subsequent events. It brought *The Family Story* up to date. The second part was intended to bring up to date *The Discipline of Law* and *The Due Process of Law* and was intended primarily for students of the law. It dealt with statutory interpretation, trade unions, commercial and procedural law. It sought to make everything as up to date as possible telling of the latest decisions up to the end of the summer term of 1983. He tried to make his meaning clear and quoted St Paul: 'For if the trumpet give an uncertain sound, who shall prepare himself to the battle? So likewise ye, except ye utter by the tongue words easy to be understood, how shall it be known what is spoken? For ye shall speak into the air.'

Landmarks in the Law, published in 1984, was a historical resumé dealing with several celebrated trials, famous lawyers and characters from literature. In his preface he wrote: 'In a way it is an anthology – a hotchpot – in which you can dip at will. You can pick it up and read a chapter or two in the train or before you go to sleep: and then put it down. It is not a connected story with a central theme.' He said that it was about those great cases of the past which have gone to make our constitution which students ought to know about. Some of the cases were from the remote past and others were more recent such as the Profumo affair.

His last book, published in 1986, was entitled *Leaves from my Library* and subtitled *An English Anthology*. The idea came from Lord Wavell's book *Other Mens' Flowers*, an anthology of his favourite poetry. Denning thought that he would gather together pieces of prose that he particularly admired and that instead of other mens' poetry he had taken other mens' stories. He quotes Montaigne who said 'I have gathered a posie of other mens' flowers and nothing but the thread that binds them is my own.' Many of the pieces had something to do with the law but he selected them mainly for their literary quality and descriptive force. He strung together prose from Winston Churchill, Lord Nelson, William Shakespeare, John Buchan, Lord Macaulay, Thomas Hardy, Lewis Carroll, John Bunyan, Charles Dickens, Anthony Trollope, Izaak Walton, Gilbert White, William Cobbett, Jane Austen and Geoffrey Chaucer. The choice gives some indication of Denning's literary taste and each piece is introduced by comment of his own.

Denning's writing falls into three main categories. Firstly he edited legal text-books for the practitioner. Secondly he put together addresses and lectures intended for young men and women at the universities and elsewhere to educate them in the law. Thirdly he produced propaganda for his views on the reform of the law. Standing apart is the report that he wrote on the Profumo affair. His style in this report has been criticised for having the style of a 'penny-dreadful' with sub-headings like 'The Borrowed Car', 'The Cup of Tea', 'The Man in the Mask' and 'The Man without a Head'.[5] It was certainly an exceptional Blue Book. The best of all his books is *The Discipline of Law*. It is divided into seven parts and is more coherent and disciplined than any of his other books. There are numbered headings and sub-headings but it is not divided into very small sections in the way that mars some of his other books. The argument is clear and it is very readable. *The Due Process of Law* is more discursive and anecdotal and does not stick to the point in the same way as the earlier book.

The Family Story contains vivid pictures of events and places and it is a valuable record of facts and memories which would otherwise be lost. Like his other books it is written in numbered paragraphs and it is somewhat disconcerting to find that Section Three 1 (1) is entitled 'Falling in Love'. There are good descriptions of the First World War and many memorable passages.

On 8 November 1918 I was taken in an ambulance train to the base hospital at Rouen. It was filled with sick men. So many that the nurses could not cope with the need. One after another died in our ward. The Armistice was 11 a.m. on 11 November 1918. There was little rejoicing in our ward. Too many were ill. There was relief. That was all.[6]

Denning's style of writing is lively and entertaining. He writes in short staccato sentences:

Mother was a different temperament from father. She got it from her father. Like him she was handsome with fine features. Very intelligent. Very hard-working. Determined to succeed in whatever she undertook. She was the driving force. Ambitious for her children. She would see that we worked to get on, as we did. Not sentimental. Not artistic. She was a foil to our father's fondness for music and poetry.[7]

The short sentences stem from his emphasis on the need for clarity in writing. He maintained that if you are to persuade your hearers in a judgment you must cultivate a style that commands attention. Your hearers must be able to understand what is said. You must not use long words unless you are sure that your hearers will be able to understand them. You must not use long sentences in case you lose your hearer. You should use plain, simple words which will be easily understood. Roundabout expressions should be avoided and, in this connection, he quotes Sir Winston Churchill. Churchill did not begin his broadcast on 17 June 1940: 'The position in regard to France is extremely serious.' Instead he began: 'The news from France is very bad.' He did not end: 'We have absolute confidence that eventually the situation will be restored.' Instead he ended: 'We are sure that in the end all will come right.'[8]

Denning's prose is taut, concrete, vigorous and clear. There is a pleasing sound to his words. Clichés are avoided. He has a horror of an unbroken page of print. The central principle of his style is that, when you write or speak, you should always be thinking of the reader or the hearer. He is a good storyteller, fond of anecdotes and makes great efforts to make his writing interesting to his readers. His best writing comes in *The Family Story* and his judgments produced some fine passages. Professor Cameron Harvey read through all Denning's reported judgments to discover the best writing. He then wrote an article about Denning's distinctive judicial writing style entitled 'It all started with Gunner James'.[9] This refers to a case heard as early as 1947. Harvey writes: 'He is an inveterate story-teller. It was his distinctive style to recount the facts in the form of a story.' Being a story-teller he tries to capture the attention of his hearers immediately: 'It happened on April 19 1964. It was bluebell time in Kent.'[10] or 'This is the case of the barmaid who was badly bitten by a dog.'[11] Harvey thinks that Denning's most memorable word sketch describes none other than old Peter Beswick:

Old Peter Beswick was a coal merchant in Eccles, Lancashire. He had no business premises. All he had was a lorry, scales and weights. He used to take the lorry to the yard of the National Coal Board, where he bagged coal and took it round to his customers in the neighbourhood. His nephew, John Joseph Beswick helped him in his business. In March 1962, old Peter Beswick and his wife were both over 70. He had had his leg amputated and was not in good health. The nephew was anxious to get hold of the business before the old man died. So they went to a solicitor, Mr Ashcroft, who drew up an agreement for them.[12]

Examples from two other judgments give the flavour of his style:

To some this may appear to be a small matter, but to Mr Harry Hook, it is very important. He is a street trader in the Barnsley market. He has been trading there for some six years without any complaint being made against him; but, nevertheless, he has now been banned from trading in the market for life. All because of a trifling incident. On Wednesday, October 16 1974, the market was closed at 5.30. So were all the lavatories, or 'toilets' as they are now called. They were locked up. Three quarters of an hour later, at 6.20, Harry Hook had an urgent call of nature. He wanted to relieve himself. He went into a side street near the market and there made water, or 'urinated' as it is now said. No one was about except one or two employees of the council, who were cleaning up. They rebuked him. He said: 'I can do it here if I like.' They reported him to a security officer who came up. The security officer reprimanded Harry Hook. We are not told the words used by the security officer. I expect they were in language which street traders understand. Harry Hook made an appropriate reply. Again we are not told the actual words, but it is not difficult to guess. I expect it was an emphatic version of 'You be off'. At any rate the security officer described them as words of abuse. Touchstone would say that the security officer gave the 'reproof valiant' and Harry Hook gave the 'counter-check quarrel-some'; *As You Like It*, Act V, Scene IV. On Thursday morning the security officer reported the incident. The market manager thought it was a serious matter. So he saw Mr Hook the next day, Friday, October 18. Mr Hook admitted it and said he was sorry for what had happened. The market manager was not satisfied to leave it there. He reported the incident to the chairman of the amenity services committee of the council. He says that the chairman agreed that 'staff should be protected from such abuse.' That very day the market manager wrote a letter to Mr Hook, banning him from trading in the market.[13]

The second judgement was given in 1977:

In summertime village cricket is a delight to everyone. Nearly every village has its own cricket field where the young men play and the old men watch. In the village of Lintz in the County of Durham they have their own ground, where they have played these last 70 years. They tend it well. The wicket area is well rolled and mown. The outfield is kept short. It has a good clubhouse for the players and seats for the onlookers. The village team play there on Saturdays and Sundays. They belong to a league, competing with the neighbouring villages. On other evenings they practise while the lights lasts. Yet now after these 70 years a judge of the High Court has ordered that they must not play any more. He has issued an injunction to stop them. He has done it at the instance of a newcomer who is no lover of cricket. This newcomer has built, or has had built for him, a house on the edge of the cricket ground which four years ago was a field where cattle grazed. The animals did not mind the cricket. But now this adjoining field has been turned into a housing estate. The newcomer bought one of the houses on the edge of the cricket field. No doubt the open space was a selling point. Now he complains that when a batsman hits a six the ball has been known to land in his garden or on or near his house. His wife has got so upset about it that they always go out at weekends. They do not go into the garden when cricket is being played. They say that this is intolerable. So they asked the judge to stop the cricket being played. And the judge, much against his will, has felt that he must order the cricket to be stopped: with the consequence, I suppose, that the Lintz Cricket Club will disappear. The cricket ground will be turned to some other use. I expect for houses or a factory. The young men will turn to other things instead of cricket. The whole village will be much poorer. And all this because of a newcomer who has just bought a house there next to the cricket ground.[14]

In *The Family Story* Denning quotes Samuel Wesley: 'Style is the dress of thought: a modest dress, neat, but not gaudy, will true critics please.'[15] There are, however, drawbacks to the staccato style. The writing does not flow and is better suited to a judgment than a book. There is little rhythm in the sentences. The style is plain and sometimes discursive, but he has an ear for the apt word and telling phrase. His style is vivid; clarity and brevity are the keynotes while his judgments are a delight to read.

Seventeen

DISASTER

A judgment too far.
The Times, 24 March 1982[1]

It is orthodox doctrine in the Christian religion that all men are equal and that the colour of a man's skin is irrelevant. As a Christian, Denning always accepted this and acted on it. He took great interest in the education of African students and made visits to Africa, India and other parts of the world. He had friends of all races and colours. As early as 1969 he had stated publicly that the greatest problem facing civilisation was the problem of colour.[2] He had been concerned with a number of decisions on immigration and deportation. As Parliament became more restrictive in its immigration policy any judgment of the courts implementing that policy might be considered by some to be racially motivated. Here Denning was in line with his brother judges in carrying out the legislative policy. His attitude to immigrants can be given in his own words:

In recent times England has been invaded – not by enemies – nor by friends – but by those who seek England as a haven. In their own countries there are poverty, disease and no homes. In England there is social security – a national health service and guaranteed housing – all to be had for the asking without payment and without working for it. Once here, each seeks to bring his relatives to join him. So they multiply exceedingly.[3]

Denning dealt with many cases of illegal immigration and wrote about the typical case of Gurbax Singh Khera:[4]

He was born in a village in the Punjab. He had an uncle in the same village. His uncle arranged with agents in India to get him to England – on payment of 15,000 rupees. He travelled by air from New Delhi to Paris. Then by car to a port on the French coast. When it was dark he embarked on a

193

small motor boat with three other Asians. The boat was manned by two white men. He was frightened because it was his first time at sea. They crossed to England. They got out on a sandy shore. The white men led them to hard ground. The Asians were put in the back of a van. They were driven for five or six hours till they arrived at Wolverhampton. He was dropped at his father's house. He soon obtained work and has continued at work ever since. Some years later he was arrested and detained as 'an illegal entrant' .... To be fair to him he seems to have behaved well and worked well. After three years, some might think that their wrongdoing could be forgiven, and that there should be an amnesty. But Parliament has decided otherwise. I think I can see why. This man, if once here by leave, will seek to bring his wife and children over. If the man is allowed to remain it will be difficult to refuse the wife and children. If this were allowed, the number of immigrants would be increased so greatly that there would not be room for everybody. Again, if an amnesty were granted, it would be an encouragement to others to follow their example: and that simply cannot be permitted. By sending back illegal entrants, it will help to deter others from trying to do the same.

One of Denning's last cases dealt with the interpretation of the Race Relations Act 1976 which made it unlawful to discriminate on racial grounds or against a racial group. It was the case of the Sikh boy's turban.[5] Mandla, a Sikh, wanted his son to go to Park Grove School, a private school in Birmingham. Mandla was interviewed by the headmaster who refused to take his son unless he complied with the school rules about dress and removed his turban. This Mandla refused to do. Mandla reported the headmaster to the Commission for Racial Equality who assisted Mandla with the proceedings against the headmaster. The Birmingham County Court judge dismissed the claim and was upheld by the Court of Appeal. The court held that the Sikhs were not a racial group. They were only distinguished from others in the Punjab by their religion and culture and this was not an ethnic difference. From the Englishman's point of view it seemed only fair that he should be able to exclude a boy from his school if the boy was not prepared to abide by the rules of the school. From the Asian's point of view it was not fair that he should be excluded from a good education because his religion and culture required him to wear a turban.

There was a great outcry from the Sikh community about this judgment. The secretary of the supreme council of Sikhs in Britain said that the ruling was absolutely outrageous and that Lord Denning was living up to his reputation as a judge who was against ethnic minorities. The Sikhs organised a protest march from Hyde Park to Downing Street and presented a petition. Commentators were quick to point out that the judgment was contrary to the intention of Parliament and referred to a White Paper which specifically mentioned the wearing of turbans as an area which would be covered by the legislation. On 1 August *The Observer* came out with a headline: 'Sikh boy: Denning thwarts Commons'. The Minister of State at the Home Office stated that the records of the House of Commons make clear that the Race Relations Act 1976 was intended to protect Sikhs from discrimination when wearing turbans. The House of Lords reversed the Court of Appeal.

On 9 July 1981 there was the usual Mansion House dinner for the judges given by the Lord Mayor of London. Unfortunately the Lord Chief Justice could not attend and it fell to Denning, as the next senior judge, to speak on behalf of the judges. He took as his subject 'Our present discontents' and the two main strands of his speech were the need to support the police and the strains now put upon the jury system. He said:

In the vital task of maintaining law and order the judges play an important part. But it must always be remembered that when it comes to dealing with mobs – with violence, with crime itself – the police are the first line of defence. All good citizens should and do support them. It is deplorable to see the way in which, on occasions, they are most unjustly attacked by vociferous groups and by the press and television .... Trial by jury is under stress. One of these strains is the right of the accused to challenge any juror – that is to say object to him – without giving any cause .... It has been resurrected in the last 25 years. Let me tell you of the riots in Bristol. It was a coloured area. A few of the good Bristol police force went to inquire into some of the wrongful acts being committed there. They were set upon by coloured people living there. Much violence. Much damage. Twelve of them were arrested and charged with riot – a riot it certainly was. So they were tried by jury. There were 12 accused. Each had three challenges. That is 36 altogether. The accused challenged the white men, but not the coloured men, nor the women. Eight were acquitted. On four the jury could not agree. The prosecution proceeded no further. The cost was £500,000. This was, in my opinion, an abuse of the right of challenge, to get a jury of their own choice.[6]

The next day, 10 July 1981, *The Times* had a comment on page 2:

'Lord Denning criticises jury vetting', saying that Denning had attacked the behaviour of defence counsel in the case of the Bristol riots and gave an accurate report of the speech so far as it related to the peremptory challenge of jurors. No protests, public or private, were made about the speech or the newspaper report.

During the long vacation of 1981 Denning worked hard on a new book entitled *What Next in the Law* and by Christmas the proofs were in the hands of the publishers. On 20 May 1982 the book was launched at a party given by Butterworths, the publishers, in Kingsway. The following day Denning signed copies of the book at Butterworths' book shop in Bell Yard. Two passages in the book gave offence to some who had come to England from overseas. One passage indicated that some of them were not suitable to serve on juries. Another that they were using the peremptory challenge so as to pack the jury with their sympathisers. Commenting on the recent riot at Bristol Denning said that there were thirty-six challenges to jurymen so as to secure as many coloured people on the jury as possible and that the police were attacked by coloured people living there who did not like their illegal activities being stopped. What he said was in essence the same as what he said at the Mansion House when there had been no adverse comment. This may have lulled him into a false sense of security.

On Saturday 22 May, there was a leading article in *The Times*, 'Denning Jury Reform Angers Black Lawyers':

Controversy erupted yesterday over Lord Denning's latest book, *What Next in the Law*, with a call from the Society of Black Lawyers for the Master of the Rolls to retire .... Mr Sibghat Kadri, the society's chairman, said the remarks were insulting and degrading and couched in terms virulent enough to destroy any remaining credibility he may have as an unbiased and impartial interpreter of the law. The society would be calling on the Lord Chancellor to ask Lord Denning politely but firmly to retire. The Standing Conference of Pakistani Organisations, of which Mr Kadri is president, is to call a meeting to start a campaign to that end.

Later on the same day Ludovic Kennedy came to 'The Lawn' to interview Denning. He referred to the offending passages and asked Denning: 'Do you stand by it?' After some hesitation Denning said that he did. It was only then that he fully realised that the passages in the book were a mistake. With regard to the suggestion that there were thirty-six challenges at the Bristol trial to enable as many coloured people as possible to be on the jury, this was based on a letter received from a barrister in Bristol. He was subsequently shown a transcript of the proceedings at the trial which showed that the challenges were quite properly used, at the invitation of the judge, so as to secure a representative jury. On Saturday evening he was telephoned by David Leigh of *The Observer* who told him that the black jurors were going to sue him and had he any comments to make? Denning replied that he had no comments but he had a sleepless night.

On Sunday 23 May, *The Observer* had a big black headline – 'Black Jurors to Sue Denning Unless' – above the article by David Leigh:

Lord Denning, the Master of the Rolls, faces a libel action from two of the black jurors in the Bristol riot case, after claiming in a book published last week that they had failed to convict guilty people because they were their own. Lord Denning, 83, gave last year's Bristol riot trial as an example of a packed jury overloaded with what he described as coloured people. He then claimed that black, coloured and brown people did not have the same standard of conduct as whites. Last night Ms Gareth Pearce of the London solicitors Birnberg & Co, said that letters had been sent to Lord Denning and to Butterworths, publishers of the book *What Next in the Law* on behalf of two black jurors in the case .... Lord Denning's account of what happened in Bristol contains a number of factual mistakes.

The article gave a detailed description of what had happened at the trial and it was clear that the newspaper was fully informed by persons present at the trial. It so happened that Denning's son Robert, and his wife Elizabeth, with their two sons, had come over for the day and Denning had the chance of talking to his son and obtaining his advice.

Denning had another sleepless night and on Monday morning, 24 May, he travelled to London from Whitchurch on his 8.25 a.m. train and opened *The Times*. There was another leading article entitled 'A Judgment Too Far'. It included these two paragraphs:

Lord Denning's ill-considered remarks on the unsuitability of many blacks for jury service have, understandably, caused considerable offence in the black community. Should he have to give judgment in a case in which race is a factor, he will be exposed to charges of prejudice and to suggestions that his decision might be affected by his personal feelings on racial matters.

Such criticism would, it is hoped and expected, be unwarranted. But Lord Denning has only himself to blame for placing himself in a position where such attacks could be made.

It was the same on issues affecting industrial relations. The accusations which the political left and many trade unionists have made against Lord Denning have only partly been based on the judgments he has given against unions in a number of court cases. Much of the feeling against him has resulted from remarks he has made in lectures and in his books.

Denning now knew that he must bow to the inevitable and retire. On arriving at his room in the Royal Courts of Justice he wrote to the Lord Chancellor and sent the letter round by hand to the House of Lords that morning. The Lord Chancellor, Lord Hailsham, replied sympathetically in his own hand and suggested that Denning should not retire at once but at the end of the summer term. Later he added that it should take effect from the end of the long vacation, on 29 September. On Friday 28 May, half an hour after the courts had risen for the Whitsun vacation, a statement was issued by Peter Post, Denning's clerk, saying that Lord Denning had intended to retire at the end of the current legal year because of his advanced age and that in the ordinary course of events the announcement would have been made in the middle of June. It added: 'In the light of recent controversy which has arisen over his latest book, which it is hoped will shortly be resolved, it has been decided to bring the announcement forward. Lord Denning will continue to sit as Master of the Rolls until the end of July.'

The Dennings were besieged by the press. Joan Denning said to the *Daily Mirror*: 'He is very distressed. He has done more for the black people in this country than any other judge. He is very upset. He realises that he has made a mistake.'[7] On 26 May Rudy Narayan, the secretary of the Society of Black Lawyers, wrote to *The Times* as follows:

Lord Denning remains one of the greatest judicial minds of this century; he was my sponsor on call to the Bar .... The remarks are clearly wrong and it is good to read Lady Denning's quoted remarks. Lord and Lady Denning have thousands of friends in Africa, Asia and the Caribbean who will be surprised at his remarks and his own and Lady Denning's distress is plain to see. A great judge has erred greatly in the intellectual loneliness of advanced years; while his remarks should be rejected and rebutted he is yet, in a personal way, entitled to draw on that reservoir of community regard which he has in many quarters and to seek understanding, if not forgiveness.

Denning had done a great deal for the students from the Commonwealth and had no colour prejudice. A couple of unguarded remarks, suggested by a letter received from a member of the Western circuit, were to cause so much anguish to Denning and his family. As he ruefully remarked: 'So there it is. All over in a fortnight.'[8]

Not only had a decision to be made on retirement but the subject of legal proceedings had to be tackled. Denning instructed Max Williams (later Sir Max Williams) of Clifford-Turner & Co, to act on his behalf. Williams briefed Mr Andrew Leggatt QC (later Lord Justice Leggatt) and David Eady. After a week of negotiations a settlement was reached. No writs were issued against Denning or Butterworths. No damages were sought. The book was withdrawn and the offending passages removed. Denning made a public apology in terms that were agreed. He wrote personally to all the jurors in the Bristol case apologising to each individually for what he had said. The book itself was re-issued in July 1982.

During that last summer term Denning was as busy as ever, talking to magistrates in the country, sitting in court all day and preparing judgments at the weekend. Dinners had to be attended most evenings and speeches to be made. The most memorable occasion was the dinner given in Denning's honour by the Speaker of the House of Commons, George Thomas (later Lord Tonypandy), on 5 July 1982. The Prime Minister, Mrs Margaret Thatcher, and many other Ministers of the Crown were present. The Speaker's House is a fitting place for a great State occasion with its impressive staircase and splendid state rooms. The dinner was held in the dining room of the Speaker's House and the portraits of previous Speakers looked down on the gathering. It was a very grand occasion and the BBC had a team there that evening to portray the dinner as an incident in the life of Parliament, which was shown on television.

Denning's valediction in the Lord Chief Justice's Court on Friday 30 July 1982, was a moving and memorable event.[9] This court was used as it is the largest in the Royal Courts of Justice. All seats were taken long before the appointed time of 2 p.m. and barristers in wig and gown pushed vainly at the swing doors to get in. The Lord Chancellor, Lord Hailsham, presided, and said that it was given to few to be a legend in their own lifetime. He said that before the war the common law had been in a period of quiescence but after the war she had awoken from her slumbers and entered upon renewed activity. He acknowledged the vast debt owed to Denning for his deep learning, powerful intellect and pungent English style. Simon Brown (later Mr Justice Brown) said: 'We shall recall that short sentences are best and that verbs are optional.' Ashe Lincoln QC, the senior practising silk, said:

In my long experience at the Bar I remember so well my first appearance as a young junior in the Court of Appeal when the presiding judge did not have your patient temperament, and I had a very rough passage indeed. It made one appreciate all the more the kindliness and humanity of Lord Denning when he presided over the Court of Appeal. So long as the common law exists, the name of Lord Denning will be revered and remembered not only in this country but throughout the world. I remember in the United States of America how greatly he is respected and how when I visited law colleges and law schools in that country I found that the students had embroidered their T-shirts with the words 'Root for Denning'. It occurred to me that it might be a useful garment to wear before the Court of Appeal![10]

In reply Denning said:

Now I have brought something to show you. A lady friend of ours, a Parsee, a member of Lincoln's Inn, has been a friend for years. On behalf of the community a case was decided by Lord Justice Ormrod and his colleagues in the Court of Appeal which won the approval of the Parsee community in Bombay; and she sent this gift for the Court of Appeal. I will tell you what she says: 'Here are seven elephants drawing a dainty silver carriage. The square piece on the rear of the carriage has the single word "Justice" inscribed on it. All the elephants are engaged in the task of pulling the carriage of "Justice" along the narrow white path, the straight and narrow road .... The great white elephant has no tusks for he does not need tusks to do his work in nature. This elephant's mind and thought force power is so highly developed in nature that he can do the work of spreading justice and maintaining the divine law and order among all souls .... This elephant represents you, Lord Denning, as the greatest force for truth and justice tempered with mercy, alive today .... I wish you would place this figure in some room in the Law Courts building where all your judges can see it, for it would serve as a constant reminder to them that justice must ever be done, and the time may come in the future when the great white elephant may no longer be in their midst.' The time has come.[11]

On the same morning, 30 July, *The Times* came out with another leading article. It said: 'Lord Denning has legal genius and he has a laudable mission to make the law accord with justice.' It continued: 'There is much to be said for a period of quiet judicial activity now, and the predictability that is afforded by a stricter regard for precedent. Lord Denning's reign was glorious, often spectacular, occasionally wayward, English law has earned a few years' rest.' *Private Eye* came out with a cartoon showing two barristers reading a headline: 'Denning to retire'. One was saying to the other: 'I expect the House of Lords will overrule his decision.' Hugo Young wrote in *The Sunday Times* on 30 May 1982:

When the Lord Chancellor considers the field of successors it is safe to say that he will choose no one like Denning. There is no such beast on the bench of judges .... When all the raucous headlines have been forgotten, and the last regrettable calamity has passed insignificantly into the dustbin, Denning's great works will endure for ever. To anyone who believes the law should liberate, not enslave, he is a beacon. He discovered that young, as a poor student in the 1920s. He is just about the only octagenarian who has never forgotten it.

Eighteen

Retirement

Lord Denning is retired and should stay that way.[1]
Water Authorities

Denning always wanted to stay on as a judge for a record period of time. In March 1980 he surpassed the English record for length of judicial service of just over thirty-six years. The previous record had been held by Lord Bramwell who had been appointed in 1856 and resigned in 1882 but sat constantly in the House of Lords until his death in 1892. Denning was one of the last judges to have a freehold. In 1960 the judges accepted a Government proposal that they should retire at seventy-five and have a contractual pension of half their final salary after fifteen years of service. This did not affect those judges appointed before 1960. A judge holding a freehold could not be compelled to retire but could keep his office for life. A pension was usually provided but it was not contractual. In the eighteenth century most office holders had a freehold but now the parson's freehold is the only well known one to survive.

Pressure for Denning's resignation came from a number of quarters. The Haldane Society at its Annual General Meeting in 1979 passed a resolution by a majority of forty to twenty demanding Denning's resignation and criticising him for his interpretation of the law relating to trade union immunity. By 1979 this Society had been taken over by left-wing members and the moderate Labour lawyers had resigned from the Society to form the Society of Labour Lawyers. Joan Denning used to ask him: 'Isn't it time for you to retire?' She had been ill in 1977 and he felt that he wanted to go on as long as her health permitted. He could never bring himself to fix a date. After a dinner at Middle Temple a Minister of the Crown took him aside and said: 'You are at the peak of your fame now. Do not go on too long.' He frequently said in public that he had all the Christian virtues except resignation.

Denning continued to go to the House of Lords until failing health prevented him from travelling to London by train. Some said that Denning was losing his grip in the last five years as a judge but others do not agree and the evidence of the law reports does not point that way. On the construction of statutes, contracts and wills he received the greatest judical and academic castigation in the 1960s. Legislation had dealt with the main problems of family law and trade unions. His disputes with the House of Lords continued to the end particularly on the question of precedent. The question at issue was not really precedent but the authority of the House of Lords.

At the time of Denning's resignation he was eighty-three and among the many celebrations to mark his retirement was a dinner given by the Lords Justices at the Inner Temple for Denning and his wife, arranged by Lord Justice John Stephenson. Denning spoke but the great applause came for the few words spoken by Joan Denning:

> I have never made an after-dinner speach in my life. Tom does all the speaking. But once he did show me a judgment he was going to give. I told him that I thought he was coming out the wrong way. He said 'Oh, do you?' and wrote the judgment the other way. The two other judges did not agree but afterwards the Lords overruled them. So he won in the Lords.[2]

The dinner was given by all who had sat with Denning during the twenty years that he had been Master of the Rolls. They numbered thirty-six.

The transition from a very active public life to the private life of retirement is not easy to make. Speaking to an interviewer in August 1982 he said: 'I don't want to be idle. I will be free to take part in political controversy which I am not at the moment, and I would like to help with legislation in the House of Lords, certainly on social matters and law reform.'[3] There are four main strands in this period of his life: he continued his role as an author; attended debates in the House of Lords; continued to interest himself in the life of Whitchurch; and dealt with a large post from the public. Three books were written after his retirement: *The Closing Chapter* was published in 1983, *Landmarks in the Law* came out in 1984 and *Leaves from my Library* in 1986.

Denning took part in more debates in the House of Lords than any other law lord. This was partly due to his long tenure as a member of the House which spanned more than thirty years. He took part in 328 debates between 1957 and 1988 and until the last year or two all the debates related to legal subjects such as Administrative Tribunals, Divorce, Domicile, Variation of Trusts, Charitable Trusts, Obscene Publications, Police, Suicide, Law Commission, Civil Evidence, Family Provision, Matrimonal Proceedings and Property, Criminal Justice and the like. He attended all debates about Public Records and the Solicitor's Profession where he felt that he had a special responsibility as Master of the Rolls. In the second reading in the debate on the Solicitors Bill 1965 he said: 'In my capacity as Master of the Rolls I have an inherent jurisdiction over solicitors – indeed, rather a paternal jurisdiction. So much so that the Master of the Rolls has been said to be the father-in-law of all solicitors.'[4]

In the five years between 1957 and 1961 he attended fifty debates but numbers tailed off after he had become Master of the Rolls in 1962. Between 1962 and 1982 he attended fifty-five debates with no attendances in 1964 and 1980. It was only after he retired that he became a regular attender; nineteen times in 1984; forty-four in 1985; seventy-five in 1986; sixty-six in 1987. Although a cross bencher he supported the Government more often than not. His voting behaviour gives some idea of his views on a variety of topics. He voted for bills relating to Charitable Trusts; Legitimacy; Police Service; Rights of Privacy; Suicide; Licensing; Legal Aid; Solicitors; Misrepresentation; Matrimonal Proceedings and Property; Supply of Goods (Implied Terms); Unfair Contract Terms; Drug Trafficking Offences; Public Order. He voted against bills on Homosexual Offences; Prostitution; Artificial Insemination of Married Women; Bill of Rights; State Immunity; Religious Cults; Shops; Human Rights and Jurisdiction; Costs of Acquitted Defendants. In the debate on Shops he moved an amendment to keep Sunday as a special day; it was defeated despite the fact that it had the support of all the bishops present. After he ceased to attend the House in 1988 he sent in questions for written answers.

Here are some examples of his interventions in debates. In the Street Offences Bill of 1959 he thought that male clients as well as the prostitutes should be prosecuted.[5] In the same year he thought that it was the greatest disservice to law and order that some people should raise calumnies against the police[6] and in the Police Service Bill 1960 that counsel often attacked the police because they felt it would ingratiate them with the jury.[7] Speaking on the Matrimonial Causes Bill 1967 he said that twenty years previously he had hoped that a Family Court would be established: a judge sitting with two lay magistrates dealing not only with divorce but with the maintenance and care of children.[8] In 1968 he thought that hearsay evidence should be admitted in civil proceedings.[9] He did not like the reduction of the age of majority from twenty-one to eighteen and thought that the change was not backed by any demand in the country.[10] He considered that majority verdicts were a great improvement but was sorry to lose the patronage of the Master of the Rolls over the appointment of Queen's Bench Masters. This passed into the hands of the Lord Chancellor.[11] He greatly applauded the Supply of Goods (Implied Terms) Bill 1972 which outlawed exemption clauses in contracts and thought that it was the most important reform of commercial law in his time.[12]

In 1976, a Bill of Rights was brought in to declare the inalienable rights and liberties of the subject. Denning took part in the second reading of the Bill on 25 March 1976. He used the 'floodgates' argument against the Bill. He asked the House to be cautious before giving the Bill a second reading. He foresaw that the Bill of Rights would be taken advantage of by crackpots and disgruntled people who would bring proceedings before the courts challenging the orderly system of our society. He said:

We may turn them down but I foresee a great deal of litigation.... It will be contrary to all our history and tradition if the courts of this country should set aside any section or part of an Act of Parliament. The supremacy of Parliament is one of the pillars of our constitution.... If judges are given power to overthrow sections of Acts of Parliament they would become political.... I hope we shall not have such conflicts in our country.[13]

He was also against incorporating the European Convention on Human Rights, in its present form, into English law. He felt that the Convention was worded in such wide terms that it was only an expression of pious hopes. For example, one of the clauses of the Convention reads: 'No person shall be denied the right to education.... The state shall respect the rights of parents to ensure such education and teaching in conformity with their own religious and philosophic convictions.' Does this mean, for example, that Muslims in Bradford would have the right to set up their own school which would be funded by the State? At the end of 1987 he intervened in a debate on human rights when a schizophrenic mother was denied access to her child by a conference of case workers. Denning emphasised the merits of the case indicating that in the circumstances access had to be denied for the welfare of the child. The Court of Human Rights had held that if access was to be denied to a parent this must be done by a court of law and not by a conference of case workers.[14] This must surely be right in principle. The Court of Human Rights gave priority to the overriding principle. It is only a court of law that can grant or deny access.

Denning had to give up attending the House of Lords in February 1988 on the grounds of health. He had, up until then, had generally good health. As a child he was regarded as the weakest member of the family and at one time it was feared that he might have heart trouble. On one occasion when he was ill as a child straw was laid in the road outside the house to deaden the sound of the horses' hooves. Late in life he suffered from arthritis in his right hip and on 1 March 1983, at the age of eighty-three, he had an operation for the replacement of a hip at King Edward VII Hospital for Officers in Beaumont Street. With increasing age a hearing aid became necessary and help was needed in getting about. An electric stair lift was installed to help him go up and down stairs.

No longer able to get to the House of Lords more time was spent in Whitchurch. Ever since he first moved to Whitchurch in 1963 he has taken a keen interest in the amenities of the town. In 1961 an old brick and timber granary standing in Parsonage Meadow became very dilapidated and was about to be pulled down as it was no longer needed for agricultural purposes. The barn had a thatched roof and wooden partitions comprising six large bins to receive the corn. It is raised on staddle stones to stop the rats getting in. Denning had the barn restored at his own expense and obtained a new lease from the landlords, the Trustees of St Cross. The Whitchurch Cricket Club have their ground in Parsonage Meadow and spectators can shelter in the barn if caught in a shower of rain. Denning was a keen supporter of the Cricket Club of which he was, of course, made President. He allowed the use of the grounds of 'The Lawn' for their Annual fête. Another barn, lying beyond their land, was derelict and intended for demolition. Denning had it removed to his meadow and reinstated. He planted poplars in the water meadows and Norway spruce and beech on a hill at Upper Wyke, three miles away. Always in the forefront of any public protest against the closure of footpaths, he appeared on television in a contest with the local authority. It was ultimately settled amicably.

Another amenity concern was the old Town Hall. When he was a boy it housed the fire engine. In 1963 it was in danger of falling down. The roof was leaking and there was doubt about ownership. The old records stated that it belonged to the freeholders of Whitchurch. A Parish Meeting was held and trustees were appointed. Later on Denning became Chairman of the Trustees and helped to raise the money for its repair. It was restored, as near as possible, to its original design. Two empty shops were acquired with some derelict property behind. The old Police Court had been held there and workmen discovered the cells beneath. When restored it was taken over by the Town Council for its own use. Whitchurch had doubled in size since Denning was young but the old town had been preserved as a conservation area.

Not only was his concern with the amenities of the town, it was also with the people who live there and in the surrounding country. He bought 'The Mount', a large house near 'The Lawn', and converted it into four flats for elderly retired couples. He also acquired six small houses in the town which he let to young married couples at modest rents. Another local interest near to his heart was to obtain the benefit of old school sites for the young people of the parish. On 2 November 1987 he wrote to *The Times* giving an example of the village of Wield, Hampshire. The local education authority closed the village school in 1963, but they continued to use the buildings for the next twenty years for their own purposes. The true owners of the school were charitable trustees, not the local education authority. In the case of Wield the trustees were known and applied to the Charity commission for a scheme. The Commission made a scheme under which the trustees sold the school for £40,000; this sum was invested to promote the education (including social and physical training) of children aged between five and eighteen years from the parish. Usually the problem was to discover who were the trustees and where the deeds were to establish the title. Denning urged villagers to search for evidence of title so that their rights should be established for the benefit of all the village.

Denning always had a great concern for the education of the young.

He spoke frequently to students in the universities and on his foreign travels. He took seriously the judge's duty to help in the legal education of law students. In 1980 a student wrote to him: 'Please do not bring up any new doctrine such as the "*Mareva*" injunction as our examinations are just around the corner.' He got on well with children and young people. He once said: 'It is not our job to tell the young what to do, but to give them their head and leave them free from direction and stand by to pick up the pieces.'[15] After his marriage to Joan, Denning he took great trouble to gain the confidence of her children. When Hazel was taking her scholarship examination for Somerville College, Oxford, he made a point of telling her that she could go to Somerville whether or not she gained a scholarship. In 1946 he took one of his stepdaughters on circuit and in 1954 his stepson, John, went with him to South Africa.

Denning always had a large post but it was boosted by an occurrence in 1983. On Sunday, 13 February 1983, Mr Patrick Evershed, a cousin of the late Lord Evershed, telephoned Denning at about lunch time.[16] It was the time of the water strike. The workers refused to repair broken or burst pipes. Mr Evershed said that his street in Pimlico had been without water for two days. Could they repair the pipes themselves or employ contractors to do it? Could they charge the expense to the water authority? It took Denning two hours to look up the authorities and at 3.30 p.m. he rang back. His answer was that the water authority was under a statutory duty to provide a supply of wholesome water in pipes to every part of their district in which there were houses and schools. It was no answer for them to say that their own men are on strike. They should employ contractors to repair the pipes. If the water authority does not fulfil its duty to the householder the latter is entitled to repair the pipes himself or employ contractors to do the repairs. On doing so he will be entitled to charge the water authority with the expense. Prima facie it is an offence to break up roads without the permission of the Highway Authority or to interfere with water pipes without the consent of the water authority, but Denning thought that the defence of necessity would avail Mr Evershed.

The newspapers and television found this a welcome diversion and on Monday 14 February the telephone at 'The Lawn' was ringing all day. Television crews came to the house and Denning went to the studio in Southampton to explain his stand. The water authorities were not amused and the Junior Minister for the Environment said in Parliament: 'With all respect to the former Master of the Rolls I must warn householders that they cannot go on digging up highways at will.' In the country some householders mended burst pipes themselves. In London expert contractors were needed, but contractors were afraid to do the work as they feared that they might be 'blacked' by the trade unions. As a result of all this publicity Denning was inundated with letters from the public seeking to obtain legal advice on their own problems. He had to reply that he did not give legal advice and that they should consult a solicitor. In February 1983 *Private Eye* had a commentary entitled 'Your legal queries answered' which ended: 'If you have a legal query you would like answered send it to Lord Denning, Dunjudgin, Whitchurch, Hants (first left past the church).'

Denning made many appearances on television and radio and proved a successful performer on these occasions. A barrister's art is in many ways connected with the art of acting and Denning's many after-dinner speeches and lectures were performances. In May 1980 he took part in 'Desert Island Discs' on BBC radio. Guided by Roy Plomley they played eight records which he would have chosen if stranded on a desert island. They were 'Greensleeves'; 'Colonel Bogey'; 'To be a pilgrim'; 'Mine eyes have seen the coming of the glory of the Lord'; 'Roses are blooming in Picardy'; *The King and I* sung by Valerie Hobson; 'The Judge's Song' in *Trial by Jury*; and 'Land of Hope and Glory' from Elgar's *Pomp and Circumstance*. The book chosen was *Palgrave's Golden Treasury* which he thought to be the best of anthologies.

In 1980 Bernard Miles wrote to him: 'I sat watching you the other evening with a band of notable thespians. The unanimous verdict – clearly a great judge – but what a terrible loss to the acting profession .... When did you take the wrong turning?'[17] Denning had a sense of mischief and a love of fun and liked to lighten his performances with jokes and anecdotes. In 1978 he reviewed David Pannick's book *Judges* on television. It is a very amusing and learned book but he had some suggestions to make about the method of appointing judges, judicial attire, legal language and publicity. Denning explained fairly what was in the book and the viewer was expecting his comments on the proposals. He explained tersely that he did not agree with any of them. One of his characteristic gestures was to put his hand on the arm of the person he was addressing. Some Benchers of Lincoln's Inn would avoid sitting by Denning, not because they were uninterested in what he had to say, but because they could not lift up their arm to get on with their lunch.

On his ninetieth birthday, 23 January 1989, Lincoln's Inn gave a dinner in his honour. Eighty-five Benchers were present including the Royal Bencher, Princess Margaret. The BBC had an item on television news interviewing Denning at home and just before the dinner. One of the dishes on the menu was 'Filet of Sole Denning'. In replying to the toast he said: 'Ninety. This is the happiest birthday I've had – so far.'

In his 92nd year Denning unwittingly became involved in controversy again. There is a rule of English law that a person charged with a crime may remain silent and cannot be called to give evidence and be cross-examined. The reason for the rule is that the prosecution must be able to prove its case independently of anything the accused says. Not only can the accused refuse to answer questions but the judge, in summing up, must not refer to the fact that the accused has remained silent. The rule was criticised by Jeremy Bentham, the legal reformer, in the early nineteenth century and has been the subject of controversy ever since. The view of those who object to the rule is very simple. An innocent man would surely have an explanation to account for his actions and that the rule as it stands is a charter for criminals. Every experienced criminal remains silent in the hope that the prosecution cannot prove its case.

On 20 October 1988 the Home Secretary, in answer to a written question in the House of Commons, announced that the Government intended to change the law on the accused's right of silence. Mr Tom King, then the Northern Ireland Secretary, was interviewed on the main news bulletin by both ITN and BBC Television, when he gave his views in favour of a change in the law. At 7 pm on Channel 4 News on the same day Denning also said that he favoured a change in the law. It so happened on that very day Lord Gifford was addressing the jury at Winchester on behalf of one of three Irish people charged with terrorist offences who had exercised their right of silence. Two of the accused had been arrested near Mr King's house in Wiltshire and one was arrested later at a camp site at Wookey Hole, Somerset. In their car, parked near the camp site, the police found false Irish driving licences and the address of the London HQ of

100th Field Regiment, Royal Artillery. In the tent on the site were lists of names and addresses of prominent Army officers and politicians who had served in Northern Ireland. The three were charged with conspiracy to murder Mr King and persons unknown. After a three-week trial all the accused were convicted and were sentenced to twenty-five years imprisonment.

There was an appeal to the Court of Appeal which was heard by Lord Justice Beldam, a very experienced Lord Justice of Appeal, and two Queen's Bench judges, Mr Justice Tucker and Mr Justice Fennell. Judgment was delivered by Lord Justice Beldam on 27 April 1990.[18] He said that the court had seen video recordings of the television programmes and was solely concerned with the possible effects they might have on the minds of the jury. He continued:

The statements of Mr King and Lord Denning, which were powerfully made, were on their face of general application, but had a particular relevance to the trial of the accused.... Their Lordships were left with the definite impression that the impact which the statements made in the television interviews might well have had on the fairness of the trial could not be overcome by any direction to the jury and that the only way in which justice could have been done and have been seen to be done was by discharging the jury and ordering a retrial.

As it was not open to the court to order a retrial the verdict of the jury was set aside and the convictions quashed.

Denning was highly incensed by the references to himself in the judgment and on Monday 30 April 1990 he wrote a letter to *The Times*. His letter was headed by the newspaper: 'In defence of freedom of speech', and he said:

In your issue of Saturday, April 28, you headlined one of your reports 'Three convictions quashed on right to silence'. You set out the reasons given by the judges of the Court of Appeal. These were that Mr Tom King, Secretary of State for Defence, and I had made statements on television which were so prejudicial to the three accused that a fair trial was impossible before the jury that was trying them. That unfairness 'could not be overcome by any direction to the jury and that the only way in which justice could be done and be obviously seen to be done was by discharging the jury and ordering a new trial'.

That pronouncement charges Mr King and me – and the television people – with a serious contempt of court. We had offended against sections 1 and 2 of the Contempt of Court Act 1981. We had been guilty of conduct which interfered with the course of justice regardless of intent to do so.

The judges of the Court of Appeal did not communicate with me before making this serious charge against me. They condemned me unheard. If I had been given an opportunity, I would have had a good defence to the charge.

'The right to silence' had been brought under public scrutiny on October 20, 1988, by a written answer by the Home Secretary to Parliament. It was a matter of general public interest on which all of us were entitled to comment. My comment on television was the same as those which I had made publicly many times before and was based on the report of the Criminal Law Committee in 1972, who proposed that the so-called right to silence enjoyed by suspects should be greatly restricted.

I knew as most people knew that three people were being tried at Winchester for conspiring to murder Mr King but I knew nothing of the course of the trial. I had read nothing of it and had no idea that it involved the right to silence. If I had been charged I should have pleaded the defence of freedom of speech given by Section 5 of the Contempt of Court Act 1981: A publication made as or as part of a discussion in good faith of public affairs or other matters of general public interest is not to be treated as contempt of court under this strict liability rule if the risk of impediment or prejudice to particular legal proceedings is merely incidental to the discussion.

That section was inserted into the statute on the recommendation of the Contempt of Court Committee supported by speeches of distinguished law lords.

Yet the judges of the Court of Appeal have condemned me without hearing my defence. They did it under the cloak of an absolute privilege. In the face of it, all I can do is to write to you.

Lord Denning also commented on the outcome of the trial and the Appeal. Rather over a year later, however, he again wrote to *The Times* acknowledging that the decision of the Court of Appeal meant that the three people tried at Winchester were not guilty and unequivocally withdrawing any implication to the contrary contained in his earlier letter.

Nineteen

Legal Influence

There is no certainty more to be deplored than the certainty of injustice.[1]
Denning

All judges know that judges change the law but in England they have always been careful not to draw attention to it. In early times they invented the legal fiction. Fictitious forms of action and practices were invented so that the appearance of continuity should prevail whilst the reality was to produce something quite new. In 1988 a Scottish Lord Chancellor was appointed and the fact that judges do change the law could be admitted. Lord Mackay has said: 'If judges are to change the law, and I see no reason to conceal the fact that they do, it must be by the development and application of fundamental principles to disputes between parties concerned about specific events which have occurred in the past.'[2] The emphasis is on the application of old principles to new situations. But the judge's power to change the law only arises in the particular case before him. It can only relate to that case and to similar cases in the future. He does not engage in wholesale reconstruction of the law as this is the task of Parliament. As Mr Justice Holmes put it: 'Judges do and must legislate but they can do this only interstitially.'[3] Denning openly stated that judges change the law when such an admission was frowned upon.

In the eighteenth century Lord Mansfield maintained that the common law courts must apply equitable principles in the same way as the Court of Chancery and whenever possible he did so. In the Supreme Court of Judicature Act 1893 the Common Law Courts were united with the Court of Chancery to form one High Court of Justice and one Court of Appeal. These courts were to exercise the powers of the former courts (s 24) but in matters not specifically provided for, or in the event of conflict, equitable rules should prevail (s 25). Denning was therefore in a stronger position than Mansfield.

He had statutory authority for applying equitable principles where there was no precedent or in the event of conflict. This is exactly what he did in the 'High Trees' case. The law said that the contract must be observed. Equity said that the landlord had promised to reduce the rent and he should keep his promise. The law gave no protection to deserted wives and equitable rules were imported to give some protection until Parliament intervened.

Equity is not a static system of law established for all time but can be adapted to any situation. It has developed from the canon law in the thirteenth century which relied on reason and conscience. It is the application to particular circumstances of the standard of what seems naturally just and right. The basis of equity is that the judge must have a discretion to do justice in individual cases as laws cannot be framed to cover all eventualities. Equity is concerned with the reality of the situation and not with the formalities. It is concerned with the substance, not the form, and with the intention of the parties. If the intention of the parties is vitiated by fraud, duress or mistake, the transaction can be rectified and set aside. It will provide for specific performance of a contract where the remedy of damages is not enough. In exercising his discretion the judge takes into consideration all relevant matters relating to the justice or injustice of granting the relief sought, delay, hardship or unfairness. The great American judge, Benjamin Cardozo, once said: 'The law has outgrown its primitive stage of formalities, when the precise word was the sovereign talisman and every slip was fatal.'[4]

Judgment is concerned with priorities which often compete with one another. For Denning, the first priority was doing justice in the individual case before him. Others gave the highest priority to sound reasoning and the observance of precedent. Denning also gave a high priority to considerations of public policy. In *Duport Steels Ltd* v *Sirs* there was a national strike in the public sector of the industry. To put pressure on the Government the union decided to extend the strike to the private sector of the steel industry although their employees had no quarrel with their employers. The Court of Appeal granted an injunction against the union to prevent them calling out the men in the private sector despite a judgment in the House of Lords that such an action was lawful. A higher priority was given to policy than to precedent.

Denning brought common sense to the interpretation of the law.

In an article in *The Times* on 17 September 1980[5] J.R. Lucas of Merton College, Oxford, said:

Although some think that the law should always be clear, in practice it is not, and we have recourse to judges for authoritative interpretations. The only question is whether in interpreting what is unclear the law should be guided by common sense and give weight to considerations of expediency, justice and morality. Lord Denning thinks it should. Others think not.[5]

Mr Lucas argued that a non-common sense decision is no more certain than one based on common sense. For the layman the law would be more predictable if based on common sense. Since laws apply to laymen there is a good argument for the development of the law to be influenced by common sense as well as legal reasoning. In a doubtful case there is a strong case for the use of common sense as it makes the law easier to predict and worthier of respect. A perceptive paragraph appeared in the *Sunday Mirror* on 16 October 1966: 'It is not that Lord Denning is excessively liberal. It is merely that he always seems to decide a case the way you or I would.... But an odd man out who has the gift of bending it [the law] in the right direction, is something for which we can be truly grateful.'

One of Denning's great ambitions was to straighten out the law. He once said: 'I prefer to straighten out the law here and now.' He liked to do it in the instant case before him and did not think that the straightening process had to be left to Parliament. He had a great sense of the importance of the present moment. He believed that a judge had to find the principle applicable to the case in hand and precedents should support the principle. The problem with the English use of precedent is that judges distinguish cases on their facts to enable justice to be done and the case law soon becomes a muddle. Denning felt that the more relaxed attitude to precedent adopted in Scotland was to be preferred to the English use. He thought that the intermingling of English and Scottish law would be for the benefit of both.[6] The Americans are keen to restate the law and the American Law Institute has published five volumes entitled *The Restatement of the Law* dealing with all branches of the law under headings such as contract, tort, agency and restitution. An attempt has been made to extract the principles of law behind each subject and set them down. Denning used this in such cases as *United Australia* v *Barclays Bank*[7] and was sometimes successful in converting the court to his way of thinking. In 1951 he wrote an article in the *American Bar Association Journal* entitled 'The Restatement in the English Courts' where he analysed the various English cases where the Restatement had been used indicating where it had been successful and where not.[8] He was eager to restate the law when in the House of Lords without any success.

Denning's contribution to the administration of justice was considerable. His method of giving judgment, the short sentences, the arresting recital of the facts, followed by a summing up of the law is a model which has been followed by others. Denning and his brother judges in the Court of Appeal pioneered the use of the '*Mareva*' injunction to prevent funds being transferred abroad before judgment. He gave judgment in German marks although fifteen years before the House of Lords, of which he was a member, had said that judgment could only be given in pounds sterling. Times change and he was prepared to adapt the law of procedure to those changes. He supported the Chancery judges who had made *Anton Pillar* orders entitling a plaintiff to enter premises and look for material infringing copyright before it could be destroyed or spirited away. He always backed those who wished to improve the procedure of the courts. He exercised the undoubted power of the Court of Appeal to make and approve changes in practice.

Denning was a great upholder of law and order and a supporter of the police. He once said: 'So you mustn't carry this human kindness too far. I've always believed that retribution is a part of the law.' In 1968 he said: 'On 2 October 1968 I went to Westminster Abbey at the opening of the legal year. As the prayer was said for the judges I felt that we had remembered that part which asks that judges should "clear the innocent" but had forgotten the part which adds that they should "convict and punish the guilty".[10] Again he said: 'The time has come when it is the duty of every responsible citizen to support the police and recognise that they are our front line of defence against violence and lawlessness; when it is the duty of every responsible newspaper and broadcasting corporation to state the case for the police and not against them.'[11] He thought that in England the police were criticised too much and thanked too little and that there was nothing more detrimental to the rule of law than that the guilty should go scot-free.

Denning was a bold judge and exercised the powers of his office as a judge to the full while other judges were more careful not to overstep the mark. One of his former pupils wondered how such a diffident man could have become such a bold judge. He did not have the duplicity of his great predeccessor, Lord Mansfield. That judges changed the law was obvious and he said so. He attacked head on what he thought to be wrong when a smoother approach might have been as successful. As early as 1951 Denning had divided his fellow judges into two categories: 'timorous souls who were fearful of allowing a new cause of action .... and bold spirits who were ready to allow it if justice so required.'[12] The power of the Chancery judges to vary trusts on behalf of infants and persons under a disability was undoubted but the House of Lords refused to exercise its powers because there was no reported decision and Parliament had to step in. The record is full of cases where Parliament had to intervene because the courts failed to exercise the powers that they had.

One of Denning's outstanding characteristics as a judge was his concern for the little man and to protect him from the power of the State, the big corporations and the trade unions. He tried to protect the war pensioner from the power of the bureaucracy, the consumer from the small print on the contract and the individual who did not want to join a trade union. This was one aspect of his concern for justice. Lord Scarman has said: 'His steadfast purpose has always been to strengthen the courts in the ordinary man's defence against abuse of power.'[13] When receiving an Honorary LLD at Cambridge on 6 June 1963 the Public Orator said: 'This man considers that the rigours of laws and precedent should be tempered by human feeling for "He who clings to the letter is clinging to a cork."' Two years later, on 23 June 1965, Oxford University conferred an Honorary DCL and the Public Orator declared: 'Equity not pedantry seems to be his motto. His respect for precedent is not excessive; he is a doughty defender of the individual and the unprivileged.'[14] He had sensitive antennae as to what ordinary people thought and had the common touch.

Denning is a religious man, a faithful member of the Church of England, and a regular communicant. He said that he had no sudden conversion but that his Christian beliefs were in part due to his upbringing, and in part what he had found out in going through life.[15] The law had been moulded for centuries by judges who had been brought up in the Christian faith and the precepts of religion, consciously or unconsciously, had been their guide in the administration of justice. Religion has been very important in Denning's life and the Christian doctrine was the basis of his legal philosophy: do not injure or cheat your neighbour and if you do so pay him compensation or make restitution. He is a humble man, prepared to change his mind if convinced by others. He has moral courage founded on his deep Christian belief.

Denning's critics are quick to point out his weaknesses. The fact that there were so many extempore judgments meant that there must be many inaccuracies and contradictions in his judgments. He had a tendency to mis-cite cases and used authorities in his judgment which had not been cited by counsel. He was a judge for so long that the risk of some of his judgments being wrong is inevitable. A serious criticism of him is that he lacked intellectual honesty; this certainly took second place to justice. He is accused of bringing unpredictability into the law; to have introduced inconsistency and uncertainty and thus encouraged appeals and increased litigation. He is said to be prepared to intervene to bend the law. Professor Atiyah has written:

Lord Denning cannot altogether escape criticism for his apparent lack of interest in the formation of genuine principles, applicable beyond the case in hand; this is, and always must be, an important part of the judicial role, and it cannot be enough for judges merely to attempt to do justice in the particular circumstances of each case without regard to the longer term effects of their decisions.[16]

Dr John Morris of Oxford University expressed the views of many when he said: 'By departing from the established rules of law the Court of Appeal seems to have usurped the functions of the legislature .... It is submitted that the rules of law binding on the court cannot be evaded by calling them technical.'[17] As a writer of textbooks Dr Morris was naturally concerned that textbooks on wills would have to be revised; but one of the happy results of the Court of Appeal's attitude to the interpretation of wills is that construction summonses in the Chancery Division have now disappeared. A more sympathetic criticism of one of his books came from the late Professor C.J. Hamson and appeared in *The Listener* on 7 January 1954. He said: 'I have the sense that the law is being wrenched out of its course and tyrannically forced into a foreign mould .... More gently taken, more sympathetically, with more regard to its native temper, the law would come almost of its own accord, almost to the conclusion of the Lord Justice.' Denning is not popular with some of the Chancery practitioners of his own Inn, Lincoln's Inn, who adopt a strictly intellectual attitude to the law.

There is no doubt that Denning was what is called a 'judicial activist' although it is difficult to define that expression. It is a positive approach to the law with a readiness to stretch the law to a certain degree so that justice can be done in the particular case. It requires judicial courage. Judges like to keep in step with their brother judges. This is an aspect of judicial comity. They may, or may not, be interested in public applause, but are deeply concerned about what other judges and the legal profession think about their judgments. It is difficult to decide how far the law may be stretched. Judicial activism includes a desire to meet the needs of the times. What is laid down in the nineteenth century is not necessarily what is wanted in the twentieth century and the law has to be adjusted to meet the different circumstances. A good description of judicial activism was given in a leading article in *The Times* on 18 December 1978:

Without usurping the function of Parliament, a judge has the duty to interpret the law as far as he can, in a way which accords with social and personal justice, which upholds rather than destroys the civil liberties of the individual, and which looks with suspicion and not equanimity, on the unnecessary encroachment of the State or other power groups on the lives of citizens. Lord Denning is the most distinguished living and Lord Mansfield the most distinguished historic example of such a judicial activist.

Denning is not an original thinker and in most respects very conservative. He adopted the principles of his parents and mirrored the ideas of the ordinary Englishman. This was one of his strengths. On one occasion he said: 'I would think that I am a conservative in behaviour if it means that I believe what most of us believe in: that is established rules of conduct. But if public opinion advances, then one should go with it.'[18] He was a 'moral' conservative. He thought that if law was divorced from morality it would lose the respect of the people. The law should reflect public opinion and he did not want to do anything which might offend public opinion. Hugo Young, writing in *The Sunday Times* Weekly Review on 17 June 1973, said: 'Yet, the most striking fact about him is that while appearing to be a disturber of the legal peace, he is at heart the most conservative of men .... There is probably no judge on the bench who is more protective of authority, more defensive of morality, or more anxious to uphold order.'

Denning, as a judge, was patient, courteous and polite to counsel, witnesses and litigants in person. He tried to help counsel and not to discourage and destroy him. He had the capacity to keep absolutely quiet so that counsel could put forward his submissions in his or her own way. In his judgments he recited the arguments of counsel correctly and they knew that the points made by them had been fully understood. Although he had a powerful intellect he was not an intellectual. The law is based on reason but there are some occasions when a rational judgment is wrong. Denning understood the limits of reason and was not afraid to contravene them. He once said: 'Beware of logic. It has misled better men than you.'[19] He gave his judgments in the pungent style he had made his own. He was very quick to take the point and was a master of extempore judgment. The fact that he served as a judge for thirty-eight years enabled him to make such a great impression on the law of his time. Such a long period of service needed great stamina and determination. To have been Master of the Rolls for the last twenty years of his service, gave him a key position in the legal hierarchy. He was a legal polymath. He had a profound knowledge of many diverse branches of the law with a mastery of case law and formidable legal learning.

What have others said about him? In 1977 Lord Scarman wrote: 'The past twenty-five years will not be forgotten in our legal history. They are the age of legal aid, law reform and Lord Denning.'[20] Lord Hailsham has said: 'Denning's strength lies in his rugged independence and unwillingness to tolerate injustice or pettifogging technicality in any form.'[21] There is always the tendency of lawyers to give the highest priority to technicalities. Professor S. Waddams, of Toronto University, writing from a Commonwealth perspective, wrote: 'The prevailing image of Lord Denning is shown by the design on the Lord Denning T-Shirt produced by students at the University of Toronto depicting Lord Denning surmounted by the words "Equity".[22] Professor Robert Stevens has written:

When the history of the 20th century judiciary comes to be written Denning's name may well be the most prominent, not so much for what he did, but for what he showed to be possible .... Judicial restraint was not something that came easily to Denning. He saw few political or intellectual reasons why, in the areas where litigation took place, the appeal judges should not be lawgivers.[23]

Roger Gray QC wrote: 'I certainly regard him as the most outstanding legal figure of this century. He was not only pre-eminent as a judge but was also a great man.'[24] There will be controversy as to whether Denning was the greatest English judge of the twentieth century but in the view of many there is little doubt about it. He was one of the makers of English law.

Notes

ABBREVIATIONS

ABAJ	*American Bar Association Journal*
AC	Appeal Cases
All ER	All England Reports
App Ca	Appeal Cases, House of Lords
Burr	Burrows Reports
Ch	Chancery
ChD	Chancery Division
Cmnd	Command Paper
Fam	Family Division Reports
HLCas	House of Lords Cases
HRO	Hampshire Record Office
ICR	Industrial Cases Reports
KB	Kings Bench
LGR	Local Government Reports
LQR	*Law Quarterly Review*
MLR	*Modern Law Review*
QB	Queens Bench
QBD	Queens Bench Division
WLR	Weekly Law Reports

Fuller references to the books mentioned can be found in the Bibliography.

CHAPTER ONE

1. Lord Atkin in *Behari* v *King Emperor* (1933) 60 LRIA 254
2. *Legal Values in Western Society* by Peter Stein and John Shand p. 59
3. Interview with Linda Rothstein in *The Advocate*, Vol 12, No 3, March–April 1978
4. *The Family Story* by Lord Denning p. 24
5. *Ibid* p. 25
6. *Ibid* p. 5
7. *Ibid* pp. 17–18
8. *Ibid* p. 19

9. *Ibid* p. 20
10. *Ibid* p. 19
11. *Ibid* p. 20
12. *Ibid* pp. 31–32
13. *Ibid* p. 22
14. *Ibid* p. 48
15. *Ibid* p. 110
16. HRO 8
17. *Idem* Box 15
18. *Idem* 8
19. *Idem* 1
20. *The Family Story* p. 36
21. *Ibid* pp. 36–37
22. HRO Box 15
23. *Idem*
24. *Idem*
25. *The Family Story* p. 38
26. *The Discipline of Law* p. 200
27. *The Family Story* p. 38
28. *Ibid* p. 240
29. *Ibid* p. 39
30. *Ibid* p. 85
31. *Ibid* p. 85
32. *Ibid* p. 86
33. HRO Box 21

CHAPTER TWO

1. HRO 54 Letter from Clauson to Denning, 1 April 1938
2. *Idem* 15
3. *Idem*
4. *Idem* Box 7
5. *Idem* 65–72 Fee Books
6. *Idem* 13
7. *Idem* 23
8. *Idem*
9. *Idem* 24
10. *Idem* Box 7
11. *Idem* 21
12. *L'Estrange* v *F. Graucob Ltd* (1934) 2 KB 399
13. *In Character* by John Mortimer
14. HRO 24
15. 'Meaning of Ecclesiastical Law' (1944) 60 *LQR* 2
16. *Beresford* v *Royal Insurance Co Ltd* (1938) AC 586
17. HRO 54: All letters of congratulation on taking silk
18. *Idem* 72
19. *United Australia* v *Barclays Bank* (1941) AC 1
20. *Lord Atkin* by Geoffrey Lewis p. 73
21. *Gold* v *Essex County Council* (1942) 2 KB 293
22. HRO 64

23. *Idem* Box 13
24. *The Family Story* p. 132
25. *Reville* v *Prudential Assurance Co Ltd* (1944) AC 135
26. *The Due Process of Law* p. 188

CHAPTER THREE

1. *The Judge* p. 3
2. *The Due Process of Law* p. 187
3. *Ibid*
4. HRO 55 Letters of congratulation on becoming a High Court Judge
5. Information in a letter from Mr A.H.Furssedonn 26 May 1989
6. *Smith* v *Smith* (1945) 1 All ER 584
7. *The Due Process of Law* p. 190
8. *The Family Story* p. 207
9. *Lloyds Bank Ltd* v *Bundy* (1975) 1 QB 326
10. *Beswick* v *Beswick* (1966) 1 Ch 538, 549
11. *Churchman* v *Churchman* (1945) P 44
12. *Fletcher* v *Fletcher* (1945) 1 All ER 582; *Smith* v *Smith* (1945) 1 All ER 584; *Norton* v *Norton* (1945) P 56
13. *Emmanuel* v *Emmanuel* (1946) P 115
14. 1945 60 *LQR* 235
15. HRO 56 Letters of congratulation on transfer to King's Bench
16. *Idem* 162 Interview in *Mail on Sunday* magazine 24 October 1982
17. *The Family Story* p. 143
18. *The Due Process of Law* p. 191
19. *Ibid*
20. Cmnd 6881
21. Cmnd 6945
22. Cmnd 7024
23. *The Due Process of Law* p. 192
24. *Ibid*
25. *Ibid* p. 201
26. HRO Box 14
27. *The Family Story* p. 165
28. *Starr* v *Minister of Pensions* (1946) 1 KB 345
29. *James* v *Minister of Pensions* (1947) 1 KB 867
30. HRO 74
31. *R* v *West* (1948) 1 KB 709
32. *Ward* v *Bradford Corporation* (1972) 70 LGR 27
33. *The Family Story* p. 162
34. *R* v *Miller* 1770 State Trials 802
35. *At the end of the day* by F.H.Maughan p. 62
36. *The Family Story* p. 165
37. HRO Box 21
38. *The Family Story* p. 164

CHAPTER FOUR

1. *The Due Process of Law* p. 245
2. *Balfour* v *Balfour* (1919) 2 KB 571, 579

3. *H* v *H* (1947) 63 TLR 645
4. *Bendall* v *McWhirter* (1952) 2 KB 466
5. 68 *LQR* 379 (1952)
6. Royal Commission on Marriage and Divorce (1956) Cmnd 9678
7. *National Westminster Bank Ltd* v *Ainsworth* (1962) AC 1175
8. HRO Box 14
9. *The Due Process of Law* p. 221
10. *Rimmer* v *Rimmer* (1953) 1 QB 63
11. *Pettitt* v *Pettitt* (1970) AC 904
12. *Gissing* v *Gissing* (1971) AC 886
13. *Heseltine* v *Heseltine* (1971) All ER 952
14. *Lord Denning : the judge and the law* by M.D.A.Freeman p. 143
15. *Hansard* 1870 3rd Series p. 600
16. *Watchel* v *Watchel* (1973) Fam 72
17. *Bernard* v *Josephs* (1982) 3 All ER 163
18. HRO Box 12
19. *Lord Denning : the judge and the law* p. 159

CHAPTER FIVE

1. *River Weir Commission* v *Adamson* (1877) 2 App Ca 743
2. *The Discipline of Law* p. 9
3. *Ibid* p. 10
4. *Davis* v *Johnson* (1949) AC 265
5. *Miller* v *Taylor* (1769) 4 Burr 2303, 2332
6. *R* v *Bishop of Oxford* (1879) 4 QBD 525
7. *S.E.Rly* v *Railway Commission* (1880) 5 QBD 217, 236
8. *Seaford Court Estates Ltd* v *Asher* (1949) 2 KB 481
9. HRO Box 17
10. *Magor & St Mellors RDC* v *Newport Corporation* (1951) 2 All ER 839, 849 and (1952) AC 189
11. *Kammins* v *Zenith Investments Ltd* (1971) AC 850, 881
12. Renton Committee on 'The preparation of legislation' Cmnd 6053 para 19.2
13. *Nothman* v *Barnet Council* (1978) 1 WLR 220
14. Coke 4 Ins 330
15. *Holy Living* by Jeremy Taylor p. 189
16. HRO Box 14
17. *Perrin* v *Morgan* (1943) AC 399
18. *Re Rowland decd* (1963) Ch 1
19. *Re Jebb decd* (1966) 1 Ch 666
20. 'Palm Tree Justice in the Court of Appeal' by John Morris (1966) 82 *LQR* 196
21. *Sydall* v *Castings Ltd* (1967) 1 QB 302

CHAPTER SIX

1. *The Discipline of Law* p. 223
2. *Lord Denning : the judge and the law* p. 29
3. *Central London Property Trust Ltd* v *High Trees House Ltd* (1947) 1 KB 130
4. *Hughes* v *Metropolitan Rly Co* (1877) 2 AC 439

5. *Birmingham & District Land Co* v *London & North Eastern Railway Co* (1888) 40 ChD 268
6. *Charles Rickards* v *Oppenheim* (1950) 1 KB 616
7. *Combe* v *Combe* (1951) 2 KB 215
8. *Lord Denning: the judge and the law* p. vi
9. *Jorden* v *Money* (1854) 5 HL Cas 185
10. *Olley* v *Marlborough Court Ltd* (1948) 1 KB 532
11. *Adler* v *Dickson* (1955) 1 KB 158
12. *Geo Mitchell (Clerkenwell) Ltd* v *Finny Seeds Ltd* (1982) 3 WLR 1036
13. *Photo Productions Ltd* v *Securicor Transport Ltd* (1978) 1 WLR 856 & (1980) AC 827
14. *Lloyds Bank Ltd* v *Bundy* (1975) QB 326
15. *National Westminster Bank Ltd* v *Morgan* (1985) 1 WLR 589
16. *Staffordshire Area Health Authority* v *South Staffordshire Water Company* (1978) 1 WLR 1387
17. *The Discipline of Law* p. 41
18. *Candler* v *Crane Christmas & Co* (1951) 2 KB 164
19. *Hedley Byrne & Co* v *Hellar & Partners* (1964) AC 465
20. *Arenson* v *Arenson* (1973) Ch 346
21. *Cassidy* v *Minister of Health* (1951) 2 KB 343
22. *Roe* v *Minister of Health* (1954) 2 QB 66
23. *Rondel* v *Worsley* (1967) 1 QB 443
24. *Saif Ali* v *Sydney Mitchell & Co* (1978) QB 95
25. *Spartan Steel & Alloys Ltd* v *Martin & Co (Contractors) Ltd* (1973) 1 QB 27
26. *Dutton* v *Bognor Regis UDC* (1972) 1 QB 373
27. *Dorset Yacht Co Ltd* v *Home Office* (1970) AC 1004
28. *Launchbury* v *Morgan* (1971) 2 QB 245 & (1973) AC 127
29. *Lord Denning: the judge and the law* p. 456

CHAPTER SEVEN

1. HRO 59 Letter from Pritt to Denning 29 April 1957
2. *The Family Story* p. 169
3. HRO 59 Letters of congratulation on appointment to the Court of Appeal
4. (1979) 95 *LQR* 446
5. HRO 75
6. *Idem* 73
7. Interview with Roger Day in *Crusader* May 1979
8. *The Family Story* p. 181
9. HRO Box 8
10. *Lord Denning: the judge and the law* p. 12
11. HRO 59 Letters of congratulation on appointment as a law lord
12. Re Parliamentary Privilege Act 1770 (1958) AC 331
13. 'Parliamentary privilege and the courts: the avoidance of conflict' by G.F.Lock in *Public Law* Spring 1985
14. *DPP* v *Smith* (1961) AC 290
15. 'Responsibility before the law' Lionel Cohen Lecture Series 7 1971. Hebrew University of Jerusalem

16. Interview with Linda Rothstein in *The Advocate* Vol 12, No 3, March–April 1978
17. *Final Appeal* by L. Blom-Cooper & G. Drewry p. 176

CHAPTER EIGHT

1. *From Precedent to Precedent* p. 5
2. *Ibid* p. 3
3. *Rust* v *Cooper* English Reports 98 p. 1279
4. *London Transport Executive* v *Betts* (1959) AC 213
5. *Ashby* v *White* 2 Ld Raymond p. 938
6. *Ostine (Inspector of Taxes)* v *Australian Mutual Provident Society* (1960) AC 459
7. *From Precedent to Precedent* p. 4
8. *Ibid* p. 15
9. *Beamish* v *Beamish* (1861) 9 HLC 274
10. *From Precedent to Precedent* p. 34
11. '*Stare decisis* in the House of Lords' by Gerald Dworkin 25 MLR 1962
    'Precedent in the Court of Appeal' by C.E.F. Rickett 43 MLR 136
    'Precedent in the Court of Appeal: Lord Denning's views explained' by Hazel Carty (1981) 1 *Legal Studies* 68
12. *Close* v *Steel Company of Wales Ltd* (1962) AC 367
13. *Young* v *Bristol Aeroplane Co Ltd* (1944) 1 KB 719
14. *The Discipline of Law* p. 297
15. *Davis* v *Johnson* (1978) 1 All ER 84
16. *B* v *B* (1975) Fam 76 and *Cantliff* v *Jenkins* (1978) 1 All ER 836
17. *Law Reform Now* by Gerald Gardiner & Andrew Martin p. 16
18. *Ibid* p. 16
19. '*Volumnes Leges Angliae Mutare*' by T.B. Smith 1959 *Scots Law Times* p. 221
20. *Conway* v *Rimmer* (1967) 1 WLR 1031
21. *Duncan* v *Cammell Laird* (1942) AC 642
22. *The Discipline of Law* p. 314
23. '*Stare decisis* in contemporary England' by Rupert Cross (1966) 82 *LQR*

CHAPTER NINE

1. *Freedom under the Law* p. 126
2. *Ibid* p. 126
3. *R* v *Northumberland Compensation Appeal Tribunal Ex parte Shaw* (1952) 1 KB 338
4. *Taylor* v *National Assistance Board* (1957) P 101, 111
5. *R* v *Medical Appeal Tribunal Ex parte Gilmore* (1957) 1 QB 574
6. *Anisminic Ltd* v *Foreign Compensation Commission* (1969) 2 AC 147
7. *R* v *Commissioner of Police for the Metropolis Ex parte Blackburn* (1968) 2 QB 118
8. *Attorney-General* v *Independent Broadcasting Authority* (1973) QB 629
9. *Gouriet's case* (1978) AC 435
10. *Metropolitan Properties Co* v *Lannon & Others*; *R* v *London Rent Assessment Committee Ex parte Metropolitan Properties Co* (1969) 1 QB 577
11. *Kanda* v *Government of Malaysia* (1962) AC 322
12. *Pitt* v *Greyhound Racing Association Ltd* (1969) 1 QB 125
13. *Enderby Town Football Club* v *Football Association Ltd* (1971) 1 Ch 591

14. *R* v *Barnsley Supplementary Benefit Appeal Tribunal Ex parte Atkinson* (1976) 1 WLR 1047
15. *Maynard* v *Osmond* (1976) QB 240
16. *Franklin* v *Minister of Town and Country Planning* (1948) AC 249
17. *Freedom under the Law* p. 122
18. *R* v *Secretary of State for Home Affairs Ex parte Hosenball* (1977) 1 WLR 766
19. *Ashridge Investments Ltd* v *Ministry of Housing* (1965) 1 WLR 1320
20. *Padfield* v *Ministry of Agriculture* (1968) AC 997
21. *Secretary of State for Education and Science* v *Tameside MBC* (1973) AC 1014
22. *Congreve* v *Home Office* (1976) 1 QB 629
23. *Laker Airways Ltd* v *Department of Trade* (1977) 1 QB 643
24. *Coleen Properties Ltd* v *Ministry of Housing and Local Government* (1971) 1 WLR 433
25. *Bromley London Borough Council* v *GLC* (1982) 2 WLR 62
26. *Abbott* v *Sullivan* (1952) 1 KB 189
27. *Taylor* v *Horden* (1757) 1 Burr 119
28. *Lee* v *The Showmen's Guild of Great Britain* (1952) 2 QB 329
29. *Freedom under the Law* p. 96

CHAPTER TEN

1. HRO 60
2. *The Family Story* p. 197
3. HRO 60 All letters of congratulation on becoming Master of the Rolls
4. Report on Committee on Legal Records 1966 Cmnd 3084
5. *The Family Story* p. 151
6. *Ibid* pp. 155, 156
7. HRO 84 Interview with *Daily Express* June 1972
8. *Idem* 85 Interview with Hugo Young *The Sunday Times* 17 June 1973
9. *Idem* 64
10. *Idem* 75
11. *Idem* 82 *The Adelaide Times* 10 July 1967
12. *Idem* 90
13. *Idem* Box 13
14. *Idem* Box 16 *Law Reporting*
15. *Idem* Letter 27 February 1982
16. *Attorney-General* v *Mulholland* (1963) 2 QB 477
17. *British Steel Corpn* v *Granada Television* (1980) 3 WLR 279
18. *What Next in the Law* p. 251
19. *Home Office* v *Harman* (1981) QB 534
20. *R* v *Commissioner of Police for the Metropolis* (1968) 2 QB 150
21. *Morris* v *Crown Office* (1970) 2 QB 114
22. HRO 85 Hugo Young in *The Sunday Times* 24 June 1973
23. *The Closing Chapter* p. 19

CHAPTER ELEVEN

1. *Landmarks in the Law* p. 359
2. *A Price too High* by Peter Rawlinson p. 93
3. *Ibid* p. 95

4. Lord Denning's Report Cmnd 2152
5. *Ibid* para 286
6. *A Price too High* p. 100
7. *Ibid* p. 111
8. *Controversial Essays* by John Sparrow 1966 p. 33
9. Denning Report para 9
10. *The Due Process of Law* p. 69
11. Royal Commission on Tribunals and Inquiries 1966 Cmnd 3121 para 21
12. *Lord Denning: The Judge and the Law* p. 16
13. HRO 72
14. *Idem* 86
15. *Macmillan 1957–1986 Vol II* by Alistair Horne p. 496

CHAPTER TWELVE

1. *Express Newspapers* v *McShane* (1979) ICR 210, 218
2. *The Closing Chapter* p. 158
3. *BBC* v *Hearn* (1977) ICR 685
4. *Heaton's Transport (St Helen's) Ltd* v *T&GWU* (1973) AC 15
5. *Churchman* v *Joint Shop Stewards Ctee* (1972) 1 WLR 1094
6. *Star Sea Transport Corpn of Moravia* v *Slater* (1979) 1 Lloyds Rep 26
7. *Express Newspapers* v *Keys* (1978) ICR 582
8. *The Closing Chapter* p. 184
9. *Duport Steels* v *Sirs* (1980) 1 WLR 142
10. HRO Box 12
11. *Hadnor Productions Ltd* v *Hamilton* (1981) 3 WLR 139
12. *Cheall* v *APEX* (1982) 2 WLR 679
13. *Taylor* v *Cooperative Retail Services* (1982) ICR 600
14. *Bonsor* v *Musicians' Union* (1954) Ch 479
15. Trade Union and Labour Relations Act 1974 s 2(1)
16. *Faramus* v *Film Artistes' Association* (1963) 2 QB 527 and (1964) AC 925
17. *Nagle* v *Fielden* (1966) 2 QB 633
18. *Dickson* v *Pharmaceutical Society* (1967) Ch 708
19. *Breen* v *AEU* (1971) 2 QB 175
20. *Emerald Construction Co* v *Lowthian* (1966) 1 WLR 691
21. *Torquay Hotel Co Ltd* v *Cousins* (1969) 2 Ch 106
22. *The Closing Chapter* p. 161
23. *Merker Island Shipping Co Ltd* v *Laughton* (1983) 2 WLR 778, 786
24. *Hubbard* v *Pitt* (1976) QB 142
25. *Langston* v *AUEW* (1974) 1 WLR 185

CHAPTER THIRTEEN

1. *Holy Living* by Jeremy Taylor p. 202
2. *Ibid*
3. *Nippon Yasen Kaisha* v *Karageorgis* (1975) 1 WLR 1093
4. *Lister* v *Stubbs* (1890) 45 ChD 1
5. *Mareva* v *International Bulkcarriers* (1975) 2 Lloyds Reports 509
6. *The Pertamina* (1978) QB 644
7. *The Siskina* (1977) 2 Lloyds Rep 230 & (1979) AC 210

8. *Schorsch Mair* v *Hennin* (1975) AC 396
9. *United Railways of Havana* v *Regis Warehouses* (1961) AC 1007
10. *The Discipline of Law* p. 305
11. *Miliangos* v *Geo Frank Textiles Ltd* (1975) 1 QB 487 and (1976) AC 413
12. *Third Chandris Corpn* v *Unimarine* (1979) 3 WLR 122
13. *Z Ltd* v *A* (1982) 1 All ER 556
14. *Chief Constable of Kent* v *Verdon-Roe* (1982) 3 WLR 462
15. *West Mercia Constabulary* v *Wagener* (1982) 1 WLR 127
16. *EMI* v *Pandit* (1975) 1 WLR 302
17. *Anton Pillar* v *Manufacturing Process Ltd* (1976) Ch 55
18. *Ex parte Island Records Ltd* (1978) 1 Ch 122
19. *Rank Film Distributors Ltd* v *Video Information Centre* (1982) AC 380
20. *Bremer Vulkan* v *South India Shipping Corpn Ltd* (1981) AC 389
21. *Andre et Co SA* v *Marine Transocean Ltd 'The Splendid Sun'* (1981) 1 QB 694
22. *Paul Wilson & Co AS* v *Par H. Blumenthal* (1982) 3 WLR 49
23. *Food Corporation of India* v *Antclizo Shipping Corporation (The Antclizo)* (1988) 1 WLR 603
24. B.J.Davenport Note in (1988) 104 *LQR* 493
25. *Re Pritchard decd* (1963) Ch 502
26. *Whistler* v *Handcock* (1898) 3 QBD 83
27. *R* v *Bloomsbury & Marylebone County Court ex parte Villerwest Ltd* (1976) 1 WLR 362
28. *American Cyanide Co* v *Ethicon Ltd* (1975) AC 396

CHAPTER FOURTEEN

1. *The Family Story* p. 174
2. *British Movietonews Ltd* v *London District Cinemas* (1951) 1 KB 190
3. *Magor & St Mellors DC* v *Newport Corporation* (1951) 2 All ER 839
4. *Chapman* v *Chapman* (1954) AC 429
5. *Re New decd* (1901) 2 Ch 534
6. Law Reform Committee Sixth Report (Cmnd) 310 p. 6
7. *Rahimtoola* v *Nizam of Hyderabad* (1958) AC 379
8. *Donoghue* v *Stevenson* (1932) AC 562
9. *The Discipline of Law* p. 289
10. *Scrutton* v *Midland Silicones Ltd* (1962) AC 446
11. *Eurymedon* (1975) AC 154
12. *Griffiths (Inspector of Taxes)* v *J.P.Harrison (Watford) Ltd* (1963) AC 1
13. *National Provincial Bank Ltd* v *Ainsworth* (1965) AC 1175
14. *Pettitt* v *Pettitt* (1970) AC 904
15. *Davis* v *Johnson* (1979) AC 264
16. *Hannah Blumenthal* (1982) 3 WLR 49
17. *Duport Steels Ltd* v *Sirs* (1980) 1 WLR 142
18. *Rank Film Distributors Ltd* v *Video Information Centre* (1982) AC 380
19. *The Nicomarchon Ethics of Aristotle* (trans F.H.Peters) 15 Ed v 10.4
20. HRO Box 21
21. *Policy Arguments for Judicial Decisions* by John Bell p. 221
22. HRO 89 Interview with Maureen Cleeve 1981
23. *Broome* v *Cassell* (1971) 2 QB 354
24. Letter received by the author from Roger Gray.

CHAPTER FIFTEEN

1. Report of the Second Commonwealth Magistrates' Conference 1972 p. 123 Speech by Sir Hugh Wooding
2. Report in *The Times* 24 June 1952
3. HRO Box 7
4. *The Future of the law in Africa: Record of Proceedings of the London Conference 28 December 1959–January 1960* Butterworths 1960
5. Report of the Committee on legal education for students from Africa 1961 Cmnd 1255
6. HRO 82
7. *Idem* Box 19
8. *Idem* Box 12
9. *Idem* 83
10. *Idem*
11. *Idem*
12. *Idem* Box 12
13. *Idem*
14. *Idem*
15. *Idem*
16. Report of Third Commonwealth Magistrates' Conference Nairobi, Kenya 26–31 August 1973 p. 30
17. *The Changing Image of the Magistracy* by Sir Thomas Skyrme p. 228
18. HRO Box 20

CHAPTER SIXTEEN

1. *In Character* by John Mortimer p. 9
2. *Freedom under the Law* p. 3
3. *Landmarks in the Law* p. 173
4. *The Changing Law* Preface p. viii
5. *Macmillan* Vol II by Alastair Horne p. 489
6. *The Family Story* p. 75
7. *Ibid* p. 15
8. *The Closing Chapter* p. 63
9. 'It all started with gunner James' by Cameron Harvey 1986 *Denning Law Journal* p. 67
10. *Hinz* v *Berry* (1970) 2 QB 40, 42
11. *Cummings* v *Granger* (1977) 1 All ER 104, 106
12. *Berwick* v *Berwick* (1966) Ch 538
13. *Ex p Hook* (1976) 1 WLR 1052, 1055
14. *Miller* v *Jackson* (1977) QB 966, 976
15. *The Family Story* p. 216

CHAPTER SEVENTEEN

1. *The Times* Leading article 24 May 1982
2. HRO Box 11
3. *The Due Process of Law* p. 155
4. *Ibid* p. 171
5. *Mandla (Sewa Singh)* v *Dowell Lea* (1982) 3 WLR 932

6. HRO Box 11
7. *The Closing Chapter* p. 11
8. *Ibid* p. 12
9. *The Times* Law Report 31 July 1982
10. *The Denning Law Journal* 1986 p. 12
11. *Ibid* pp. 14, 15

CHAPTER EIGHTEEN

1. *The Closing Chapter* p. 73
2. *Ibid* p. 37
3. HRO 161 Interview with Editor of *Financial Times* European Law Letter
4. House of Lords Debates 262 2 February 1965
5. *Idem* 216 5 May 1959
6. *Idem* 219 5 November 1959
7. *Idem* 220 17 January 1960
8. *Idem* 280 14 February 1967
9. *Idem* 288 8 February 1968
10. *Idem* 297 26 November 1968
11. *Idem* 312 19 November 1970 Supporting Beeching Commission
12. *Idem* 336 16 November 1978
13. *Idem* 339 25 March 1976
14. *Idem* 491 16 December 1987
15. HRO Box 17
16. *The Closing Chapter* p. 67
17. HRO Box 20
18. *R* v *Cullen*
    R v *McCann*
    R v *Shanahan* Law Report in *The Times* 1 May 1990

CHAPTER NINETEEN

1. Profile in *The Sunday Times* by Hugo Young 24 April 1973
2. Lord Mackay. 1987 Maccabean Lecture in Jurisprudence 'Can judges change the law'
3. *Policy arguments: judicial decisions* by John Bell p. 226
4. *Wood* v *Lucy* 222 NY 88.90
5. 'Common sense before the law' Article by J.R.Lucas in *The Times* 17 September 1980
6. 'Borrowing from Scotland' Lecture at Glasgow University 5 May 1961
7. *United Australia* v *Barclays Bank* (1941) AC 1
8. 'The Restatement in the English Courts' Article in (1951) 37 *ABAJ* 329
9. HRO 87 Profile by Joan Bakewell in *The Law Society's Gazette*
10. HRO 133
11. *Idem* Box 14
12. *Candler* v *Crane, Christmas & Co* (1951) 2 KB 164, 178
13. 95 *LQR* 1979 p. 445
14. HRO Box 7
15. *Idem* 91 Talk BBC Home Service 14 September 1943
16. *Lord Denning: the judge and the law* p. 30
17. 82 *LQR* 1966 p. 202

18. HRO 90
19. *The Family Story* p. 170
20. Article in *The Times* by Lord Scarman 5 January 1977
21. Review of *The Discipline of Law* in *Books and Bookmen* April 1979
22. *Lord Denning: the judge and the law* p. 472
23. *Law and Politics* by Robert Stevens p. 505
24. Letter from Robert Gray QC to the author

Bibliography

Bell, John, *Policy Arguments in Judicial Decisions* (OUP, 1983)

Blom-Cooper, Louis and Gavin Drewry, *Final Appeal: A study of the House of Lords in its judicial capacity* (OUP, 1972)

Bresler, Fenton, *Lord Goddard* (Harrap, 1977)

Denning, A.T., *Freedom under the Law* (Stevens, 1949); *The Changing Law* (Stevens, 1953); *The Road to Justice* (Stevens, 1955); *The Discipline of Law* (Butterworths, 1979); *The Due Process of Law* (Butterworths, 1980); *The Family Story* (Butterworths, 1981); *What Next in the Law* (Butterworths, 1982); *The Closing Chapter* (Butterworths, 1983); *Landmarks in the Law* (Butterworths, 1984); *Leaves from my Library* (Butterworths, 1986).

Denning Law Journal (University of Buckingham, 1986)

Devlin, Patrick, *The Judge* (OUP, 1979)

Goldstein, L. (Ed), *Precedent in Law* (OUP, 1987)

Harwood, Antony, *Circuit Ghosts: A Western Circuit Miscellany* (Winchester, 1980)

Honoré, Tony, *Making Law Bind* (OUP, 1987)

Horne, Alastair, *Macmillan* Vol 2 1957–1986 (Macmillan, 1989)

Howard, Anthony, *The Life of R. A. Butler* (Cape, 1987)

Hyde, H. Montgomery, *Norman Birkett* (Hamish Hamilton, 1964) *Sir Patrick Hastings* (Heinemann, 1960)

Jowell, J.L. and J.P.W. McAuslan (Eds), *Lord Denning: The Judge and the Law* (Sweet & Maxwell, 1984)

Kennedy, Ludovic, *The Trial of Stephen Ward* (Gollancz, 1964)

Knightley, Phillip and Caroline Kennedy, *An Affair of State* (Cape, 1987)

Marjoribanks, Edward, *The Life of Sir Edward Marshall Hall* (Gollancz, 1953)

Maugham, F. H., *At the End of the Day* (Heinemann, 1954)

Mortimer, John, *In Character* (Penguin, 1984)

Parmiter, Geoffrey, *Edmund Plowden* (Catholic Record Sty, 1987)

Paterson, Alan, *The Law Lords* (Macmillan, 1982)

Rawlinson, Peter, *A Price too High* (Weidenfeld & Nicolson, 1989)

Robson, Peter and Paul Watchman (Eds), *Justice: Lord Denning & the Constitution* (Guildford, 1981)

Sainty, John, *A list of English Law Officers, King's Counsel and holders of patents of precedence* (Selden Society, 1987)

Skyrme, Thomas, *The Changing Face of the Magistracy* (2nd Edition, Macmillan, 1979)

Smith, Arthur, *Lord Goddard* (Weidenfeld & Nicolson, 1959)

Smith, T.B., *British Justice: The Scottish Contribution* (Stevens, 1961)

Stein, Peter and John Shand, *Legal Values in Western Society* (Edinburgh University Press, 1974)

Stevens, Robert, *Law and Politics: The House of Lords as a Judicial Body 1800–1976* (Weidenfeld & Nicolson, 1979)

Walker-Smith, Derek and Edward Clarke, *The Life of Sir Edward Clarke* (Butterworths, 1939)

Index

Abbreviation used: D =
Lord Denning (Denning,
Baron Alfred Thompson,
of Whitchurch)

abuse of power, 99–109
Ackner, Lord (Desmond
Ackner), 111
Adler v *Dickson*, 70–1
Adoption of Children Act
1926, 64
advocacy, art of, 23–4
Africa, development of
law in, 173–5, 180
age of majority, 205
Aldous, Guy, 34
Allen, Professor C.K., 86
American Bar
Association, 173, 175
Anderson, Professor
J.N.D., 174
Andover Grammar
School, 6–7, 10
'Anton Pillar' orders, 156,
157, 158, 160, 168, 216
APEX, 143
Appellate Jurisdiction Act
1876, 85, 97, 170
arbitrations, 157–8; D as
arbitrator, 176–80
Arenson v *Arenson*, 74
Asquith, Lord Justice, 60
assets, seizure of, 151–5
Astor, Lord, 124–5, 127
Athenaeum Club, 35
Atiyah, Professor, 67–8,
218

Atkin, Lord, 30, 63, 80,
164–5
Attorney-General and
'relator' actions, 101–2,
109
Australia, D in, 175, 181

Bacon, Sir Francis, 80
Baker, Sir George, 96
Banner, Josephine, 84
Bathurst, Sir Maurice,
QC, 172
BBC v *Hearn*, 135
Beldam, Lord Justice, 211
Bellew, Arthur Grattan,
25
Bendall v *McWhirter*, 50
Beney, F.W. KC, 78
Bernard v *Josephs*, 56
Beswick v *Beswick*, 37–8,
190
Bevan, Stuart, 21
Bill of Rights (1976), 205
Birbeck College, D
President of, 82
Birkett, Norman, 29
Bishop, R.O.
(Headmaster, Andover
Grammar School), 7
Bishop, W. (solicitor for
Southern Railway), 21,
23, 29
Blackburn, Raymond,
101
Bligh, Tim, 127
Bonsor case (1954), 144
Boots Ltd, 146

Bowen, Lord Justice, 68,
159
Braddell Memorial
Lecture, 181
Bramwell, Lord, 202
breach of contract
(commercial), 147–9
Breen v *AEU*, 146
Bremer Vulkan case
(1981), 157–9
Bridges, Edward, 13
Bridlington Principles of
the TUC, 142–4
Bristol riot case, and black
jurors, 195–7, 199
British Institute of
International and
Comparative Law, 172
British Legion, the, 45
British Movietone News v
*London District
Cinemas*, 73
British Steel Corporation,
140
Bromley Borough Council
and London Transport
fares (1982), 107
Broome v *Cassell*, 170
Brown, Mr Justice (Simon
Brown), 200
Buckley, Sir Denys, 112
Buckmaster, Lord, 165
Byrne, Mr Justice, 48

Cairns, Lord Justice
(David Scott Cairns),
39, 55, 68, 85

Callaghan, James, 101, 133
Canada, D in, 173, 176, 184
Candler v *Crane Christmas & Co*, 73, 77
capital punishment, 47–8
Caplan, Leonard, 111
Cardozo, Benjamin, 214
Cassels, Mr Justice, 35, 39
Cassidy case (1951), 74
certiorari, writ of, 99, 100
Chalfont, Lord, 178
Chancery Division, 28, 42, 219; equitable remedies, 101; ex parte, 155–6; matrimonial law, 51, 55; precedent, 72–3; variation of trusts, 163–4, 217
Changing Law, The (Denning), 184
Chapman v *Chapman*, 162–4
Charles, Mr Justice, 32, 39
Cheall v *APEX*, 143
Cheshire, Professor Geoffrey, 14–15, 83–4
Cheshire, Group Captain Leonard VC, 83, 84
Cheshire Homes, D Chairman of Trustees of, 83–4
Chitty, A.J.M., 130
Chitty, Sir Thomas Willes, 24
Chobham Farm case (1972), 137
Chrysler Company, 148–9
Church of England, 27, 35, 217–18; law and religion, 82–3
Churchill, Sir Winston, 189
Churchman case (1972), 137
Cinematographic Film (Control) Order 1943, 161
Civil Jurisdiction and Judgments Act 1982, 154, 169
Clifford, John, 27

Clogg, Derek, 126, 127
'closed shop', 144–5
Closing Chapter, The (Denning), 187, 203
co-habitation and family law, 56
Cobbett, William, 2
Coke, Sir Edward, 62, 85
College of Arms, 85
Combe v *Combe*, 69
Commission for Racial Equality, 194
common law, 28, 67–77
common sense and the law, 215–16
Commonwealth Magistrates' Conference, 180–1
construction: statutes, 58–63, 162, 168–9; wills, 63–6
consumer affairs, 70–1, 217
contract, 67–73, 147–9, 161–2, 165–6, 168, 205
Cook, E.R., 22
Cotton, Lord Justice, 151
Court of Appeal, 28, 31–2; Appeal judge, 78–81; Criminal Appeal, 89; Master of the Rolls, 95–7, 110–13, 115–17; precedent, 69–70, 95–8; statutory interpretation, 62; 'substantial evidence' test, 107; *see also individual cases*
Criminal Justice Act 1967, 89
Criminal Justice Bill and press reporting, 117
criminal law, 28, 32–3, 46, 89
Critchley, T.A., 130
Cross, Professor Rupert, 98
Crossman, Richard: 'Crossman's catalogue', 59
Crown privilege, 97–8
Crown Proceedings Act 1947, 82
Cuckfield, 17–18, 40, 114

Cumberland Lodge 83, 84
Cutter v *Powell*, 24

Daily Express, 138–9, 140
Daily Mirror, 139
Davies, Lord Justice Arthian, 121
Davies, David, 176
Davis v *Johnson*, 95–6, 167–8
declarations, applicants for, 101, 102
Denning, Baron Alfred Thompson, of Whitchurch: on abuse of power, 101–9, 217; on adultery, 43–4; Appeal judge, 78–81; on art of advocacy, 23–4; author, 183–92; Bar practice, 19–33; capital punishment, 47–8; character, 19, 23, 27, 41, 87, 115, 123, 220; childhood, 2, 3–7; Commissioner of Assize, 33; common law judgments, 67–8; contract and new circumstances, 72–3; divorce law, 34–9, 41–4; ecclesiastical law, 27; his education, 6–7, 10, 12–13, 14–15; legal education, 173–5, 185, 207–8; exemption clauses, 70–1, 205; fair trial, 45–6; fees and earnings, 21–2, 23, 26, 29, 31; Fiji Sugar arbitration, 176–8; gardening, 114–15; 'High Trees', 68–70, 214; honours, 121–2, 139, 169, 173, 217; appointed to House of Lords, 84–90; conflicts with House of Lords, 161–71, 203; House of Lords debates, 203–6; inequality of bargaining power, 71–2; Jamaican Bananas and Fyffes,

Denning, Baron Alfred
Thompson—(*contd*.)
178–80; Appeal judge,
78–81; trial judge, 33–9,
46, 48, 216–17, 220;
'judicial activist', 219;
justice, love of, 1, 2,
145, 161, 214–15;
King's Bench Division,
39, 44; lecturer, 81–3,
89, 92–3, 175, 181,
183–5; first marriage,
15–18, 31; second
marriage, 39–41, 208;
Master of the Rolls, 95,
110–14, 115–17;
matrimonial law, 49–57,
166–7; law of
negligence, 73–7;
Pensions Appeals,
44–5; precedent, 91–8,
167–8, 169–70, 185,
203; and Press, 117–20,
139; Profumo inquiry,
125, 127, 130–3, 188;
prose style, 189–92;
pupil master, 26–7; race
relations, 193–9;
Recorder of Plymouth,
33; reform of practice,
151–60, 215; religion,
217–18; retirement,
198–203, 206–7; 'right
to silence', 210–12; silk,
28–9; statutory
interpretation, 58–63;
on summing up, 46–7;
T-shirts, 122–3, 220;
teacher, 13–14; trade
unions, 134–49; travels,
172–6, 180–2; trial by
jury, 32–3, 46, 47; TV
and radio broadcasts,
208–10; war service,
10–12; wartime Legal
Adviser, 30; water
authorities, 208; wills,
63–6
Denning, Charles (D's
father), 3–5, 31
Denning, Clara (née
Thompson) (D's
mother), 3–4, 5

Denning, Gordon (D's
brother), 4, 6, 7, 8–9
Denning, Joan (Joan
Stuart, D's second
wife), 39–41, 48,
114–15, 181–2, 198, 202,
203
Denning, John Edward
Newdigate (Jack, D's
brother), 4, 6, 7–8, 12
Denning, Marjorie
Evelina (D's sister), 4, 5,
7, 114
Denning, Mary (Mary
Harvey, D's first wife),
15–18, 31
Denning, Norman Egbert
(D's brother), 4, 9
Denning, Reginald
Francis Stewart (Reg,
D's brother), 4, 6, 8, 14,
20
Denning, Robert (D's son),
15, 17, 29, 31, 39, 197
Denning, Thomas
Newdigate Poyntz (D's
great-grandfather), 3
Denning, William (D's
grandfather), 3
Devlin, Lord (Patrick
Devlin), 34, 69
Dickson v *Pharmaceutical
Society*, 146
Diplock, Lord (Sir
Kenneth Diplock):
'Bremer', 159; Express
Newspapers, 139, 141;
trusts, law of, 54;
mentioned, 61, 65, 96,
100, 174
Discipline of Law, The
(Denning), 185–6, 187,
188
dissenting opinion,
expression of, 88–9
dividend stripping, 166
divorce law, 34–9, 41–4,
see also matrimonial law
Dixon, Sir Owen, 89
domestic tribunals, 107–8,
109, 146
Domestic Violence Act
1976, 95

Donaldson, Lord Justice
(Sir John Donaldson),
118, 135, 155, 158
Donoghue v *Stevenson*, 165
Donovan, Lord (Terence
Donovan), 41
Dorset yacht case (1970),
76–7
Douglas-Home, Sir Alec,
179
DPP v *Smith*, 89
*Due Process of the Law,
The* (Denning), 186,
187, 188
Duncan v *Cammell Laird*,
97–8
Duport Steels Ltd v *Sirs*,
140–1, 168, 214
Dutton v *Bognor Regis
UDC*, 76

Eady, David, 199
Earl Grey Lecture (1953),
82
East Africa, D in, 174,
180
ecclesiastical law, 27
economic loss, damages
for, 75–6
Edgecombe, John, 125,
127
education, 173–5, 185,
207–8; D's, 6–7, 10,
12–13, 14–15
Eldon Scholarship, 14
Ellingham, Marjorie, 176
Elwyn-Jones, Lord, 97,
181
Employment Acts, 142,
144, 169
equity, 57, 213–14;
'deserted wife's equity',
51, 166–7
Essex County Hospital
case (1942), 31–2
estoppel, promissory,
68–70
European Convention on
Human Rights, 144,
205–6
European Court of
Justice: statutory
interpretation, 62

Eve, Sir Malcolm
Trustram (Eve
Commission), 176, 177
Evershed, Lord, 97, 110
Evershed, Patrick, 208
ex parte injunctions,
151–2, 155, 156–7
exemption clauses, 70–1,
205
Express Newspapers Ltd v
McShane, 138–9, 140
Express Newspapers v
Keys, 139

fair trial, 45–6
'family assets', 54
family law, 49–57
Family Story, The
(Denning), 186–7,
188–92
Faramus v *Film Artistes'*
Association, 144–5
Fennell, Mr Justice, 211
Fifoot, Cecil, 78, 112
Fiji Sugar Arbitration,
176–8
Fitzmaurice, Sir Gerald,
QC, 172
flogging, 47
'floodgates' argument,
75–6, 205
Foot, Sir Dingle, 110
Foot, Michael, 140
Foreign Compensation
Act 1950, 100
foreign currencies,
judgments state in, 154,
216
Foster, Sir John, 41
Fox, Lady (D's step-
daughter), 172
Fox, Michael, 40
Fox's Libel Act 1792, 47
France, war service in,
11–12
Freeman, Professor
M.D.A., 57
Fyffes Group, 178–80

gaming clubs, licensing of,
101
Gardiner, Lord, 94, 95, 97
Geer, Charles Henry, 6

Ghana, University of, 174
Gibson, Mr Justice (Peter
Gibson), 157
Gifford, Lord, 210
giving of reasons, 146
Glyn-Jones, H. KC, 39
Goddard, Rayner, 29
Gorman, Mr Justice, 118
Gouriet case (1977), 101–2
Granada Television case
(1980), 118–19
Graveson, Professor
R.H., 172
Gray, Roger QC, 170–1,
221
Greater London Council
and London Transport
(1982), 107
Greene, Lord, 60
Griffiths (Inspector of
Taxes) v *J.P. Harrison*
(Watford) Ltd, 166

Hadnor Productions Ltd v
Hamilton, 142
Hailsham, Lord (Quintin
Hogg): appraisal of D,
199–200, 220; D's
retirement, 198; House
of Lords, authority of,
170; *Punch* criticism of
court, 119–20; Rules of
Court, 153; *mentioned*
122, 131, 150, 178, 198
Haldane Memorial
Lecture (1953), 82
Haldane Society, The, 202
Hamlyn Lecture (1949),
81, 99, 104, 183–4
Hamson, Professor C.J.,
78, 85–6, 218–19
hanging, 47
'Hannah Blumenthal' case
(1982), 158, 168
Hansard as tool in
interpretation of
statutes, 58–9, 62
Harman, Harriet, 119
Harvey, Professor
Cameron, 189–90
Harvey, Cyril, 24
Harvey, Rev Frank, 15,
17

Harvey, Mary *see*
Denning, Mary
Havana case (1961), 154
Haynes, John E. (D's
brother-in-law), 7
Heaton's (road haulage)
case (1972), 135–6
Hedley Byrne & Co v
Hellar & Partners Ltd,
73, 75
Henn Collins, Pamela, 34
Henn Collins, Stephen,
19, 20, 21, 25, 78–9, 116
Herbert, Sir Edwin (Lord
Tangley), 41
Heseltine v *Heseltine*, 54
Heuston, Professor
R.F.V., 132
Higgs and Hill case
(1966), 147
'High Trees' case (1947),
68–70, 77, 214
Hill, Mavis, 86
Hobson, Sir John, 126,
131
Hodson, Lord, 52
Hogg, Quintin *see*
Hailsham, Lord
Holmes, Mr Justice, 213
Holt, Sir John, 92
Home Office v *Harman*,
119
Hook, Harry, 190–1
House of Lords, 28, 30–1;
D in conflict with,
161–71; debates in,
203–6; *Hansard*, 58–9;
Lord of Appeal in
Ordinary, 84–90; *see*
also individual cases
Housing Act 1957, 107
human rights debate,
205–6
Hurst, Judge Gerald, 86

illegitimacy and
interpretation of wills,
65–6
immigration, 193–4
Imperial Hotel (Torquay)
case (1969), 147–8
indemnity clauses, 70–1
India, D in, 176

industrial relations,
134–49, 198
Industrial Relations Act
1971, 135, 143, 149
inequality of bargaining
power, 71–2
injunctions, applicants
for, 101, 102
International Federation
of Seamen's Union,
137–8
interpretation (of statutes:
wills) *see* construction
Israel, D in, 173, 175
Ivanov, Captain, 124

Jamaica Banana Board,
178–80
James v *Ministry of
Pensions*, 44–5
Jarman on Wills, 65–6
Jenkins, Roy, 106
Jockey Club, 145
Jones, Mr Justice
Kenneth, 141
journalists: and justice,
117–20; labour
relations, 138–9
Jowitt, Lord (Sir William
Jowitt), 22, 28, 39, 41,
122, 184
Judges (D. Pannick), 209
Judicature Acts *see*
Supreme Court of
Judicature Acts
jury, trial by, 32–3, 46,
195–6

Kanda v *Government of
Malaya*, 103
Karminski, Sir Seymour,
174
Keeler, Christine, 124–8
passim
Keith, Lord, 90
Kennedy, Ludovic, 196
Kenya, D in, 174, 180
Kerr, J., 152
Khera, Gurbax Singh,
193–4
King, Tom, 210–12
King's Bench Division: D
appointed to, 39, 68;

prerogative writs, 99,
see also Queen's Bench
Division

Laddie, Hugh, 156
Laker, Freddie, and
'Skytrain' case, 106–7
Lambard, William, 113
Lamplugh v *Braithwaite*,
24
Land Charges Registry,
52–3
Landmarks in the Law
(Denning), 187–8, 203
Langston v *AUEW*, 148–9
language: D's prose style,
189–92; statutory, 60,
93, 162, 214; in wills, 63
Lannon case (1969), 102–3
Latey, William, 79
Launchbury v *Morgan*, 77
Law Commission, the, 94
law and order, 195, 204–5,
216
Law of Property Act 1925,
63, 65
Law Reform Committee,
163–4
Law Reform Now
(Gardiner/Martin eds),
94
Lawton, Lord Justice,
120, 140, 153
Lawyers Christian
Fellowship, 83
Leaves from my Library
(Denning), 188, 203
Leeds, D wartime Legal
Adviser in, 30, 31
legal education, 173–5,
185, 207–8
legal fiction, the, 213
legal records, 112
legal representation and
right to be heard, 103
Leggatt, Lord Justice
(Andrew Leggatt QC),
199
Leigh, David, 197
L'Estrange v *F. Graucob
Ltd*, 26
Levin, Bernard, 106
Lincoln, Ashe, QC, 200

Lincoln's Inn, D at,
19–21, 34, 113–14, 210,
219
Lionel Cohen Lecture
(1961), 89, 175
Lloyd, Mr Justice, 158
Lloyds Bank Ltd v *Bundy*,
36–7, 71–2
local government, D's
views on, 81
locus standi, 101, 102
London Electricity Board,
87
Lucas, J.R., 215
Luxmore, Mr Justice, 35
Lynskey, George, KC, 33

MacDermott, Lord, 60
Mackay, Lord, 213
Macleod, Ian, 131
Macmillan, Harold, 127,
129, 130, 131, 133,
170–1
McNeill, Robert, 176
McWhirter, Ross, 101
Magdalen College,
Oxford, D at, 10, 12–13,
14–15
Magna Carta Trust, 175
*Magor and St Mellors
Rural District Councils*
v *Newport Corporation*,
61
majority verdicts, 205
Malaysia, D in, 181
mandamus, 99
Mandla case (1982), 194–5
Mann, Paul, 127
manorial records, 112
Mansfield, Lord, 46, 69,
85, 92, 217
Mareva v *International
Bulkcarriers*, 151–3,
154–5, 160, 216
Marriage Guidance
Council, 43, 83
Marriage Welfare Service,
42
Married Women's
Property Act 1882,
49–50, 53–4, 56, 167
Marshall, Dr Geoffrey, 16,
17

Matrimonial Causes Act 1973, 55, 169
Matrimonial Homes Act 1967, 53
matrimonial law, 49–57, 166–7, 205, *see also* divorce law
Matrimonial Proceedings and Property Act 1970, 54–5, 167
Matthew, Theobald, 25
Maudling, Reginald, 87
Maxwell, Sir Alexander, 30
medical profession and negligence, 74
Megarry, Sir Robert, 51, 79
Merriman, Lord (Frank Merriman), 20, 42
Middle Temple, D member of, 25
Miles, Bernard, 209
Miliangos case (1976), 154
ministerial discretion, 104–7, 108
Moberly, Sir Walter, 84
Moccatta, Mr Justice, 152, 153
Moir, Anthony, 23
Morris of Borth-y-Gest, Lord, 87
Morris, Dr John, 64–5, 218
motion as access to law, 150
Musician's Union, 144

Nagle v *Fielden*, 145–6
Narayan, Rudy, 198–9
National Industrial Relations Court, 135
National Marriage Guidance Council *see* Marriage Guidance Council
National Provincial Bank Ltd v *Ainsworth*, 52, 166
National Union of Journalists, 138, 139
natural justice, 46, 102, 103, 104
'Nazi Parson', the, 30
negligence, law of, 73–7, 164–5

Nelly, P.J., 78
New Zealand, D in, 175–6, 181
News of the World and Profumo affair, 129
Nigeria, D in, 174
Normanbrook, Lord (Sir Norman Brook), 126

Oaksey, Lord, 85
Observer, The, 195, 197
O'Connor, Martin, 25
O'Hagan, Henry, 20, 25
O'Malley, Leonard, 86
'ouster clauses', ministerial, 100
'Outpost Emmaus', 84
Oxford University, D at, 10, 12–13, 14–15

Pacific Islands Monthly, 177
Pacific Review, 178
Padfield v *Ministry of Agriculture*, 104–5
Pain, Peter, 137
Pakistan, D in, 175, 176
Parker, Roger, 106
parliamentary privilege, 87–8
Patel, A.D., 178
Pedder, A.L., 10
Pension Appeals, 44–5, 78, 217
Pettitt v *Pettitt*, 54, 167
picketing, 136, 137, 141–2, 147, 148
Plomley, Roy, 209
Poland, D in, 173
police, law and order and the, 195, 204–5, 216
Post, Peter, 140, 198
Post Office Union, 101
power, State exercise of, 99–109, 134, 184
Poyntz family, 2–3
precedent, 91–8, 214, 215; D's differences with House of Lords, 167–8, 169–70, 203; *Precedents for Pleadings in the King's Bench Division*

(Bullen & Leake), 25, 183; 'Romanes' lecture, 185
prerogative writs, 99, 100–1, 102, 108
Press, the, D's relation with, 117–20, 139
Press Association, 138
'presumed intent', principle of, 72–3
Pritt, D.N., 21, 23, 29
Private Eye, 201, 209
Privy Council cases, 87–9
Probate, Admiralty and Divorce Division, D at, 34–9
professional negligence, 31–2, 74–7
Profumo affair, 113, 124–33
promissory estoppel, 68–70
property, sharing proceeds of matrimonial, 53–7, 167
public inquiries and natural justice, 104
Public Record Office, 112–13

Queen Elizabeth College, Greenwich, 113
Queen's Bench Division, 105, *see also* King's Bench Division

R v *Commissioner of Police for the Metropolis*, 119–20
R v *Miller*, 46–7
race relations, 193–9
Radcliffe, Cyril, 86, 133
Radcliffe inquiry (Vassal, 1963), 118
Rahimtoola v *Nizam of Hyderabad*, 90, 164
railway affairs, D and, 21
Rank Film Distributors v *Video Information Centre*, 157
Rawlinson, Lord (Sir Peter Rawlinson), 126–7, 131

Re Jebb decd, 64
Re Pritchard decd, 159
Re Rowland decd, 63–4
records, legal and State,
112–13
Redmayne, Martin, 127,
128
Registrar of Civic
Appeals, 116
Reid, Lord, 86, 166
'relator' actions, 101–2,
109
religion, influence of, on
law, 82–3, 217–18
Renton Report on
statutory interpretation,
61, 62–3
reporting and justice,
117–20
restatement of law,
215–16
Rice-Davies, Mandy, 123
Riches, Robert, 111
right of silence, accused's,
210–12
right to work, 145–6
Road to Justice, The
(Denning), 184–5
Roe, John, 6
Roe, Mrs John, 5
Romanes Lecture (1959),
92–3, 185
Romer, Charles, 30
Rondel v *Worsley*, 75
Rooks v *Barnard*, 170
Rowlatt, Sir Sidney, 27
Royal Commissions:
Historical Manuscripts,
112; Marriage and
Divorce (1956), 51;
Tribunals and Inquiries
(1966), 132
'Rule in Shelley's case', 65
Rules of Court and leave
of writ, 152–3

Salmon, Lord Justice, 118,
121, 132
Scarman, Lord (Leslie
Scarman), 59, 72, 80–1,
110, 217, 220
Schorsch Meir v *Hennin*,
154

Schreiner, Mr Justice
Oliver, 86
Scottish Law, 215
Scruttons Ltd v *Midland
Silicones Ltd*, 165–6
Seaford Court Estates Ltd
v *Asher*, 59–60
secondary picketing,
141–2
*Secretary of State for
Education and Science* v
Tameside MBC, 105
Segar, Robert, 14
seizure of assets, 151–5
Selborne, Lord, 85
self-incrimination, 157,
168
sequestration, writs of, 149
Shaw, Thomas, case of
(1952), 99–100
Shawcross, Lord (Sir
Hartley Shawcross) 30,
131, 172
Sikh community, 194–5
Simon, Lord, 33, 63, 78,
162
Simonds, Lord (Gavin
Simonds): construction
of statutes, 162;
dividend stripping, 166;
Lord Chancellor, 60–1,
94; relationship with D,
90, 122, 165; *mentioned*
86, 163
Siskana, The, case of, 152
Skyrme, Sir Thomas, 41,
180
Slade, Lord Justice, 155
Smith, Professor T.B., 97
Smith's Leading Cases, D
edits, 24–5, 28, 183
Soames, Edwards & Jones
(solicitors), 22
Society of Labour
Lawyers, 202
SOGAT, 139
Solicitors Bill 1965, 204
Soskice, Sir Frank, 111
South Africa, D in, 172–3,
181, 184
South America, D in, 175
Southern Railway, 21
Sparrow, John, 132

'Splendid Sun' case (1981),
158
*Staffordshire Area Health
Authority* v *South
Staffordshire Water Co.*,
72–3
Starr v *Ministry of
Pensions*, 44
State Immunity Act 1978,
169
state and individual,
99–109, 217
statutes, construction of,
58–63, 162, 168–9
steel industry, 140–1
Stein, Professor Peter, 1
Stephenson, Lord Justice
John, 203
Stevens, Professor Robert,
220–1
Stevenson, Mr Justice
Melford, 110–11
strikes, 138, 139, 140–1,
208, 214
Stuart, Hazel, 39, 40, 208
Stuart, J.M.B., 39–40
Stuart, John, 39, 40, 208
Stuart, Pauline, 39, 40
'substantial evidence' test,
107
suicide and the law, 28
Summerskill, Baroness, 52
Sunday Mirror, 215
Sunday Pictorial and
Profumo affair, 126
Sunday Times, The, 201,
219–20
Supply of Goods (Implied
Terms) Bill 1972, 205
Supreme Court of
Judicature Acts: 1873,
57, 85, 97, 160, 213;
1981, 157, 160, 169
Swan, M.F.V., 34–5
Sydall v *Castings Ltd*,
65–6

Tameside schools: case of,
105
Tangley, Lord, 41
Taylor, Jeremy, 62, 150
Taylor case (T&GWU and
USDAW) (1982), 143–4

Taylor v *Caldwell*, 24
television licence fees case
  (1976), 105–6
Temple, William, 82, 83
Templeman, Lord, 156
terms of art in wills, 65
Thames Television, 142
Thankerton, Lord, 104
Thatcher, Margaret, 199
Third Chandris
  Corporation v
  Unimarine, 154
third parties, contracts
  benefiting, 165–6
Thompson, John Thomas
  (D's maternal
  grandfather), 3
time limit on actions,
  159–60
Times, The: black jurors,
  195–6, 197–8; D and
  unions, 136; D's
  retirement, 201; 'In
  defence of freedom of
  speech', 211–12;
  judicial activism, 219;
  'leaky umbrella' (House
  of Lords), 140, 168,
  171; *mentioned*, 144
Tonypandy, Lord (George
  Thomas), 199
tort, 73–7
Trade Union and Labour
  Relations (Amendment)
  Act 1976, 137, 168
trade unions, 134–49;
  domestic tribunals,
  107–8, 109; Gouriet
  case, 101–2; legislation,
  168; *mentioned*, 186,
  202, 217

Transport and General
  Workers' Union, 136,
  137, 143, 147
Trinidad and Tobago, D
  in, 181
trusts, law of, 54
TUC, Bridlington
  Principles of the, 142–4
Tucker, Mr Justice, 211
Turner Memorial Lecture,
  175

Unfair Contract Terms
  Act 1977, 71
United States of America,
  D in, 173, 175, 184
'unlawful means', 147–8
Upjohn, Lord, 54, 159
USDAW, 143

Vaisey, Harry, 35
variation of trusts, 162–4,
  169
Vassal affair, 118

Wachtel v *Wachtel*, 55–6
Waddams, Professor S.,
  220
Wade, Professor H.W.R.,
  111
Ward, Stephen, 124–31
  passim
Ward v *Bradford*
  Corporation, 46
wards of court, 42
Warren, Sir Herbert, 10, 14
water authorities'
  statutory duties, 208–9
Welsh Circuit, 48
Welsh student protest
  (1970), 120–1

Wensleydale, Lord, 58
Western Circuit, 21, 23, 48
What Next in the Law
  (Denning), 118–19, 187,
  196, 199
Whitchurch (Hants): D's
  childhood in, 2, 3–7;
  'The Lawn', 114–15,
  206–7
Whitford, Mr Justice
  (John Whitford), 29,
  157, 158
Wield (Hants) village
  school, 207
Wigg, George MP, 128
Wilberforce, Lord
  (Richard Wilberforce),
  166
Willes, J., 59
Williams, Professor
  Glanville, 170
Williams, Sir Max, 199
wills, interpretation of,
  63–6, 218
Wilson, Harold, 129;
  Wilson report on Public
  Records, 113
Winchester College, D
  teaches at, 13–14
Winchester trial case
  (1988), 210–12
Windward Islands, 178–9
Winfield, Professor Percy,
  78
Winn, Lord Justice
  (Rodger Winn), 64, 86
Woodham, T.H., 21
Wright, Lord, 161

Young, Hugo, 201,
  219–20